High
Country
Hunting

High Country Hunting

Hunter's Information Series ®
North American Hunting Club
Minneapolis, Minnesota

High Country Hunting

Library of Congress Catalog Card Number 89-63098
ISBN 0-914697-26-9

Printed in U.S.A.

10   11   12   13   14   15   16   17   18   19

Caution

Contents

Acknowledgements

In my mind, not since Jack O'Connor's *Sheep And Sheep Hunting*, published in 1974, has there been a more complete and up-to-date book about hunting sheep and mountain goats. *High Country Hunting* is packed with hard-won hunting techniques and entertaining campfire stories. This is a good book.

For their behind the scenes work, special thanks to: NAHC Senior Vice President Mark LaBarbera, Associate Editor Dan Dietrich, Editorial Assistant Karyl Dodge, Member Products Manager Mike Vail and Special Projects Coordinator Linda Kalinowski.

Steven F. Burke, President
North American Hunting Club

Photo Credits

Photos in this book were provided by the author. In addition to examples of his own talent, he has included photos from Chuck Adams, Patrick Allen, Galen D. Clark, David Fox, Charlie Gephart, H. Grounds, Mike Hamrick, Don Harrell, Ed Huxen, Arnie Johns, T.S. Marcum, Bill Miller, Leland Speakes, Jr., Wilson Stout and Robert Strong.

About The Author

L loyd Bare spent much of his childhood hunting pheasants with his father in Iowa cornfields. As a teenager, he and his father, Jack, hunted mule deer and antelope in Wyoming on family vacations.

Lloyd earned a degree in pharmacology from the University of Iowa. After graduation he moved to Michigan to pursue his career. He did not, however, leave his love for hunting behind. In Michigan he hunted white-tailed deer and upland birds.

"The Disaster Year," as Lloyd calls it, was 1971. In the fall of that year, Lloyd and Jack were on their first mixed bag hunt in British Columbia. Their elk, moose and caribou hunt with Don Peck Outfitters was successful. The campfire tales, however, centered around sheep hunting, around the close calls and exciting stalks at the top of the world. Lloyd's interest was sparked.

The stories and tales in this book explain how completely Lloyd was smitten with sheep fever—that obsession to hunt wild sheep near the precipitous peaks and shear cliffs in North America's most rugged, desolate country.

Those campfire tales prompted Lloyd to book his first sheep hunt with Don Peck Outfitters in British Columbia. Although Lloyd did not return from that 1973 hunt with a sheep, he did return with the burning desire to hunt sheep and mountain goats. He was hooked.

Lloyd's love for hunting the high country grew. He partici-
pated in the first official meeting of the Foundation for North
American Wild Sheep in 1978. Since that first meeting in Detroit,
Michigan, Lloyd has served on the Foundation's Board of
Directors, as well as serving as the organizations secretary for a
number of years.

Lloyd has completed his Grand Slam of North American wild
sheep, and shoulder mounts of his Rocky Mountain bighorn, desert
bighorn, Dall and Stone sheep grace his trophy room. His big
game hunting adventures have taken him from Canada's
westernmost province of British Columbia, to its easternmost
province of Quebec. He has hunted from as far south as New
Mexico, to as far north as Alaska.

Lloyd has also hunted Rocky Mountain goats, which may be
North America's most underrated species. He has hunted mountain
goats in Canada and the U.S., including Alaska and British
Columbia.

After one particularly exciting high country hunt, Lloyd made
the commitment to share his experiences with other hunters. In
1978 he began to write about sheep and goat hunting.

Today he writes 40 to 50 hunting stories each year. His stories
appear in all the major outdoor magazines, including *North American Hunter*.

Dedication

This book must be dedicated to all high country hunters and outfitters of the past, present and most importantly, the future. The hunters and outfitters of the past instilled in us the wonders of sheep and goat hunting. They made us dream and hope. We must remember such men as Charles Sheldon, Dr. W.T. Hornaday, William A. Baillie-Grahman, Theodore Roosevelt, John Phillips, William Beachy, James L. Clark, General Richard Mellon, Donald Hopkins, Colonel Harry Snyder, George Parker, Herb Klein, Colonel Wilson Potter, John Batton, Roy Hargreaves and Bert Rigall.

Also, I must thank several people: My long-suffering wife Kathy must rank first on this list. She does possess the patience of Job. She does understand that high country hunters don't always return home on the scheduled date. She does understand that when spring arrives, just as sure as sap rises in maples, I develop a terrible case of cabin fever. She does realize that when I kick the dog, cuss at her and yell at the kids, that I really still love them but I must get away to the mountains.

At times, she and my sons might have survived with last year's coats or shoes so I could climb the high ridges into the high basins. She spends days and nights alone while I watch the rams battle, the eagles soar and the marmots preach. Without her, I could not enjoy the high country.

I must thank my dad, Jack, for introducing me at a young age to his love of hunting and all wild creatures. Also, for accompanying me on so many wonderful hunts. I must thank mother for being mother.

Thank you, outfitters and guides who have taught me, suffered with me, climbed with me and who have become wonderful friends: Dewey Browning, the late Don Peck, Ross Peck, Gary LaRose, Jerry Hughes, David Welch, Dale Gunn and Joe D'Errico.

Thank you, writers and editors for early books on mountain hunting. These books set hunters' hearts thumping and minds dreaming; *Alaska Yukon Trophies Won And Lost*, by G.O. Young; *North American Head Hunting*, by Grancel Fitz; *The Best Of Sheep Hunting* put together by John Batten; *Hunting Big Game*, by Tom Brakefield; *Grand Slam Of North American Wild Sheep*, edited by Bob Householder.

Jack O'Connor must be thanked in a category all by himself. He would be included in the dedication list, in the early writer list and in the story list. O'Connor above all others instilled a dream of climbing to the high basins and ridges in all readers with his wonderful magazine articles and books. He hunted sheep before it became fashionable. Without a doubt, he knew more about sheep hunting than any other hunter of his time.

I must thank Linda Strong, David Onerheim, Dr. Robert Broadbent, Dr. Roy Schultz, B.J. Galvin and Jerry Owen for sharing their marvelous stories of the high country.

Tom Tietz and Chuck Adams, thank you for your expert information on bowhunting the creatures of the high country.

And finally I must thank all my friends in the Foundation for North American Wild Sheep for their help collecting the photos for this book. A special thanks to my close friends and fellow board of directors for the many hours of telling hunting tales and hard work helping the wild sheep: Jerry Christian, John and Jane Babler, Francis Stubbs, Jim Froelich, Dr. Roy Schultz, Duane Smelser, Bill Walters, Michael Valencia, Paul Asper, Dr. James "Red" Duke, Dr. Jerry Waite, Lanny Wilson, Harvey Kadlec, Arnie Johns, Lowell Baier and Fred McMurray.

1

The Mystique Of
Hunting Mountain Game

His nine companions started feeding nearly an hour ago but the old ram remains in his shale bed. For the first time in his life he feels old and tired. His joints need to absorb the sun's warmth before he can join the younger rams for breakfast. Finally he stands and stretches to soothe the remaining stiffness.

Even though his teeth hurt and his knees ache, the old monarch holds his head high as he marches across the shale to nibble course yellow grass in the alpine basin. He will not let the other rams know how bad he feels. To them the 12-year-old will remain king of the mountain.

Just behind the basin, rugged crags soar toward fleecy clouds. A vein of water trickles through the boulder-strewn meadow like a silver ribbon before cascading 100 feet down the cliff. Below the basin towering spruce stand like dark green, almost black sentinels. Unseen from above, deadfalls make the spruce nearly impregnable to common man. Toward the head of the canyon, an eagle swoops and soars effortlessly on thermals.

Suddenly tension grips the mountainside. The rams stop eating and stare at two eight-year-olds standing rigidly beside each other. The darker ram stretches his neck low and turns his head slightly. His neck muscles bulge and his ears lay back. The ram's right front leg whips up into the other's chest.

One ram walks uphill 20 feet, turns and glares back at the

other, eyes red. Dirt and grass fly as both rams paw the ground and charge. As they near one another, each rears up on his back legs and lunges, head tilted sideways. As the bodies come down, two heads rush toward each other until two rough horn edges meet with a resounding blow. Immediately each ram twists his head to bring the other horn into contact.

As the crash echoes through the canyons, the two rams recoil, each slightly dazed. The basin becomes strangely quiet until the two great rams suddenly lunge again, horn meeting horn with the force of two enraged bulls. The lighter ram tries a quick butt to the ribs but the darker ram slips aside.

The old monarch loses interest. He has seen and participated in many such battles over his 12 years. The two younger and nearly equal rams fight for their rightful rank just below his acknowledged leadership in the rigid ram hierarchy. After five more violent crashes, the lighter colored ram lowers his head and walks away, leaving the winner to his hard-earned victory.

Unseen by the rams, two sets of human eyes watch every move from behind a rock ledge across the canyon. The hunters sit silent, mesmerized by the battle. Between crashes, they hear only the gentle whisper of wind through the tops of stunted firs. The same breeze caresses their sweat-covered foreheads.

About 10 a.m. the old ram strides back to the shale, kicks a few rocks from his bed and lies down. One or two at a time, the other rams find beds. Finally all 10 sheep are lying down, each looking in a different direction. One of the rams lets his horns rest on the shale, but not the big old boy.

Taking turns, the two hunters check the old ram one last time in the 20x spotting scope. His heavy, dark horns curve well below his jaw before turning up above the scarred nose. The broomed tips look as thick as a man's wrist. Neither hunter speaks but both know they gaze upon a trophy of a lifetime.

"They should stay down until mid-afternoon," my guide, Dewey, whispers from our hidden viewpoint. "They might get up for a bite or to find a softer bed but they won't move far. We should have plenty of time to make a stalk."

After stowing the spotting scope and slipping our packs on, we scoot behind the rock ledge and creep into the timber. An hour later we reach a small stream in the canyon bottom. The icy water tastes like nectar from heaven on my parched tongue.

Shortly after we start up the other side toward the rams, my lungs burn and my legs quiver but we push ever upward. Every

Stunning scenery may be the cause of sheep fever, that obsession that fills otherwise sane NAHC members with the desire to climb precipitous ridges and lofty peaks to hunt sheep and mountain goats. You'll find no country more beautiful in all of North America.

dozen or so steps, I stop to rest my aching legs. How I envy Dewey's rock-hard body and seemingly undefeatable lungs.

Two hours later we approach the ram's level. Dewey rechecks the wind as we make our way through the timber. Finally he decides we are above the rams, so we slip out of our packs. An eagle screeches his displeasure at something far below as he soars on the wind.

A quick glance from behind the last tree confirms that the rams have not moved. We crawl over the sharp shale to a position behind some low juniper. The rock scrapes my knees and elbows but I feel nothing except my thumping heart. A trickle of sweat leaves a salty trail down my forehead, nose and lips.

After my heart slows to a normal rhythm and my breathing calms, I slip my .300 Win. Mag. over a cushioning juniper, center the crosshairs in the magnificent ram's chest and gently squeeze the trigger. Somehow, the shot seems anticlimactic.

Another Mountain, Another Day

Guide Dale Gunn and I ride horseback to the tree line on the gently sloping backside of a mountain in British Columbia. We tie the horses to some scrub junipers, then hike to the top on foot. Again my lungs burn and legs drag as Dale scampers up. At last I gasp up the final few feet to the top.

Catching my breath, we sit just below the ridge top. I marvel at the gorgeous scene painted before me. This is not sheep country, I think, but rather rugged rock, steep cliffs and practically no vegetation. As I soak in the beauty, a mountain goat tiptoes out from behind a boulder. His pure white coat gleams against the reddish-gray rocks behind his stocky body.

The billy stands out of range and fortunately does not spot us. In fact, the goat ambles *toward* us. To my untrained eye, he appears to walk on the side of a sheer cliff with no visible means of support. With my compact binoculars I find the narrow crack which offers the goat footing. At one point the billy comes to a dead end. At least it looks like a dead end. With no apparent concern, the beautiful animal thrusts his front feet upward, catches a ledge several feet above and pulls himself up with only his front feet.

Occasionally the goat stops to graze on something. I can only see hard rock. His long, thick mane and chaps make the stocky body seem even heavier as the old billy nears my position. Finally Dale nods at me. I slip behind my rifle, take careful aim and squeeze the trigger. Rock flies just over the goat's back. Twice more I fire with similar results.

After my goat disappears over the ridge, I ponder my poor shooting. "How far was he," I ask.

"Not more than 100 yards. Why'd you shoot over his back?"

This is my first high country hunt. Amid the vastness of this beautiful country I completely overestimated the distance. Thinking the goat stood at least 300 yards away, I aimed over his back on purpose.

Dale hopes we might find the goat again so we slip and slide down the rock until we find another excellent vantage point. We're lucky. The billy pokes his head out from a narrow chimney in the rock but does not offer a target. He looks right and left but cannot see us against the sun. After what seems like an hour, my trophy takes another step or two out, exposing his chest.

This time I hold the crosshairs on his chest and squeeze. Absolutely nothing happens. He doesn't flinch, turn his head or even twitch his nose. A second shot: the same results. Then, as I squeeze a third time, the goat's knees buckle and he tumbles off his perch as if in slow motion, and lands 200 feet below.

Many sportsmen agree that sheep hunting ranks at the very apex of the outdoor experience. The animal itself with its regal bearing is the reason for the lofty rank.

After two hours of the toughest climb down I've ever encountered we inspect my trophy. Luckily the fall didn't damage the horns or cape. I could cover the three bullet holes in his chest with a tin cup.

After caping the luxurious hide Dale announces that we will have to climb back to the top and get the horses down the backside. Looking down, I see the creek and know camp is just downstream, an easy walk. Ignorant of mountains, I suggest that perhaps Dale can go over the top and get the horse while I climb down to the creek and meet him at camp.

"That's OK with me. Better stay to the right. I think you'll run into a dry waterfall on the left that you can't get down over," he says as he packs the hide and horns and starts up.

For a time I made progress. The going is tough in places but not impossible. Then I learn the truth about mountains: You can't see what problems you might face from above, you only find them as you reach them. Several times the only way down a ledge is to hang by my hands and drop a few inches to rock below.

Finally I reach a long ledge with no apparent way off. Both ends meet straight slick cliffs and the ledge is about 15 or 20 feet above the shale slide below. If I can reach the slide, it angles gently down to the creek. But it is too far to hang and fall without harm. After walking the ledge both ways three times with no luck I sit down defeated.

A terrible thirst develops in my poor old body, perhaps from work, perhaps from fear. Whatever the reason I must drink. I find a few blue colored berries but have no idea if they are poisonous.

Suddenly the sun peaks out of the clouds behind my precarious perch and paints a rainbow on the mountain across the creek. Not just any rainbow, but the most vivid colors I've ever seen. My spirits soar like an eagle. I sense that the Gods of the hunt stand with me. Looking carefully along the ledge again, I find a narrow chimney. Using elbows and knees, I creep down the chasm until my tired feet hit the welcome shale below.

Although terrified by the entire experience, I fall in love with these mountains. I find a serene beauty here unmatched in other wildlife habitat. The vastness and stillness etch an indelible impression on my soul. In short, I am hooked on the mountains.

Afflicted With Sheep Fever

Why do otherwise sane men and women torment their bodies climbing up to the wild rams and goats of North America? Throughout the length and depth of our country, we find many dedicated hunters. Some stalk the wary whitetail, some thrill to the bull elk's eerie bugle, others sit freezing in a duck blind beside a sleek black lab. But the dedication of sheep and goat hunters goes far beyond that of any other hunters. Some even say high country hunters are possessed.

A true sheep hunter, one smitten with the dread disease, "Ovis Pyrexia" or sheep fever, possesses a drive, perhaps an obsession, to climb the steep ridges up to the high basins just to be with the sheep. Those afflicted with the disease are restless when not on a sheep mountain or talking sheep with other hunters. They drive many miles and spend many dollars on the phone just to talk with other sheep hunters. They attend meetings with sheep hunters and read all the available sheep stories, but nothing short of getting up there with the rams seems to help.

As to the cause of this dread disease, I have heard many and different theories. Some praise the magnificent country sheep

Mountain goats truly live at the top of the world. While sheep prefer grassy basins, goats stay in the rocks where one wonders what they eat. Goats seldom panic or run. Rather, they walk from danger to where no predator, except an accurate, well-placed shot from a hunter, can follow.

inhabit, others the gut-busting ordeal to reach them. Some tell of the wonderful companionship around the campfire and some insist it is the feeling of being on top the world when sitting high on a sheep mountain. But no, the cause must be something else since you can experience all these things on hunts for other game. For me, the animal itself causes the terrible condition.

The magnificent ram is unlike any other wild game. He strides across his mountain kingdom, head erect, self-assured, almost arrogant. His horns crown the ram monarch of the mountains. These massive horns weigh more than any other North American headgear—save that of the mighty moose. If straightened, they would reach some 40 inches above his head with their 15- to 16-inch bases.

A ram's great curling horns, which grow until his death, tell the story of his life. During the mid-winter time of little feed and a slight hormonal change, a yearly ring forms, much like a tree trunk ring. Less noticeable rings form during the rest of the year depending on food conditions. During years of plenty, more horn growth occurs; during lean years, less growth shows on the horns.

Horns of a mature ram often have chunks missing, the result of clashes with other rams. Desert sheep horns are very brittle and large missing chunks are not unusual. Rams use their horns as protection and as weapons but they also display them as a symbol of rank in the ram hierarchy. Each ram in a bachelor band knows his place in the pecking order and in most cases accepts that place. Newcomers and equals spar most often. More serious fighting takes place during the annual rut.

Sheep and goat hunting can be the physically toughest hunting of all, but the rewards are beyond belief.

Sheep Hunting In Alaska

My guide and I sit beside the Russell Glacier between two towering Alaskan mountains. Seven Dall rams keep us pinned down. That morning we stripped from the waist down to cross an icy ribbon of glacial water. The first barefoot step sent chills raging through my entire body. On the second step, I felt sharp rocks, but by the third step my feet felt nothing.

At long last a rain squall moves in and the rams climb up and out of sight. We dash across the flat and start up a ravine toward a plateau 200 feet above. Slipping on wet rock makes progress tough but finally we come out on the flat. Alas, the sheep have disappeared. "Damn, where did they go?" my guide mutters.

While standing in the middle of the plateau, we spot the rams high above at the same time they spot us and scamper even higher. We slip behind a large boulder to plan our next move and watch the sheep. Finally they bed down high in the peaks.

A thick-furred marmot mounts a nearby rock and stares at us from a position on his haunches. He soon decides we can't be trusted and his long string of shrill chatter shatters the silence. He reminds me of a miniature Churchill ranting at Parliament.

About 300 yards to the left we find a deep drywash to cover our climb toward the rams. Other than panting and puffing, the first 1,000 feet or so prove an easy climb. Then we run into the steep face of a dry waterfall. I watch as my guide climbs the treacherous rock on the left of the cliff. When at last he reaches the top, he shakes his head no and points to the other side.

I start up the right side but soon find myself on hands and knees. My fingers grasp tiny cracks in the rock as my toes desperately search for support. Then I push up to the next crack in the rock. Worse than the solid rock is loose rock on the hard surface. One slip would mean a fall of several hundred feet. The sweat of absolute fear trickles down my back.

At long last my raw fingers haul me over the top. My chest feels like it will burst at any minute, but we have no time to rest. A half hour later we reach the ridge where we last saw the rams. Joe creeps to the edge. My heart sinks when he motions me up. The Dall rams have moved even higher.

One more ridge, just one more I tell myself. One more turns into four more, each higher than the last. Finally, Joe turns and makes a curling motion around his head. Rams! The sun peeks out from behind a cloud. Sunlight bathes the crags. I made it.

Why Hunt The High Country?

Whenever I look at that Alaskan ram on my wall with its golden, flaring horns, memories rush back of the hard work and terrifying climb. But I also remember the exaltation when I looked down on the rams from my position on top of the world.

The actual shooting rates secondary on nearly all big game hunts and sheep hunting offers no exception. In fact, the shooting is probably less important on sheep hunts than any others. How else can we explain the fact that each year hundreds of sane men and women hunt Montana's unlimited sheep areas when they know these areas are among the toughest to hunt and that only two to three percent of the hunters will take a ram?

Success like this can lead to a bad case of sheep fever. David Onerheim took this record book bighorn ram in 1987. It scored 201¹/₈ Boone & Crockett points, and is the third largest bighorn ram taken since 1924.

I know one Alberta sheep hunt ranks at the top of my memory cabinet and I never fired a shot. I did see many rams and had the privilege of seeing a ram that would rank high in the record book. I sat on the high ridges watching undisturbed rams battle each other. We saw eagles soar and marmots scurry.

True sheep hunters even delight in the sight of ewes and lambs. One particularly hot Alberta day the flies bothered the sheep and the hunters. A band of rams contained no trophies so Dewey and I set a spotting scope up on three ewes and two lambs grazing in a grassy basin. One ewe decided she had enough of the sun and flies.

David Onerheim was hunting in British Columbia's Cross River Drainage when he took this record book bighorn. British Columbia continues to produce big, record book animals.

She walked toward the shady rock ledges but paused under a long overhanging ledge just the right height to scratch her back. I could see the relief and pleasure on her face.

A lamb tried the same but was too short. So it reached up with a hind leg and scratched like a dog. After each ewe gave its tormented skin a good scratch, they progressed along a narrow ledge until the lead ewe found herself rimmed out. She looked around, wanting to back out, but found the ledge blocked with other sheep. She paused a moment then slid down 20 feet to the shale slide and shade. The others calmly followed.

High country and high country hunting offers a beauty and quiet serenity not available on other hunts. This is not to say that the quiet stalk of a whitetail in a northern woods is not a wonderful experience. Likewise, no sound in nature quite compares with a bull elk bugling his high country challenge. But almost all hunters, who are not after sheep or goats, move most of the time, stillhunting or stalking their quarry.

Not so the NAHC member who hunts mountain game.

Once the high country hunter reaches the ridges and basins, he sits and glasses hour after hour. Sheep and goat hunting demands no rush, no hurry. He has time to think, time to relax and air out his spirit. The sheep hunter atop the highest ridge puts day to day stress out of his mind and soaks up the clean air and the sights and sounds found only in the mountains. An Alberta outfitter tells about a priest who, when the outfitter returned from a short scouting walk, lay spread-eagle on the coarse mountain grass, clad only in his boxer shorts, simply enjoying the solitude and soaking up the sun's warmth.

Most dedicated high country hunters exhibit an intense hatred for crowds. Such times as opening day of the deer season, with its invading hordes, repulse them quicker than the smell of rotten eggs. High country hunters much prefer the solitude of a lonely mountain. High on a sheep or goat mountain you seldom, if ever see another hunter.

God must have been in a wonderful mood when he made sheep and goat mountains. As I rounded the last bend in Alberta's Washout Creek, I entered paradise. Steep cliffs towered above the little basin on two sides. Thick stands of stately spruce guarded the other two. Several old white moose antlers set off the lush green meadow grass where a silver ribbon of water seeped from a high spring. Even though the basin held no sheep, I sat and enjoyed the meadow for an hour.

Although some good sheep country holds no goats and some good goat country holds no sheep, you often find both species in the same area and even on the same mountain. However, each species inhabits a different niche. You'll find rams in high grassy basins, often just under rugged peaks which they use for escape. Sheep prefer the country between tree line and the crags.

Goats on the other hand, hang out in the steepest, roughest rocks and the absolute tops of the peaks. They travel with ease where no sane sheep would tread. Often one side of a mountain slopes gently down through meadows and basins while the other drops precipitously with cliffs and rocks. Look for sheep on the meadow side and goats on the rocks.

Throughout this book, I'll mention the term "Sheep Mountain." Although a sheep hunter can easily recognize a sheep mountain, they're not all alike. Nor can I simply define a sheep mountain. They just possess some indescribable quality that stands out to the man who climbs the high ridges searching for the magnificent ram.

If you look up and see a mountain heavily forested almost to the top, that's probably not a sheep mountain. If you look at an exceptionally steep mountain with little vegetation, that's probably not a sheep mountain. But if you look at a mountain with rolling basins or meadows with boulders and perhaps a trickle of water high above the trees, one with rugged peaks above the basins, you're probably looking at a fine sheep mountain. One thing is certain, all sheep mountains are beautiful.

At first glance, most desert sheep country looks barren and foreboding. Up close, however, you find hundreds of wild flowers and cactus blooms. The ride back to camp one Nevada evening reminded me of the wonderful experience sheep hunting offers, even in the desert. We saw over 30 sheep. I drank from a cold, clear spring in the middle of a desert. I marveled at the gnarled trunks of bristle cone pines. I watched a bluebird flit from tree to tree atop the 10,000-foot Mount Hayford.

As we rode horseback through the towering ponderosa pine coming down the mountain, the shadows lengthened and the first cool evening breeze soothed our faces. When we emerged from the trees, the last light intensified the cactus' fiery red blooms. Above, the arms of a Joshua tree framed the blue sky.

As we approached the last ridge before camp, Jerry pointed upward. There, silhouetted against the violet clouds, stood a yearling ram like a sentinel in the sky. When we reached camp

A rustic hunting camp high in the mountains adds to the mystique and pleasure of a high country hunt.

neither of us spoke a word for several minutes, each lost in the grandeur and awe of sheep country.

So what does it take to be a high country hunter? Being a little crazy helps as does having an understanding spouse. In case your spouse doesn't want to accompany you chasing about the mountains, he or she must possess the patience of Job, the understanding that sheep hunters don't always return home on the scheduled date, and the security to know that when spring arrives, just as sure as sap rises in maples, you will develop a terrible case of cabin fever.

My good friend, sheep hunter and past president of the Foundation for North American Wild Sheep, Dr. Roy Schultz, sums up, "To know the lofty peaks where the eagle rides the rising thermals; to smell the pugnacious pitch of the stunted spruce as it brushes my face; to taste the cool water from a refreshing rivulet in my parched mouth; to view the majestic beauty and serenity of a full curl ram chewing his cud, bedded down in a hidden basin. These are just a few of the rewards, granted to those who have been there."

2

The History
Of Sheep Hunting

"**B**efore me was the main object of my trip to those northern wilds; beautiful they were, glistening white in the sun not withstanding a brownish stain and game in every motion. Most of them carried fair horns, well spread, and all had black tails. They fed nervously and kept constantly on the move, a few often running with alertness, and every moment one or another would throw its head to look, either up or down. I remained motionless, flat on the ground, among some rocks, watching every movement. How to stalk them was a puzzle.

"Only those who have been high up above the valleys and woods, among the peaks and crags, and there have seen the mountain ram in his element, can appreciate the sight or realize the emotion surging through me as I beheld them. They stood like marble silhouettes, erect, rigid, on the sky-line of that wonderful landscape—the essence of boldness, grace, energy, self-confidence, wildness! For five minutes they stood motionless, sweeping the country below with their keen eyes. Unless hidden from sight I do not believe any moving object could have escaped them.

"After the excitement of the hunt the vast panorama of mountains about me never seemed so beautiful. Directly below were the bare, steep slopes extending to the timber which bordered the creek. Beyond, lay the valley of the west fork, fringed green by the spruces, while the waters of the creek were shining and glistening in the rays of the setting sun, which tinted with gold the heavy clouds on the horizon. The lofty mountain behind camp stood out boldly, its high-turreted rock and rough peaks forming fantastic shapes against the skyline and at its base our camp fire burned brightly. Behind, stretching far away, were the bewildering masses of the main Ogilvie ranges, the varied rocks blending colors and fading like a wavy ocean merging into the soft, dull blue of the sky beyond. A large ram lay at my feet.''

Charles Sheldon wrote these words over 60 years ago about a hunt that occurred over 80 years ago in his book, *Wilderness Of The Upper Yukon*. According to most experts, Sheldon was the first sportsman to hunt sheep in the far north country. He also accurately recorded all the known sheep ranges of Alaska and the Yukon and recorded the different horn configurations, hair color and other distinguishing factors among the Dall and Stone sheep of the north. His records hold true today.

Sheep hunters of today exclaim the same thoughts about the majestic ram and its habitat that Sheldon did just after the turn of the century. Tom Brakefield in his *Hunting Big Game Trophies*, published in 1976, perhaps best sums up the thoughts of sheep hunters: ''Rams stand at the very pinnacle of big game. By any ratio of horn length to body height or horn mass to body weight, no other animals in the world of either antlered or horned persuasions, carry such massive indicators of their maleness.''

The earliest sheep hunters in North America pursued sheep for meat or occasionally for ceremonial purposes. Native tribes such as the Hareskins, Slaveys and Kootenais in the north, the Sioux in the plains and the Pimce and Papago in the south, all left recorded evidence of sheep hunting.

John Clark of the Lewis and Clark expedition hunted bighorns near Yellowstone as early as 1805 with his U.S. Harper's Ferry model in .54 caliber. Although he mentions the ram's wonderful horns he no doubt hunted for food. The same can be said of frontiersman John Fremont on his hunts in Colorado in 1842.

Dall sheep were first classified from a specimen collected by an old pioneer in the winter of 1879. During Alaska's gold rush days starting in 1896, many prospectors and others in the area shot Dall sheep for food. Not until 1904 did Sheldon first sport hunt the beautiful, pure white animals.

Jack O'Connor reported that men accompanying Spanish explorer Francisco Coronado first saw desert sheep in 1540 and reported them as having large horns and little tails. However, other than natives, settlers and early explorers who shot sheep for meat, no one hunted desert sheep for sport or trophies until Dr. W.T. Hornaday, a hunter, naturalist and director of the Bronx Zoo, hunted sheep in Sonora in 1906.

Because of their extremely remote habitat, the Stone sheep of northern British Columbia may be the only species first hunted by sportsmen. A few may have been shot by natives for meat or by the first explorers through the country, but until the 20th century, Stone sheep country was a vast, mostly unexplored region.

Only a few dedicated mountain hunters actively pursued wild sheep in the years before World War II. The few who did were most enthusiastic. Such names as Charles Sheldon, William A. Baillie-Grohman, Theodore Roosevelt, W.T. Hornaday, John C. Phillips, William Beach, William J. Morden, James L. Clark, General Richard Mellon, Donald Hopkins, Colonel Harry Snyder, George Parker, Jack O'Connor, Herb Klein, Grancel Fitz and Colonel Wilson Potter crop up in almost any literature about early, dedicated sheep hunters.

In these early days a sheep hunt required much planning and money. The treks lasted from six to twelve weeks by the time you spent a week or two on a train and steamer and five to fifteen days by pack train just to reach the northern hunting grounds. Although a few ''sheep nuts'' hunted primarily for sheep, most early sheep hunts were part of general bag hunts. Very few hunters ever shot all four species of North American wild sheep before the 1950s.

Some of the earliest trophy sheep hunts ended up offering hardship at best and danger at worst as well as awesome beauty and excitement. Other than Sheldon, a group of three American hunters undertook one of the first major expeditions into the Dall sheep area of Alaska and the Yukon in 1919. One of the men, G.O. Young, wrote a book about the hunt, *Alaska-Yukon Trophies Won And Lost*, published in 1947.

Young teamed up with Dr. A.H. Evans and J.C. Snyder on the memorable hunt. They contracted with outfitters Morley Bones and Gene Jacquots. In 1945, Jack O'Connor hunted much of the same area with Jacquots and I was fortunate enough to hunt on a bit of the same ground in 1977.

After taking a steamer from Seattle to Cordova, Alaska, Young's group took a trail to Chitina, Alaska, and then McCarthy, Alaska, where they met Bones. They were to hunt on foot and horseback to the White River in the Yukon. There the hunt would end when the hunters, Bones and their trophies floated in a scow built of whipsawed lumber down the White River to the Yukon River, where they would hail a steamer bound for Whitehorse, Alaska. The plan worked to perfection until the party reached the White River. The return can best be described as a nightmare. However, before the troubles, the hunt offered the same memories and excitement of a modern day hunt.

The traveling portion of Young's hunt was on horseback. Their horse problems sound just like modern packtrip horses: "We traveled in single file. I afterwards observed that it was impossible to make those cayuses travel in any other manner, even when on a wide river bar. At times some of us wished to engage in conversation and would endeavor to ride side by side, in an attempt to do so; but invariably one of the horses would force its way forward or drop to its accustomed place."

The party experienced the normal problems crossing enumerable river channels with pack horses, including losing some horses and dropping packs. Horses on ice is something I've never experienced but according to Young, they often cut footholds in ice for horses when crossing glaciers. Horses also fell into small crevasses.

Formed by the Russell Glacier on one side, and foothills of the high mountains extending on the other sides, the Skolai Basin stands as one of the most stunning places on Earth. I camped at the same place as Young's party with a magnificent view of Castle Mountain (where I took a full curl Dall) on one side and the Seven Sisters peaks on the other. "There one may watch the colors come and go on the cheeks of the Seven Sisters as the sun plays peek-a-boo around old Castle Mountain. While sitting there you can see numerous bands of mountain sheep," Young wrote.

These men experienced the same thrills but also the same exhaustion modern hunters do. After climbing up, down and around a mountain all day chasing a particular ram, Young reached the creek about dark but the horses had broken free and disappeared. In the book, Young admitted to becoming weak from hunger and total exhaustion but he didn't want to admit it to Bones. Since they couldn't find their party at night with no horses, they built a fire and stayed the night.

Young again and again experienced events and scenes so etched in the minds of all sheep hunters: "A small glacier overhung the crest a short distance from where I stood, with its color in sharp contrast to the rich red of the iron-stained cliffs

Although the great sheep hunters and outfitters have gone to that land where all rams wear 40-inch horns, you can still hunt the areas they opened up. Here guide Robert Napoleon looks over the famous Scoop Lake area of British Columbia.

directly beneath. I stood just below the crest of the mountain where I was protected from the wind. Not a sound reached my ear, except the trickle of water from the ice and snow. The sky was cloudless; the whole landscape appeared to be hushed and still, and a deep peace breathed over the entire region. I experienced a sense of loneliness as I gazed upon that immense chasm and the multitude of towering heights beyond. But it was a joyful loneliness brought about by the silence and the indescribable desolation. I felt a great desire that all my friends and comrades of the outdoors might share with me the deep emotion of the moment.''

After building a scow (more like a raft with sides) for the trip down the White River, Jacquot and the Indian guides headed on horseback for Bone's cabin on the south end of Kluane Lake. Bones was to take the hunters down the White on the scow and then pick up a steamer on the Yukon to Whitehorse. Unfortunately the over-laden scow ran into driftwood lodged against the shore. The boat soon capsized in the water and ice. The men managed to save only a gun, precious little food and blankets. The churning water claimed practically all of the 60-plus trophies (sheep, moose, caribou, bear).

The hunters ended up on a small island some 350 miles from Whitehorse with food for only four or five days. Due to Dr. Evan's poor physical condition they could not walk out and try to find help. Bones left the hunters, promising to return with help.

Fortunately Bones found another hunting party and returned for Young and his companions the next day. Rather than be safe, their troubles had just begun. The early winter killed and covered any available horse food. They had enumerable streams to ford and mountains to cross before they reached the trail to Jacquot's cabin on the north end of Kluane Lake.

Before reaching the lake, the now large party practically exhausted the little food supply. They existed on dirty rice (taken for dog food) fried in caribou fat. Game was not plentiful without traveling some distance and they could not afford the time.

At long last they arrived at Jacquot's homestead where they took a boat to Bone's place on Kluane Lake's south end. From there the trip was uneventful by wagon to Whitehorse and rail to Skagway. In all, four months passed from the time Young left home until he returned.

Young and his party suffered terrible hardships on this early trek to the northern sheep country but afterwards Young relished every moment: "We had gone far beyond the beaten trail and looked upon a great wilderness undefaced by the hands of man. I trust that I will always keep fresh the memory of the Northern Lights, the azure skies, the glorious sunsets and the beautiful mountain sheep as they grazed so peacefully on plots of green or wound their way over lofty crests."

As well as his early hunts in the north country, Charles Sheldon broke ground hunting desert sheep in the southwest. He hunted sheep in Mexico in the years 1898-1902 but did not keep a journal. He did, however, keep an excellent journal during the years 1912-1922.

G.O. Young hunted Castle Mountain in Alaska's Wrangell Range in 1919. The author killed his first Dall ram on the same mountain. Knowing you have stepped in the tracks of the early hunters makes one pause and remember.

Hunting along the Colorado River in 1912, Sheldon wrote, "Besides the magnificent views of perpendicular walled canyons and cliffs, I was most impressed with the profound silence. There were no murmurs of insects, not a falling rock—silence absolute."

Sheldon made good use of natives in the area as guides. The old Havasupai hunter, Sinyala, showed Sheldon blinds near the rim where a long time ago Indians used to lie and shoot sheep as they passed from the head of one canyon to another. Sheldon commented several times how rough and very dangerous the country was to hunt.

In 1913 Sheldon hunted the Gila Range in southern Arizona. They hunted from horseback and used a horse-drawn cart for supplies. One morning the wagon broke down but they repaired it with wire. Soon after, they ran into 30 fully armed men sitting around a fire. These Mexican revolutionists were as relieved that

Sheldon was only hunting sheep as Sheldon was that the Mexicans would not bother them.

One day Sheldon descended the far side of a range, "so steep as to be dangerous." After dark he traveled along the range until he felt horse tracks with his feet. Three hours later he reached camp. "My feet and legs were full of cactus thorns, but I found it glorious to be again in the mountains with all the beauty of the landscape."

A few days later Sheldon dropped three desert rams within minutes of each other. (This was before modern game laws were enacted.) After spotting four rams some half-mile in the distance, Sheldon stalked them much like a modern hunter would. He used a dry wash to cover part of the stalk and he walked with great caution. Alas, the rams had moved when he slowly crawled up the last ridge.

Sheldon found the rams across the next gully. He descended the perpendicular side of the small canyon and climbed the opposite side slowly so as to keep his breath. "Cocking my rifle, I worked around on my back and slowly rose in sitting posture with elbows on knees. The largest ram was a hundred feet above the others, standing on a rock, looking over the country—what a wonderful sight. The other three were feeding below."

One shot brought down the biggest ram. A second shot dropped another and a third one more. Sheldon felt the fourth too small to shoot.

Sheldon, not a biologist or anthropologist, was a careful observer and competent naturalist. His journals bulge with sightings and comments about all of nature from plant life, to small birds, to the largest mammals he encountered on his hunting trips. He represents a far different man from one L.S. Chadwick who, in 1936, took North America's longest-horned ram.

Chadwick, a rich sportsman hired Frank Golata and Curley Cochrane, about the only men who could take him into the game-rich east side of the Rockies in northern British Columbia. Chadwick had hunted with the famous Roy Hargreaves in Alberta in the past and took him along to be certain he had an expert sheep hunter with him.

In those days a long pack trip from Fort St. John was necessary to reach British Columbia's Prophet-Muskwa River. In all, the hunt lasted 60 days. One day Chadwick, Hargreaves and Golata left their camp to shoot a ram or perhaps a moose for camp meat. They spotted a large Stone ram at great distance but Chadwick took a shot with his .404 Jeffrey Magnum. The ram scampered off but

Chadwick said he thought he had hit it and told Hargreaves to go after the wounded ram.

Hargreaves took his .30-06 and found the ram. The initial wound proved superficial and did nothing more than draw a little blood. Although small of body, the ram's horns were magnificent. One horn measured 50⅛ inches long and the other 51⅝ with bases of nearly 15 inches. To date this is the only North American ram carrying horns over 50 inches. It was Hargreaves shot that finished off the record Chadwick ram. Many sportsmen, especially sheep hunters, consider the Chadwick ram the greatest big game trophy ever taken in North America. All that without the normal exciting, lung-busting stalk.

Since those days, many sportsmen have hunted the same area. In 1946, Jack O'Connor camped in the same spot as Chadwick and saw the same stump where they placed the head to be photographed. I hunted within 10 miles of the spot in the early 1970s.

Other than trappers and settlers who hunted for meat, the earliest sheep hunters in the American west were Europeans. One such hunter was William A. Baillie-Grohman, who grew up in the European Alps. After his hunt in the late 1870s Baillie-Grohman wrote, "The one or two specimens of bighorn I had seen in European collections, and especially some heads friends brought from the American wilds, had roused in me the wish to go and do likewise."

Braillie-Grohman bagged at least 70 or 80 rams one of which, he wrote, measured 19 inches at the base. He claimed to have seen an even larger ram. Like all sheep hunters, this European was most impressed by the sheep and the country they inhabit. "The bold and majestic ram, standing motionless on yonder giddy shelf, showing in perfect repose the classic outline of his noble head against the blue of the Rocky Mountain sky, as if cut in cameo fashion by the deft hand of a Grecian sculptor. He looks the emblem, not of agility as does the chamois, but of proud endurance. He is the truest type of the Rockies grand solitude and barren vastness."

The European stalked his largest ram for two days. After spotting him with other lesser rams, Braillie-Grohman decided he couldn't stalk them without spooking the sheep. He lay for more than an hour behind a stunted sagebrush waiting for the sheep to graze toward him. Just as he about gave up, the ram's head appeared 25 yards away looking right at the sagebrush.

With his gun beside him on the ground Braillie-Grohman could do nothing but wait. Other sheep appeared but left in a few minutes. As dusk approached, the giant sheep head disappeared from view. But where did it go? The hunter knew he couldn't find his horse and equipment in the dark so he elected to spend the night on the rocks and hunt the big ram the next morning.

After much climbing and walking the next morning, Braillie-Grohman at last found the huge ram again directly below, grazing at the foot of the precipice. One shot broke his backbone and the ram fell.

John Batten also hunted sheep long before sheep hunting became the ''in'' thing to do. He took his first ram in 1928 at the age of 16 and was still hunting in the late 1970s, perhaps longer. I suspect that Batten actively hunted sheep more years than anyone in North America and perhaps the world.

In 1924, Martin Bovey dropped the huge bighorn that, for many years, topped the record book. He was hunting with renown sheep outfitter Bert Riggall in Alberta. Andy Russell hunted and worked as a guide for Riggall starting in 1936. Grancel Fitz bagged his first desert ram in 1935 and his first Stone sheep in 1946. Jack O'Connor took his first ram, a desert, in 1934 and his last, a Stone sheep, more than 40 years later.

But with a few notable exceptions none of the early hunters took monster rams. In fact most bagged rams that would be considered average or even below average today. Young wrote of rams 34 or 35 inches on the curl as being large. Sheldon wrote of 35-inch desert sheep being the best he took. The list goes on. I firmly believe this says something about modern biologists and game managers since we take rams much larger than that today.

Modern sheep hunting and its tremendous popularity after World War II probably started with Jack O'Connor's wonderful magazine articles on sheep hunting. He wrote while still a professor of journalism at the University of Arizona and continued with several major outdoor magazines until his death. Jack wrote exciting and unforgettable accounts of hunting sheep all over North America in that particular style unmatched before or since.

After the war, the Alcan Highway opened Stone sheep country up to hunters with less time and less money than required by the long pack trips. O'Connor was one of the first to take advantage of the new highway (actually a dirt and gravel road). O'Connor's wife and hunting companion, Eleanor, was one of the first women sheep hunters and his son, Bradford, accompanied O'Connor on many

In nearly 50 years, no one has taken a ram with horns larger than this Chadwick ram, which breaks the 50-inch plus mark. Unfortunately, over the years the Stone ram has taken on a bighorn-like color due to age and dirt.

memorable hunts. Because of the Alcan most of the best known hunts and trophies for Stone sheep occurred after the war.

In direct contrast, the most memorable bighorn hunts occurred between 1900 and 1945 in Alberta and British Columbia just outside the two great Canadian national parks, Banff and Jasper. The railroad to Lake Louise acted as the jumping-off point for most hunts. Alberta was also home to the most famous old-time sheep guides. Bert Riggall guided Martin Bovey to his great ram. Other respected guides included, Ray Mustard, Roy and Jack Hargreaves, the Brewster brothers and Jack Browning.

Today, jets, Beavers, Otters and Super Cubs have opened even the remotest sheep country to time-conscious sheep hunters. Unfortunately our fast-paced living severely limits the time most modern hunters think they should spare away from business. Today, sheep hunts may last only a week or two. These hunters do miss a great deal by not using the time consuming pack trains.

Back in the late 1940s, writer, hunter, Grancel Fitz coined the term ''Grand Slam''—the taking of all four species of North American wild sheep. According to Fitz, Charles Sheldon collected the first grand slam. Colonel Wilson Potter of Philadelphia was the second to accomplish the feat and Dr. Wilson L. DuComb of Illinois the third. Ernst von Lengerke of New York and O'Connor rated fourth and fifth, and they may have completed their slams on exactly the same day in 1946.

Until his death, O'Connor berated his friend Fitz for using the term grand slam. O'Connor felt that the term and its publicity caused the obtaining of all four sheep species to be the most prestigious thing a big game hunter could do. O'Connor believed you should hunt sheep for the love of the animals and the beautiful country they inhabit. O'Connor was right, of course, but he must share some of the responsibility because of the many exciting articles he wrote on sheep hunting.

In 1957, Bob Housholder, a part-time desert sheep guide from Arizona assembled the names of some 50 hunters who had taken the four species. In 1967 he began sending out a newsletter to members who paid $20 per year to belong to the Grand Slam Club. Today the club lists 400 members (the author is number 273). There are, no doubt, more than 400 people worthy of membership, as you must pay annually to be recognized.

The past 15 years or so have produced many remarkable, and some would say disgusting, events by those wishing to join the ''elite.'' Several hunters have taken the entire slam in one season.

The author's grand slam of North American wild rams. The slam, when taken in the true spirit of sheep hunting, represents the highest honor for a North American sheep hunter.

If memory serves me right, one took the slam in one month.

While I agree with O'Connor's sentiments to a great extent, I also know that today many hunters still feel about their sport as the old-timers did. They hunt sheep because they love sheep, they love to be up on those high wind-swept ridges with the rams, the grizzly, the marmot, the eagle. They bring back memories of gut-busting climbs, of the wonderful aroma of fir and spruce, of sparkling streams and of winds so strong a man can't stand upright.

Most early grand slam takers loved the sheep and the country and were in no hurry to take their slam. Arvid Benson took his first ram in 1956 and completed the slam in 1961. Alex Cox dropped his first in 1948 but didn't complete his slam until 1966. Chris Klineburger hunted between 1957 and 1966 to fill his slam.

To many hunters, the term grand slam represents a well-deserved reward to the man who truly loves sheep and sheep hunting. He hunts for the love of the hunt, not for recognition. Only a few never hunt sheep again.

Today two of the four species are not too tough to obtain—the Dall and the Stone sheep. Rocky Mountain bighorns and the desert rams are much tougher. All desert sheep permits and most bighorn are allocated by a drawing. Alberta allocates a limited number of permits to each licensed bighorn outfitter so if you book a hunt with one of them you obtain the permit through him. Montana offers unlimited licenses in a few areas but these are tough to hunt and they close hunting within 48 hours after reaching a quota.

Alaska, the Yukon and the Northwest Territories all offer essentially unlimited Dall permits and anyone in decent shape should be able to take a good ram. Steve Peterson, Senior Staff Biologist with the Alaska Department of Fish & Game reports, "Anyone going sheep hunting should be able to walk 10 miles a day in tough terrain with up to a 60-pound pack on your back—often in rainy, snowy, windy and cold conditions. None of it is flat walking." British Columbia puts a quota on each licensed outfitter and again a hunter in decent shape should take a good Stone ram.

Other than Alberta, Wyoming offers the most bighorn permits to both residents and non-residents. Hunting can be tough and bighorn hunters show the lowest hunter success rate of all four species. Nevada offers the most desert sheep permits and taking a good desert sheep anywhere is easier than getting a good bighorn. Obtaining a permit is the hardest part of the hunt.

The best advice I can offer the potential sheep hunter is to apply for permits in all states offering a drawing. You may go years without drawing out but then someone must win and you can't win if you don't apply.

3

Wild Sheep
Of North America

According to biologists, only two species of wild sheep make their home in North America; the thinhorns, *Ovis dalli* and the bighorns, *Ovis canadensis*. Americans, being great dividers, have come up with a host of subspecies. However, for general use as well as official record keeping, we divide wild sheep into four groups: the Dall, *Ovis dalli dalli*; the Stone, *Ovis dalli stonei*; the Rocky Mountain bighorn, *Ovis canadensis canadensis* and the desert, *Ovis canadensis nelsoni* and related species.

Some people still insist that *Ovis dalli kenaiensis*—sheep from Alaska's Kenai Peninsula—should be separate, but they are classed as Dall sheep. Similarly, some insist that a separate subspecies *Ovis dalli fannini*, or fannin sheep, exists between the true Dall and the Stone sheep. According to the record book, any sheep with black hairs, other than tail (i.e. the fannin) are classed as Stone sheep. The fannin is usually lighter in color than the true Stone and may show only a dark saddle. They probably exist due to crossbreeding between Dalls and Stones.

Likewise many sportsmen, biologists and game departments list a separate bighorn, *Ovis canadensis californiana* or California bighorn. You'll find these sheep in Idaho, the Dakotas, British Columbia, Oregon, Washington, California and Nevada with limited numbers in other states. The Boone & Crockett Club insists these somewhat smaller sheep be classed with the true Rocky

Mountain bighorns, although many think they were originally a desert species from southern California. Today, biologists use the California bighorn extensively in transplant projects.

Although all are recorded as desert sheep, biologists list at least four subspecies: *Ovis c. nelsoni, mexicana, cremnobates* and *weemsi*. In general you'll find *nelsoni* in Nevada, *mexicana* in Arizona and Mexico and *cremnobates* and *weemsi* in Mexico.

For the remainder of this book we'll consider only the four species recognized by Boone & Crockett and Pope & Young and include all subspecies or invented names in one of the four. Also for the sake of simplicity I'll refer to the Rocky Mountain species (*O. c. canadensis*) as bighorns. So we will consider Dall, Stone, bighorn and desert sheep.

According to William Wishart, wildlife research biologist with Alberta's Fish and Wildlife Division, Asia is generally accepted as the ancestral home of North American sheep. Our sheep show characteristics closely related to the primitive Siberian snow sheep of northeastern Asia. They reached North America by way of the Bering Strait land bridge during the Pleistocene epoch.

Biologists offer various theories as to the causes for the evolution of the two species of North American wild sheep, the thinhorns and the bighorns. Some theorize that all the sheep came across during one land bridge.

Then with the coming of the great ice sheets, some moved farther south and eventually developed into bighorns. The others retreated north to Alaska's Brooks Range, where the snowfall was not heavy enough to form large masses of ice. These, they theorize, developed into the thinhorns.

Other respected scientists believe the sheep that evolved into bighorns came across before the great ice masses and moved south as far as Baja California.

Later, they maintain, some of the sheep moved north to become thinhorns. Others believe thinhorns evolved from sheep that came over during one of the last land bridges.

Today, the wide Peace River in British Columbia and Alberta, and the low, wet, heavy forests of British Columbia's Skeena Valley act as a formidable barrier to wandering sheep. We find no bighorns above the Peace River and no thinhorns below it.

Other than the pure white Dall sheep, great color variation exists within each species. In general, however, desert sheep are a lighter brown than the bighorns and Stone sheep run more to salt and pepper black or gray.

It is also possible to distinguish species by horn configuration. Dall and Stone sheep usually sport widespread horns and horns of the "argali" type that pinch in close to the face and then flare out. Bighorns normally produce a tighter or closer curl. Also, thinhorn sheep produce horns which are more triangular in cross-section, with a ledge or ridge on the outside of the horn. Bighorns and desert rams more normally are rounded in cross section and don't exhibit the ridge.

In practice, however, many thinhorns show round or tight horns and many bighorns have triangular or flaring horns. My desert ram (*nelsoni*) shows a ridge as prominent as my Dall. My desert also has a flaring horn. O'Connor repeatedly described Stone sheep with rounded horns and bighorns with flaring or argali horns.

Weight between individual sheep within a species also varies a great deal depending on genetics, food source and mineral content of the habitat. However, bighorns generally grow to the largest body weight, followed by the Stone, Dall and desert sheep.

Desert Sheep

Undoubtedly, desert sheep were the first wild sheep seen by Europeans in North America. In 1540, Pedro de Castadena, of Coronado's expedition, sighted sheep at the confluence of the Gila and San Francisco rivers in Arizona. "Sheep as big as a horse, with very large horns and little tails," Pedro wrote. Another soldier wrote in more detail, "found a ram's horn that was six feet long and as thick at the base as a man's thigh." We must pardon this hardy soul for slight exaggeration, but no doubt the rams looked huge compared with domestic sheep. The more northern species were not discovered for another 250 years.

According to Wishart, desert bighorn rams weigh between 127 and 190 pounds and adult ewes between 74 and 114 pounds. As with all animals, the desert sheep exhibit large differences in weight. Most biologists say the *nelsoni* and *weemsi* run smaller than the *mexicana*, but my *nelsoni* ram from Nevada weighed nearly as much as most bighorns and looked much larger than a number of Arizona *mexicana* rams I've seen.

While John Batten actively hunted sheep for more years than anyone, Jack O'Connor probably viewed and hunted more desert rams than anyone. O'Connor reported that desert bighorns were smaller than Rocky Mountain bighorns. Further, O'Connor reported seeing desert rams that would weigh between 215 and 220 on the hoof. Several other desert rams have been reported over 200 pounds. Desert rams also stand shorter at the shoulder than the bighorns of the north.

Desert sheep grow longer, more pointed ears than the northern species and generally have a longer tail. According to Lanny Wilson, wildlife biologist with the Bureau of Land Management (BLM) and one of the foremost sheep biologists in North America, desert sheep in Nevada, unlike other species, may exhibit pink, black or even polka-dot tongues. The tongue color, Wilson says, can further be associated with horn configuration, body shape and temperament.

Most desert sheep are tawny or buff in color, much lighter than northern bighorns. However, some run as dark or darker than bighorns. I've seen many bighorns with an almost buckskin hide that looked much lighter than my own desert ram. On the other hand my desert ram is lighter than any of my bighorns. All sheep show lighter color in fall and winter after their summer coat has been exposed to the sun for several months.

Even though desert ram horns normally run shorter around the curve than the northern rams, they may look much bigger due to the desert ram's thin neck, narrow body and shorter hair. Even a fair desert ram looks huge, especially on a skyline, to the hunter accustomed to bighorns. Desert ewes definitely grow much longer horns than their northern counterparts. The first desert ewe I ever saw looked much like a two-year-old (sometimes referred to as a sickle-head) ram.

Although you'll find several exceptions such as the 10,000-foot Mt. Hayford in Nevada, desert sheep usually inhabit much lower country than their northern cousins. In Sonora, Mexico, rams live on steep, rugged but relatively low mountains—from a few hundred to 4,000 feet above sea level. Desert sheep country can also be extremely hot during the day but become bitterly cold at night.

Natives, trappers and meat hunters shot by far the most desert sheep in the early days. When the first game laws were enacted all desert sheep were strictly protected.

During the 1930s and 1940s the Mexican government issued a few permits for museum or biological collecting. Jack O'Connor, Grancel Fitz and several other notable hunters obtained rams with these special permits.

In April, 1952, Nevada opened the first legal sheep season since modern game laws were written. Forty-six hunters took 15

Most desert bighorn sheep are tawny or buff in color. Horns on a desert ram may look tremendous in size, however, this is often due to the ram's thick neck, narrow body and short hair.

Huntable bighorn sheep populations can be found in mountainous areas from Alberta and British Columbia down through Idaho, Montana, Wyoming, Colorado and New Mexico. The older ram at right just approaches real trophy size. He needs another two years.

rams on this hunt. In January, 1953, Arizona issued 20 permits. Since that time Nevada, Arizona, Utah and New Mexico have offered permits for desert rams.

Rocky Mountain Bighorn Sheep

Franciscan missionaries on the California peninsula described bighorns in 1702. However, not until 1800 did Duncan McGillivray kill and preserve a bighorn in Banff, Alberta. The Royal Society of London named the new species *Ovis canadensis canadensis* in 1804, about the same time that Lewis and Clark expedition members hunted them near what is now Yellowstone National Park. Trappers, mountain men and a few hardy sportsmen hunted bighorns throughout the 19th century.

The heaviest of all wild sheep, a mature bighorn weighs between 160 and 315 pounds with ewes between 117 and 200 pounds. A California subspecies ram weighs less at 181 to 205 pounds. You may distinguish a bighorn from desert species by their shorter ears and shorter rows of teeth.

Like the desert sheep, a bighorn's coat color varies from dark brown to light or grayish brown with a white strip outlining the back of all four legs. O'Connor reported that, in general, bighorn coats lighten as the season progresses but darken with age. Apparently genetics or food have little to do with coat color since I've seen bighorn rams as dark as Stone sheep beside light colored, buckskin rams on the same mountain in Alberta. Everybody has their own taste but the most beautiful ram I ever saw had a dark chocolate body with a face nearly as black as a Stone sheep's body and dark, broomed, close curled horns.

Horns of adult bighorn rams generally are longer, more massive and less divergent than those of the desert and California rams. In the record books, bighorn rams score higher than any other sheep species. Since bighorns normally sport a tight curl close to the head, they are more apt to be broomed than the horns of other species. Given a choice, most trophy hunters prefer a well broomed ram to one with perfect points.

Bighorn rams carry the massiveness of their horns out farther on the curve than other species. In fact, in the case of gold rams, the first quarter circumference may be larger than the base. I've seen and taped many rams that measure the same at the base and first quarter.

Today, you'll find Rocky Mountain bighorns in mountainous areas from Alberta and British Columbia down through Idaho, Montana, Wyoming, Colorado and northern New Mexico. Nevada contains a huntable herd of bighorns as well as California and desert rams. Due to transplants and restocking, you'll find California sheep in Washington, Oregon, Idaho, British Columbia, California and the Dakotas. These states now offer some bighorn hunting. Wyoming, to the best of my knowledge, is the only state that has offered bighorn permits since their first game laws were enacted.

Stone Sheep

Due to their isolated habitat, the Stone sheep was the last of our North American wild sheep to be classified. In 1897, an American from Montana named Andrew Stone shot three of these beautiful rams in the Cassiar Mountains near the Stikine River in northern British Columbia. Because of the gold strikes, no doubt, some miners had shot and eaten stone sheep but didn't know they were an unlisted species.

Stone sheep undoubtedly show the greatest variation in color of the four species. They run from almost pure white to gray/brown, to a charcoal or blue/gray to nearly black. Typically, a Stone sheep's belly is white, legs are black/brown faced with white, rump is pure white and tail is black. In general, Stone rams are much darker at the southern part of their range and much lighter at the northernmost habitat. Salt and pepper best describes the head and saddle of typical Stone sheep.

Like all species of sheep, Stone sheep vary a great deal in weight. According to Wishart the average mature stone ram weighs 220 to 230 pounds with a few over 250 pounds. O'Connor wrote of taking little, mature rams in the Atlin Lake, British Columbia area that wouldn't dress out at more than 120 pounds.

The amber-brown horns of Stone sheep are generally thinner but longer than those of bighorns. They run thicker and heavier than the average Dall ram. Many Stone rams show an argali curl or wide spread. Some show a curl nearly as tight as a bighorn. Most, however, show a greater tip to tip measurement than the horn edge to horn edge measurement.

Chadwick's Stone ram, taken near the Muskwa-Prophet River, still ranks as the only ram in North America ever taken with horns measuring over 50 inches on the curl. This beautiful ram exhibits a typical argali configuration. The horns pinch in toward the jaw and then flare out past the horn edges.

Stone sheep range from the Peace River in British Columbia north into southcentral and southeast Yukon with perhaps a few found in the extreme southwest part of the Northwest Territories. Outfitters for Stone sheep receive quotas based on average kill and population estimates for all nonresident hunters.

Dall Sheep

To many sportsmen, the pure white Dall ram with its golden, flaring horns is the most striking wild sheep. L.M. McQueston, an early frontiersman in Alaska, collected a specimen in the winter of 1879-80 which was the first Dall classified. These sheep contrast with their habitat much better than the brown or gray sheep to the south. Spotting their white coats against the treeless green of their summer and early fall alpine environment is easy for neophyte and expert alike. Only when snow falls does the white coat offer protection for the sheep. These sheep grow a much thicker fine wool undercoat than the more southern species.

On the average, Dall rams don't grow as heavy as Stone rams. Wishart puts the average weight of Dall rams at 180 to 220 pounds

Called the fannin sheep by some, this beautiful ram is actually a Stone sheep. Note the steep, rugged terrain that is typical of good Stone sheep habitat. Because of its isolated habitat, the Stone sheep was the last North American wild sheep to be classified.

and ewes between 100 and 124 pounds. To prove the exceptions, O'Connor reports once shooting a 13-year-old Dall ram that didn't weigh 135 pounds.

One fact is certain: Dall sheep are the most plentiful of the four types of wild sheep in North America. Fortunately in many areas civilization has not affected Dall sheep populations as much as the other species.

Dull gold or faded lemon best describes the color of Dall horns. Most exhibit a definite ridge on the outside of the horn. Dall horns are much more apt to pass the magic 40-inch mark than any other species. Also, due to their normal wide flare or argali curl, Dall sheep are much more apt to have perfect points. Normally only close curl horns show much brooming. In my experience, the farther north you go the less sparring exists between rams which can break points. You won't find nearly as heavy a horn or as large a circumference on Dalls as the southern sheep.

In the latest record book, a Dall taken in Alaska's Wrangell Mountains by Harry L. Swank, Jr., topped the list, scoring 189⅝ points. Second place is still held by Frank Cooke's 185⅝-point ram. The Cooke ram almost made the super 50-inch mark and probably did when green. Dry, one horn measured 49⅘ inches.

Dall sheep range from the far northernmost mountains of Alaska, through the Yukon and into the westernmost range of the Northwest Territories. You'll also find huntable Dall populations in extreme northwest British Columbia.

Ram's Headgear

Since a ram's headgear is true horn compared with the antlers of the deer family, they continue to grow throughout the ram's lifetime. These great horns also tell the story of the ram's life, his age, his battles, his good years, his bad and to a certain extent, his species. No two sets of horns look exactly alike and hard-core sheep hunters can recognize a particular set of horns years later.

Horn shape and configuration give a good indication of what region the ram came from. BLM wildlife biologist Lanny Wilson can usually pinpoint within a few miles exactly what mountain a given ram came from. My Nevada *nelsoni* ram looks much more like the flaring curl typical of *mexicana* rams than the tighter curl *nelsoni*. Wilson knew I shot a desert ram but didn't know what state it came from. However, upon seeing the horns he told me it came from Sheep Peak, in the Sheep Range of the Desert National

Only when snow falls does the white coat of a Dall sheep offer protection. For neophyte and expert alike, spotting these sheep against the treeless green of their summer and early fall alpine environment is easy.

Wildlife Range, Nevada. He missed by only two or three miles.

A ram's horns grow by pushing up from the base. As the ram ages, the horn grows longer and larger at the base. With few exceptions the horn puts on much more length as a youngster, then less and less each year. A slight hormonal change and the time of little food in the winter causes a temporary stoppage of horn growth and an annual ring forms much like the rings on a tree. Lesser rings form due to diet changes during the year.

Some horns, especially those on younger rams, are easy to age by the annual rings. Others, particularly old rams, are tougher. The rings near the base of old rams are close together and hard to distinguish. Also, older rams may have broomed or otherwise lost much of the horn tips. Very often you can age rams with broken horns by starting at the third or fourth year ring. Two or three slight rings most often make up the third year ring and the fourth year ring is normally the deepest.

Actually any ram shot in the fall will not be six or seven or whatever years old. Rather he will be 6½ or 7½ since the lambs are born in the spring. Because bighorn and Stone rams rub their horns on resinous trees more than the desert or Dall species, they become darker in color and tougher to age. The youngest ram I ever shot was 5½ years old (my first) and the oldest 11½ (my last).

Most dedicated trophy hunters believe an old ram, especially a desert or bighorn, with well-broomed tips represents a much finer trophy than one with perfect tips. These rams look bigger, look tougher and look older.

Brooming simply means a horn has been broken or rubbed off. I've seen many horns with all their lamb year broomed off and a few with both the lamb year and yearling year missing. If more horn is missing the ram probably broke the horn rather than broomed it on purpose.

The exact cause of brooming brings up more arguments among hunters than anything else about wild sheep. Some maintain that fighting causes the brooming. Others insist that they lose horn tips from falling. At the present time most knowledgeable sportsmen and biologists believe the rams rub their horn tips on rocks and gravel for better side vision.

In all probability, all three theories contribute to broken or broomed horn tips. When rams fight the horn bases do not come in direct contact with each other as might be expected. Rather the first blow is with tilted heads so the base of one may contact the tip of the other. Rams do take bad falls. Sure-footed as wild sheep are,

This young ram will start brooming his horns in another year or two. Note how the tips would otherwise grow beside his eyes and block peripheral vision.

they live in a rugged country and do experience falls.

Most horns with missing tips show them rubbed off smooth and round. I've seen some broomed back far enough from the tip that the stub looked as big around as a man's wrist. These tips were not broken from fighting or a fall. They must have been rubbed off on purpose. Bighorn rams, somewhat more than desert sheep and much more than the Stone and Dall sheep, grow a tight curl horn, one that does not flare out or go on a wide curl. Look at an old broomed bighorn ram from the side and you'll see the ram has much better side vision with the horn tip broomed back. In fact, many old rams could not see sideways without the brooming.

Many mature rams, especially desert and bighorns, have chips or great chunks missing from their horns. This most often occurs at that point on the horn where they meet another horn in battle or sparring. Since desert sheep habitat is arid the horns are more brittle and therefore they show more missing chunks than the other species. A large chunk missing near the first quarter measurement cost me nearly two inches in scoring and would have cost more if it had come at exactly the first quarter.

Although all four species will show actual brooming and chips, Dall and Stone sheep normally have more perfect points and very few chips out of the horn. In my experience the northern sheep fight less than the southern sheep.

In October, northern rams start looking for the ewes they moved away from last winter. Their necks begin to swell with the rut and the semi-friendly sparring of summer and early fall turns into serious battles. Sometimes two rams only interlock horns and twist, but usually they charge and hit head on. When you consider that two large rams charging at perhaps 20 miles per hour can produce over a ton of impact, you can understand the source of the phrase "battering ram."

The rut for northern sheep peaks in November and December so the ewes drop their lambs in late May and June when conditions are best for survival. Desert sheep mate during August and September, therefore, the births occur in February and March when vegetation is greening from winter rains.

Rams do not gather harems as elk do. Nor do they stay with a single female like moose. Promiscuous best describes the wild ram. Normally the heaviest horned ram breeds most of the ewes. However, smaller rams complete the breeding while the older rams occupy themselves breeding or fighting. Often smaller rams do not compete because of previous order of male dominance in the strict

The annual rut is the only time that bighorn rams will be found near ewes and lambs. Special bow seasons open during the rut offer bowhunters a tremendous opportunity.

ram hierarchy (more on this later). After breeding, the rams separate from the ewes and wander off alone or in bachelor bands.

Ewes of all species prefer to drop their lambs in a hidden or rough spot such as a ledge, the base of a steep cliff or in a shallow cave. Young sheep can run within a few days of birth. The ewe usually weans the lamb in two months, about the same time, horns begin to sprout. Lambs normally stay with the ewes year-round until they are two or three years old when the young rams leave to find other males about the same age.

Young rams and even older rams that for some reason migrate and join other bands, must find their rightful place in the social hierarchy. The system of rank and dominance is vigorously upheld in every ram band. The rank depends on strength and horn size. As rams mature they display their horns to other rams as symbols of dominance. Normally only rams of similar size do real battle for rank. Others often spar playfully but not with the intensity of equal rams.

Watching equal rams battle is a sight a hunter will never forget. The rams paw at one another and perform several other dominance rituals accurately described by Dr. Valerius Geist in his work *Mountain Sheep—A Study In Behavior And Evolution*, including horn displays, low stretch, twist, head shakes, rubbing and nuzzling. Then comes the actual clash.

The ram initiating the clash faces his opponent, lifts one front leg and tilts his head sideways. If he tilts his head to the left, the left horn will make first contact. His eyes stay wide open, looking at the opponent, and his ears lay back flat. The ram rises on his hind legs and the front legs rear up. With eyes fixed on his opponent, the ram charges forward. As the body straightens out and begins to fall, the head and neck are propelled toward the target faster than the body.

Rather than meet full on base to base, the ram turns his head so the narrow edge of one horn meets the other with much more force pinpointed in a small area. He then rotates the head to bring the other horn into contact. The clash echoes through the mountains and may be heard over a mile away. Rams soon learn their rank in the hierarchy.

Sometimes several rams take part in a sort of melee. I really believe this type of behavior is more play than serious dominance battles. Once in Alberta my outfitter, Dewey Browning, and I heard several clashes but couldn't find the sheep. Finally Dewey said he found them but couldn't put his binoculars down long enough to show me or he'd lose track of the rams. With his excellent directions, I finally located the rams in a tiny opening in heavy timber across the canyon.

The opening could only hold two rams at a time. Due to considerable difference in color and horn size we put together a picture of rams at play. Two rams would clash, shake their heads and back out of the opening. Then two different rams entered the arena and clashed. Each pair took turns until at least eight different rams took part and they started over again. The show lasted at least two hours before silence again overtook the mountains. Dewey and I just looked at each other. No words were needed.

Favorite Sheep Habitat

Depending on habitat, weather and hunting pressure, wild rams can live to be 12 or 13 years old. My oldest ram spent 12 summers in the high basins but a friend bagged a ram they aged at 13½ years. A few have been known to live over 15 years in semi-captivity on preserves.

All mountain sheep require a dry climate, sufficient feed and rough country for protection from predators. North America's wild sheep have found these needs in areas that reach 80 degrees below zero in the winter and in areas that reach 125 degrees in the summer.

Sheep do not do well in areas of heavy rainfall, deep snow and heavy timber. Both O'Connor and Geist report that sheep do not like timber and in fact will go to extreme measures to avoid timber. Geist even reports their heart rate jumps if they are forced into timber.

I hesitate to disagree with such respected sheep authorities but I have seen sheep go into timber for no apparent reason and even bed in timber. Perhaps sheep in certain areas have taken more to the timber because of hunting pressure or advancing civilization.

One day in Alberta, Dewey and I sat quietly eating lunch in a little basin right at the edge of the trees just off Alberta's Forbidden Creek. We'd built a small fire for warmth and to heat sandwiches. Suddenly Dewey pointed and I looked up to see a ewe and lamb come down off the huge rock field. They walked into the timber followed by at least 18 others. They not only marched calmly into the timber but came within 30 yards of our fire. They stayed in the timber for nearly an hour before going out the other side to graze in a little pasture.

Another time we found sheep beds in lush grass in dense timber where a spring seeped forth its cool water. The sheep not only came into the timber to drink but also to loaf and sleep.

Actually, wild sheep inhabit a great variety of terrain. But one thing is common to all sheep habitat: rough country. Although sheep prefer gentle slopes and large basins, they know they can traverse over rock slides and steep cliffs better than their soft-footed predators.

Sheep in nearly all areas inhabit different feeding grounds in winter than during the rest of the year. This winter ground may be higher or lower than the summer range depending on snow depth and available feed. In some areas, high winds keep the highest ridges and plateaus free of snow, whereas snow may clog the lower country.

Dall sheep habitat is typically alpine, steep, open grasslands interspersed with broken cliffs and shale slopes on recently glaciated mountains. Most are located above timberline which in most areas means above 2,500 feet.

Typical Stone sheep habitat is somewhat more sub-alpine in nature with more precipitation than Dall habitat. You'll find the open basins smaller with more thickets of dwarf birch and alpine fir. Below the sheep basins you'll find aspen, Engelmann spruce and lodgepole pine, often in large stands.

The mountains in bighorn habitat usually stand taller and bigger than other sheep habitat. Peaks soar to 11,000 feet or better with timberline much higher than sheep country farther north or south. Basins tend to be smaller and sheep are found in smaller bands.

Desert sheep country is much rougher and contains much less vegetation than more northern sheep country. Sheep often feed down in the valleys and then wander to higher country to bed down. I've hunted desert sheep country where you didn't get off a horse all day except to glass the basins, and I've hunted desert country where a horse could break a neck in the first steps. Some desert country holds little vegetation and in others you'll find huge trees. Vegetation in the Desert National Wildlife Refuge grows just the opposite than in north country mountains. At the bottom only cactus, Joshua, yucca and other desert plants grow. As you ride higher, you find pinyon and juniper stands before you run into huge stands of ponderosa pine. Near the tops of the peaks, only stunted, centuries-old bristle cone pine grow. In the north, vegetation thins as you progress up the mountains.

4

Hunting Dall Sheep

"Come on Lloyd! Joe spotted four rams. Two look pretty good," my dad whispered as loud as he could. His eyes sparkled as I grabbed my rifle and met him. We'd seen several different ram bands that day but the sheep either looked too small or they avoided our stalks. We had taken a break for peaches and tea at the tent high atop Chitistone Mountain in Alaska's Wrangell Range when the action started.

After reaching Joe we watched the rams feed in a small basin across the canyon to see if they would stay put. Our guides, Joe D'Errico and Jim Houston, decided the best two rams would measure 37 or 38 inches.

The rams laid down about 6:30 p.m. Dad decided the hike around the head of the canyon to get above and close to the rams was too far, as tired as he felt at this late hour. Since we were only a short walk from camp, we stayed to put the rams to bed. We'd know where to start the next day.

One of the smaller rams rose and ambled away but returned to the others when none followed him. A few minutes later the other small ram wandered off but like his companion, he too returned when nobody followed. Just about the time we decided these Dall sheep were down for the night, all four rams rose and marched single file toward the saddle at the end of the basin.

"Come on. Maybe we can cut them off," Joe ordered.

As usual the rams made much better time than four huffing and puffing humans. The beautiful white creatures went over the top at least 10 minutes before we got within range. Going on to the saddle, we passed our favorite spot on the mountain. Light from the sun, low in the west, made the remaining ice on the little indigo lake shine like a mirror. At 8 p.m. we spotted two of the sheep far below in the bottom of a large basin. After a freeze-dried supper cooked on our tiny backpack stove we snuggled into our down bags near midnight.

Early the next morning we made a quick breakfast with water carefully saved from the night before. The tiny rivulet we used as a water source always dried up during the cold night and flowed again only after the sun melted a little snow or ice. Four well-camouflaged ptarmigan in their half white, half brown autumn plumage, scampered away as we started up the hill. (I have yet to see a ptarmigan fly).

After hiking uphill past our shimmering lake we reached the ridge above the basin in an hour. Three of the four rams lay in the shale over 1,000 feet below us. Apparently one of the larger rams had left the little band. Although the largest ram wasn't far away in a horizontal plane, he was at the extreme limit of dad's range or perhaps a little past, almost straight down. With no certain prospects for a better shot, dad decided to try from there.

"Hold low on his back, almost to his tail or you'll shoot high," I recommended. The ram lay facing away from us. Dad scooted to the edge of the rim and laid his .30-06 Remington over a down vest. Jim held his legs. Dad's back expanded as he took a deep breath and squeezed. Rocks spattered just above the ram's nose. The ram leaped and sprinted away almost in one motion. Dad tried a shot at the running ram but without success.

The two smaller rams also trotted off but strangely none of the three rams ran far. In fact the big one lay down again and the other two grazed. I'm sure they didn't know where the shots came from and when they could find no danger, continued with their routine. We waited to see if they would stay put.

An hour later Joe said we should work down a dry wash out of sight and then climb back up the ridge to a position beside the basin. The slippery talus-covered ridge was too steep to walk down. Near the bottom we had to climb down a steep white cliff one at a time. When Jim disappeared from sight, we heard rocks falling and a terrible thud. Fortunately, it was only his pack.

Going up the ridge proved much tougher than coming down.

Bill Hutchens and his fine Dall sheep taken in the Wood River area of northern Alaska. Bill's ram sports the thin horns and wide spread typical of sheep from that area.

Most of the way Dad and I could only trudge eight or ten steps before resting our throbbing legs. It seemed nearly straight up. By the time we crept over the edge every muscle in my legs screamed for relief and my chest felt like someone had beat on it.

One sickle-head ram appeared below, but we couldn't see the others. Jim inched his way around the corner to get a different line of sight. Spotting another ram, he crabbed his way back to Dad. While they crept into position, the ram wandered beneath Joe and I. Dad returned just in time to lay down and take the ram with one shot.

After the required back slapping, whooping and hand shaking, Dad and I looked for an easier route back to the top while the guides caped the ram. Hopefully we would not have to climb down and back up, retracing our earlier steps. By staying on a sheep trail right on the very edge of the ridge we avoided the slippery talus.

Three hours later Dad and I arrived at our favorite lake just above camp, dog tired and foot sore but elated. Joe and Jim appeared over the top only a few minutes after we sat down. After stuffing ourselves on delectable backstrap we sat back and watched the magenta sunset paint a spectacular rose hue across the canyons and mountaintops at twilight.

Jack O'Connor once wrote, "The principles of sheep hunting are really very simple. The hunter must see the sheep before the sheep sees him. Then he must select a route where the wind is right and where he can stay out of sight of the sheep. Then he sneaks up and shoots the sheep."

O'Connor recommended exactly the right theory. However, in practice, each situation is a bit different requiring a bit different strategy. If there is such a thing as a typical Dall sheep hunt, Dad's ram in Alaska provided a typical hunt. Later in the hunt my ram offered a completely different plan.

Many Dall hunts start from the mountaintops or at least near the tops rather than from the bottoms as is more usual with Stone or bighorn hunts. Since you may camp high up with the sheep you need not hurry a late afternoon stalk or even start a stalk that darkness might overtake. You actually start hunting the minute you step out of the tent. In fact, on that particular hunt, we hunted so close to camp that we could return for a bite to eat or drink without loosing any time.

However, the experience also points out one trait that Dall rams exhibit much more than the species farther south. While other rams stay in a given basin no less than all day and in most cases several days, Dall sheep move quite often between basins. They'll stay on the same mountain or group of mountains, but they do move. I remember one band of bighorns in Alberta that stayed in the exact same basin at least five days in a row.

Even though we camped within a couple hundred feet of the top of Chitistone, we still had to make arduous climbs up and down on the final stalk. Deep, straight-walled canyons cut Dall country just as they do most good sheep habitat. G.O. Young experienced many such climbs up, down and around the ridges to get within range of his largest Dall back in 1919.

Other than climbing to the high basins and the final stalk, most sheep hunting involves much more sitting and looking than any other big game hunting. You spend hours with your binoculars searching for rams. Although you still spend time with binoculars and certainly you spend a lot of time with a spotting scope, Dall

While other sheep often stay in one basin for several days, Dall sheep move between basins. They may stay on the same mountain or group of mountains, but they are not stationary. A mobile backpack camp is often the best way to stick with these sheep.

sheep hunting involves much less binocular time than southern sheep hunts.

Unless you hunt late in the season or have unexpected early snows, the pure white Dalls against the lush green alpine carpet stand out like a diamond in a coal bin. Even neophytes can spot the beautiful sheep almost as quick as a veteran guide. In contrast, you can often spend hours with binoculars trying to find a well-camouflaged desert sheep in its gray and brown habitat.

You will use a spotting scope as much on a Dall hunt as any other sheep hunt. I can't count the number of miles or the number of tough climbs my spotting scope has saved over the years. In Dall country you can estimate the horns from a great distance after you spot a ram with your eyes or binoculars. Then you need only make that agonizing climb if the ram is worthwhile. Normally, I only carry one spotting scope between the guide and myself, so my binoculars get a lot of use just admiring the sheep while the guide uses the scope.

Sometimes you get so discouraged you try to make sheep grow

in the spotting scope. On one Alaska trip, we fought our way up the mountain from the gravel bar through a jungle of willow and alder. A machete would have been handy. The thick, tall brush all grew pointing downhill so we continually had brush poke us. According to my daily notebook, the five-hour climb was the toughest I ever made.

After spending the night in backpack tents, we walked the top ridge the next morning. By this time I'd climbed up, down and around every mountain in the neighborhood. We spotted two half-hook rams on the next ridge beside a prominent butterfly-shaped patch of snow. As the afternoon wore on, we couldn't find any other rams. Every half hour or so I turned the spotting scope back on the two rams. Each time I thought they looked bigger. By evening I was almost ready to shoot one. Fortunately I came to my senses.

Each and every stalk on wild sheep is different, but in general you want to find the sheep, let them lie down around mid-morning and then stalk them. If possible all sheep hunters should end the stalk above the trophy. While rams, like all animals, do look uphill, they don't expect danger from above and often never look that direction.

On a stalk, you may be out of sight of the rams for several hours. If you start the stalk while the sheep graze, they may wander quite a distance while you make the stalk. But if you wait until they lay down for their mid-morning siesta, the rams are much more apt to be very near where you last saw them. Rams may get up and stretch a bit or kick a rock out of their beds, but they stay quite close until they get up to feed again late in the afternoon.

Not waiting for them to bed down nearly cost me a fine trophy on the same Alaska hunt when Dad killed his ram in 1977. The hunt started and progressed much differently than Dad's hunt, but it ended in "typical" fashion, with a climb to near exhaustion before I shot a ram.

After landing in the Super Cub on a rough gravel bar near Russell Glacier, I spotted seven rams in a mile wide area of moraine and icy creeks. While waiting for outfitter Gary LaRose to fly my guide, Joe, in, I watched the rams feed on the side of the mountain not 200 feet above the moraine. They disappeared for a time but reappeared in a few minutes. Joe and I pitched our tent on a mossy knoll above a little glacial stream and watched the rams until the sun set.

Most sheep hunting involves much more sitting and glassing than any other big game hunting. Once you find the sheep, let them lie down before you begin the stalk. If possible, end your stalk above the ram.

It is illegal to hunt the same day you're airborne in Alaska, so I fell asleep dreaming of easy sheep horns and delicious sheep steaks.

The next morning we walked down to the first fast-moving creek. But how could we cross the stream, and the mile flat without the sheep seeing us? The sheep fed even lower on the mountain than before, so we crossed the creek after first taking our boots and pants off.

Soon after crossing, we discovered we could not progress across the flat without spooking the rams. Ancient glaciers had pushed the moraine into a few little hills but not nearly enough to hide a stalk. We watched the rams all day with binoculars and a spotting scope. We did learn one ram carried a fine curl and a quarter set of horns, but we could do nothing but watch. When we crawled into the tent the rams still fed low on the mountain.

We decided to get up before sunrise the next morning and race across the flat before the rams had enough light to see us. Unfortunately, the sun gave off enough light on our arising at 4 a.m. to foil our plans. After crossing the creek, we waited until the rams slipped into a little cut out of sight. We made it about halfway before they came out and pinned us down again. We ate a hasty breakfast and waited.

Clouds came in and dropped light sprinkles on us. About the same time, the rams went into another cut higher up and clouds offered some cover. We hurried to the base of the mountain and found another icy stream to cross. This time, I took my only dry socks off, put my boots back on and laced them as tight as possible. On the other side, the dry socks quickly absorbed the little moisture I took in the boots.

We slipped and slid up a steep, wet draw to reach the little plateau where we last saw the sheep. We huddled behind a huge boulder to keep out of the rain and strong wind. Between wet outer clothes from the rain and wet inner clothes from sweating, I nearly froze waiting for the weather to clear.

Alas, we could not find the rams on the plateau. Starting toward the rim to check below we saw rams above us. The sheep spotted us and sprinted even higher on the mountain. We huddled behind a large rock until they settled again, then crept down and across a deep ravine and out of sight. After the four-hour heartbreaking and gut-busting climb, much of it on hands and knees, we found the rams about 300 yards below us. I looked up and found we were near the top of the mountain. Somehow the shot seemed anticlimactic. But my dreams of an easy sheep hunt certainly proved untrue.

Unpredictable weather is guaranteed on Dall sheep hunts. You must prepare for any weather even on July or August hunts. Dr. Robert Broadbent, of Reno, Nevada, learned this on his 1959 hunt in the Wrangells: "We spent a week hunting sheep out of that spike camp and it rained every day. It didn't always rain hard. Some days it rained harder. When the clouds lifted sufficiently for us to locate a band of sheep on a mountainside, the animals would invariably become shrouded once more in the wet and gloom by the time we'd make our climb. I kept the muzzle of my rifle taped to keep the water from running down the barrel!"

Dr. Roy Schultz, found cold, wet, miserable conditions on his Dall sheep hunt: "I climbed my first sheep mountain in the Yukon during the fall of 1967. The day I killed my sheep, the weather was as rough as it comes. It rained in the morning when my guide and I rode our horses as far as they could go up a mountain. Then we started climbing on foot. Halfway to the peak we were stopped by fog so thick that we could see nothing. Finally it cleared, but by the

Leland Speakes is shown here with his Dall ram taken while hunting in the Yukon. Yukon's Pelly Mountains offers more vegetation and more gently sloping mountains than Alaska's Wrangells and Chugach areas.

time we were three-fourths of the way to the top, wind-driven hail and snow belted us.''

"We kept going, even up one cliff that we had to climb by finding handholds in rock crevices. At the crest we spotted a basin that held 18 sheep, including three good heads. We had worked up a sweat climbing the mountain, but after stalking to within 300 yards of the Dalls we were so cold in the bitter wind that we couldn't hold our binoculars steady.

"My guide finally picked out the best ram and told me to nail him. I was shaking a little from both cold and excitement, so I rested my .300 Wthby Mag. on a rock. My first slug went over the sheep's back, but the second dropped him,'' concluded Schultz.

Depending on the location, Dall sheep hunts are conducted using a variety of methods. In many areas, especially in Alaska, so little natural horse food exists that using horses is impractical. Mountains in such areas as the Wrangells rise too steeply for even the most sure-footed horses.

Small planes such as Super Cubs with balloon tires do much of the work of horses and trucks in Alaska. Most often your outfitter flies you in to a gravel bar at the base of a mountain or a ridge. Then you either hunt from base camps and climb each day or climb with backpack camps and hunt from higher on the mountain. With backpack camps you can move and change camps at will.

I've been dropped off as low as 500 feet above sea level and climbed with a backpack camp to over 6,000 feet and I've been dropped off as high as 5,000 feet and made camp right there. However, hunting from a base camp and climbing each day offers the advantage of larger tents and a better food supply. Backpack camp food must, by necessity, consist mostly of lightweight freeze-dried food. Some outfitters attempt air-drops after you've been high on a mountain a few days. By packing canned goods around paper towel rolls outfitters can push boxes out of the slow moving planes at low altitudes.

In other areas, notably certain areas in the Yukon, enough natural horse food exists to sustain a few horses. In these areas you can ride partway up the more gently sloping mountains and therefore hunt out of well set up base camps. Or you can ride quite a distance from base and hunt from spike camps but with much more substantial food than hunting from backpack camps.

Backpack camps without a doubt offer more mobility than any other camp. However, at my age I look for a bit more comfort and the great help horses offer. Younger men may opt for the exciting

A few outfitters, especially in the Northwest Territories, use pack dogs to take the load off hunters on backpack hunts. These two fine dogs belong to outfitter Greg Williams.

backpack hunts and in certain areas they offer about the only means of locating the big old rams that have learned to avoid habitat near airplanes and horses.

A few outfitters, especially in the Northwest Territories, offer a unique backpack hunt. One such outfitter, Greg Williams, of Nahanni Butte, developed pack dogs to help take the weight off of his guides and hunters on long, rough backpack trips.

These dogs fit in the back of a Super Cub for the flight into the hunting area. Then the dogs carry much of the hunter's gear and equipment. I'd think you could move much farther each day with the dogs' help. The stout dogs can pack out a sheep and a half of boned meat over 20 miles of talus slides, cliffs and rivers.

Greg's dogs are very well-mannered and have yet to spook a ram. Veteran hunter Bob Strong used the pack dogs on his wife's archery Dall hunt. "Pack dogs have to be a coming thing in all kinds of mountain hunting," said Strong.

"Typical" Dall sheep country perhaps varies more than any other sheep country, but all is gorgeous beyond belief. In Alaska's far north Brooks Range, you'll find rolling mountains between 2,000 and 3,000 feet and little vegetation other than low grass, moss and lichens. The Alaska Range in central Alaska offers a stark contrast to the more northern areas. Here you find towering peaks such as the 20,000-foot Mt. McKinley.

Glaciers cut the Wrangells and Chugach ranges in the southeastern part of Alaska's sheep country. When viewed from backpack camps in the high country, these glaciers look much like multi-lane super highways. As small glaciers unite to form larger ones, the dirt and rock they dig from the side of mountains forms lines in the larger ice flow which resemble the lane dividers in a highway.

The Yukon's Pelly Mountains offers more vegetation, especially more horse food and more gently sloping mountains than the Wrangells and Chugach areas. The great Mackenzie Range in the Northwest Territories offers too much variety to really classify. It ranges from low rolling mountains to high rugged peaks. Actually all Dall sheep areas vary greatly, but the above generalizations hold true in most cases.

Recommending the best area to hunt any wild sheep brings about many arguments. Perhaps the answer is for each sheep hunter to first decide what he wants.

Does he want an area with the most rams? Does he want an area with the best chance at a real trophy ram? Often a trophy area may not hold as many sheep. Does he want a backpack hunt, a horseback hunt or a base camp hunt? Does he want to fish and hunt other species?

Because of the vast, remote wilderness areas involved, even local fish and game departments can't offer accurate population estimates for Dall sheep. However, most experts agree that 30,000 to 50,000 sheep make their homes in Alaska's mountainous areas. According to Donald E. McKnight, acting Deputy Director of the Alaska's Department of Fish and Game, sportsmen harvest 1,000 to 1,100 rams each year. The Brooks Range in the far north and the Alaska Range in the center of the state, no doubt, contain the largest sheep herds.

You'll find somewhat fewer sheep in the Wrangells and Chugach, but on the average, rams from these southeastern ranges grow more massive horns than those in the north. Often Brooks and Alaska Range rams grow long horns but they normally don't

Recommending the best area to hunt Dall sheep brings about many arguments. Perhaps the answer is for each sheep hunter to first decide what he wants. Is he interested in a good chance for a ram, or a good chance for a trophy ram? This respectable Dall ram was taken by Wilson Stout.

measure nearly as big around the base or the quarters as the southeastern sheep. Dall sheep also make their home in Alaska's Talkeetna Mountains and in parts of the Kenai Peninsula.

Although various biologists and game managers disagree on the figure, the Yukon probably holds somewhere in the neighborhood of 18,000 to 20,000 sheep. Hunters harvest about 250 to 300 each year. Due to the difference in size, the Yukon holds many more sheep per square mile than Alaska. Yukon rams are more apt to grow heavy horns like those from the Wrangells or Chugach than the northern Alaska rams. You can also find many more Yukon outfitters using horses than Alaska outfitters.

The Mackenzie Mountains of extreme western Northwest Territories (NWT) probably hold 3,000 to 8,000 Dall sheep, although biologists there don't offer any specific figures. Some 150 to 200 rams are taken in the NWT each year by nonresidents, along with 20 to 25 by resident hunters. Not long ago only one or two outfitters offered hunting in the Territories but now the government lists eight outfitters operating in the Mackenzies. Older sheep literature claims that rams taken from the NWT run smaller and thinner horned than those from Alaska and the Yukon. However, the new outfitters go into areas previously not hunted and bring out some fantastic rams. In fact, for the last several years, NWT rams have taken most of the awards at the Foundation for North American Wild Sheep competition.

Getting into Dall sheep country can be easy or tough depending on where you live and where you hunt. Most Brooks Range hunters fly into Fairbanks or Kotzebue via Seattle depending on the hunt area. Alaska Range hunters use Fairbanks or Anchorage. Wrangell or Chugach hunters start from Anchorage. From any of these major airports, you fly into small jumping-off towns such as McCarthy, Glennallen and Valdez.

Yukon hunters generally end up at Watson Lake, Dawson or Whitehorse. Many flights to Watson Lake or Dawson layover in Whitehorse. All flights into hunting country are by small plane and each outfitter uses a different departure point, so rely on your outfitter's advice.

Watson Lake is also used as the destination for many hunts in the Northwest Territories. Outfitters there use Norman Wells, Ft. Simpson and other outpost towns as a jumping-off point. Hunters with plenty of time may consider the Alaskan Highway rather than jets to reach the jumping-off points. The U.S. Army constructed this marvelous engineering feat during WW II when they feared the

Backpacking into Dall sheep country offers the most mobility. Plus, you start hunting the minute you step out of the tent. Above, Jack Bare, the author's father, climbs Chitistone Mountain in Alaska's Wrangell Mountains.

sea lanes to Alaska would be cut off. The actual Alaskan Highway starts at Dawson Creek, British Columbia, goes through Watson Lake, Yukon, and to both Fairbanks and Anchorage, Alaska.

Highways 16 leads out of Prince George, B.C., and runs into highway 37 which joins the Alaskan Highway at Watson Lake. This route offers a beautiful alternative to the Dawson Creek to Watson Lake segment. Either way, you'll view stunning country on the way to your Dall hunt.

Part of your decision on where to hunt Dall sheep may involve other game to hunt, photograph or just view. Many outfitters offer fantastic combination hunts but to save money, you may opt to just take photos and watch the other magnificent creatures in the area.

In nearly all Alaska sheep areas you will probably see plenty of caribou and goats. Many times you'll get a chance to spot black bear and an occasional grizzly. Yukon hunters will most likely spot similar game on sheep hunts. In the Territories, you'll see caribou and bear but not many goats. Write the game departments of Alaska, Yukon and the Northwest Territories (see Appendix 1) for information on license applications and season dates.

All sheep hunters, and in fact all hunters, have their own idea of what constitutes a wonderful trophy. Although Dall rams don't carry massive horns like the bighorns and desert sheep, I know of nothing which strikes the eye quite like golden, flaring horns atop a pure white ram.

5

Hunting Stone Sheep

Stepping off the pontoon plane at Tuchodi Lake, British Columbia, we gazed at the most beautiful country in the world: sheep country. On the north side of the lake rugged peaks rose from sloping spruce-covered bases to their snow-capped tops. On the south, cliffs rose nearly straight up to even rougher peaks.

A couple of hours later I saw three Stone sheep. The small rams stood on a white, mineral lick cliff staring down at two strange looking creatures in a boat. We fished all afternoon and caught no fish but we did see rams and I knew at once our decision to go sheep hunting ranked as the best decision I ever made.

Dad and I along with a good friend, Dr. "Mac" McLaughlin, hunted elk, moose and caribou in the lower Tuchodi Valley two years previously with outfitter Don Peck. Much of the supper table and campfire talk revolved around sheep hunting. Although we had an excellent antlered hunt, the sheep hunting sounded even better. Little did I know. Two years later that first sight of sheep from the boat convinced me and somewhere during the hunt I came down with an incurable case of "Ovis Pyrexia," sheep fever. O'Connor once wrote that after a sportsman goes on his first sheep hunt he either never again sets foot on a sheep mountain or he becomes completely addicted.

I'm afraid many more hunters fall into the second category than the first.

Stone sheep hunters use horses much more than those pursuing Dall sheep. In fact nearly all Stone outfitters use horses to some extent. Part of my first Stone hunt proved different. After hunting from horseback and/or resting my blistered feet for nine days we decided to take the boat up the lake and then backpack up Standard Draw for two days. We took sleeping bags but no tents and only enough lightweight food for a couple of snacks and one evening meal. Again, I saw young rams on the mineral lick above the lake. Soon after leaving the boat we found goat hair on a spruce limb, quite a surprising place for a goat at the bottom of the mountain. After crisscrossing the stream and climbing up the draw, we trudged up a steep ridge.

Unfortunately, while crossing the creek the final time, I slipped on a wet rock and nearly lost my glasses. I did dunk my rifle. The ridge offered good footing but my flatlander lungs demanded a rest more often than Dale liked.

Shortly before noon we stopped our climb for a bite to eat. I spotted four goats on the opposite side of the canyon near the top of the mountain below Merchant Saylors Peaks. As we watched the goats with passing interest, Dale's sharp eyes found three rams in a draw south of the goats.

"Let's move out. Those rams look good from here," Dale said.

Like most sheep hunting we had to slip and slide down one side of the canyon and struggle up the other. I never seem to find rams on the same side I'm on. Unlike many mountains, the toughest part of the climb came near the bottom. The wide draw we started up narrowed and eventually we ran into a dry waterfall which we scaled on hands and knees. At times, I could push my legs up only eight or ten steps at a time before they turned to rubber and demanded a rest. At long last we arrived at the large location-marking boulder, but no rams.

Staying out of sight we crept higher. Every few steps Dale slipped his hat off and inched his head over a rim. We thread our way back and forth as we climbed higher. From the other side, we thought the rams were grazing in a large open basin. However, ravines and side canyons cut the basin, making it hard to see everywhere without moving. To make our task tougher, snow and fog moved in.

Dale slid to another edge.

"There's the rams," he whispered. "They're quite a distance away yet. Come on up."

Stone sheep have excellent eyesight and an extraordinary sense of smell. However, they will not spook at the sound of falling rocks. Also, sheep are unable to count; in this chapter the author shows you how nimrods use that fact to their advantage.

By now the four rams had turned into eight. Under cover of snow, we stalked closer, keeping tight to the rocks. When the snow moved out, we counted 12 sheep feeding or resting. We heard the rams bleat. I selected what appeared to be a nice ram and was ready to shoulder my gun when Dale put his hand on my shoulder and pointed. Farther away and a little higher lay a larger ram. Once again we crept higher under the cover of snow.

When we crawled into a good position above the ram, I discovered the fall in the creek had fogged my scope.

Desperately I tried to take it apart and dry the glass but to no avail. Between my wet scope, the fog and the snow, I became frustrated trying to line up on the ram. We would have to wait until the fog and snow lifted to have any chance using the wet scope.

Suddenly my ram rose from his bed and strutted toward a lighter colored ram. After staring at each other for several minutes, they backed off, reared and lunged. The crash echoed off the rock walls and died. The snow increased, pushed by a slanting wind. Clash after clash reached our ears out of the snow but we could see nothing.

At about 5:30 p.m. the snow disappeared over the ridge and the fog lifted enough to try a shot. I leaned back against the overhanging ridge and rested my .300 Win. Mag. Browning on my knees. Although the scope remained foggy, I could make out the ram's outline enough to center the crosshairs on his chest. As the snap of my rifle sounded, 14 other rams sprinted away. Mine buckled his knees and fell.

Rushing down to my ram I recalled reading about full curl rams and what a wonderful trophy they made. I tugged a tape measure out of my pocket as I slipped and slid down the basin. The measurement dropped my spirits almost as fast as the shot raised them. Only 32 inches on the outer curve. The ram had a large body but miniature head.

Although he carried a full curl, it came around too tight to measure the normal 37 or 38 inches. Today, I would know the difference, but on that first sheep hunt the ram fooled me badly. But at least I had my first ram and caught the deadly fever.

For the most part, this stalk proved typical. We spotted the sheep from across the canyon, climbed down and back up and got above the ram. We had marked their position well. Although the rams moved a bit while we were out of sight, they didn't leave the basin. We stalked with the wind blowing in our faces and shot from above.

While we caped the ram, the snow turned to rain. We didn't reach the boat until after dark but our cook, Patty, heard the motor and flashed a light every few minutes to guide us back to camp. We arrived at "Lac A Nookie" cold, wet to the skin and tired but extremely happy.

Wild sheep are not the smartest of all wildlife but their eyesight is phenomenal. You also need to make your stalk into or with a quartering wind. But the noise of slipping or falling rocks doesn't seem to bother rams.

After all, they live in a world of falling rock. Sheep also don't seem to be able to count; good hunters take advantage of that fact.

On that same 1973 trip to Tuchodi, my dad, Jack, took a beautiful 42-inch ram. He and his guide Raymond Stump rounded

Jack Bare with his trophy Stone ram. The typical Stone sheep country in the background is above the Tuchodi Valley in northeastern British Columbia.

a corner and saw the ram up the slope on the other side. The ram saw them at the same time but didn't seem concerned since he stood over a half mile away. However, because of the terrain, Dad and Raymond couldn't go behind or above the ram.

A deep draw ran from in front of the hunters to a position just below and to the right of the huge ram. Raymond expressed the fear that the minute the two hunters dropped into the draw and out of the ram's sight it would go over the top. Most wildlife stays put if they see the danger at a distance, but spook if they can no longer see what's bothering them.

While Raymond stood in plain sight, Dad crawled into the draw and out of sight. As Dad stalked up the draw he looked back at Raymond several times to make certain the ram had not moved. Raymond continued to just look around, never staring right at the ram. The draw didn't allow Dad to get above the ram but he did get close enough to poke his rifle over the edge from about 150 yards and take his fine ram with one shot.

Dr. Roy Schultz took a record book Stone with a typical stalk and restalk hunt. He and his guide, Bill Napoleon, spotted the old ram on the skyline after they'd rode about five miles from camp. Even from 1½ miles away, the ram looked tremendous. They climbed above and around, until they were behind the ram, According to Schultz, rimrock that didn't look too bad from below became an impossible situation. They climbed hand and foot through several chimneys and over ledges.

When Schultz and Napoleon peeked over the edge they saw three rams, calmly chewing their cud while bedded down on the black shale. The largest ram had a light gray face and massive horns broomed at the end. Schultz soon discovered a problem, however.

"We were near the summit of Goat Mountain between the Muskwa and Prophet rivers in British Columbia. From our lofty position, we could see the Muskwa River on our right appearing as a thin silvery ribbon. On our left the Prophet glistened in the bright sunlight and the Muskwa-Prophet Bench now turned shades of red and gold as the dwarf arctic birch and aspen responded to an early autumn frost.

"Our problem was that the ram faced directly toward us. I would risk ruining a trophy if I shot from my position, as the bullet might knock a horn off," Schultz told me.

Napoleon suggested they go over the saddle and get a side shot. They inched back from the peak and lowered themselves to a ledge on the opposite side of the ridge from the rams. Schultz clung tightly to the rocks as he followed the Cree guide along the ledge. When they reached the saddle they couldn't see the rams so they crawled toward a small rocky ridge.

Sliding up behind the rock pile, Schultz saw his trophy not over 125 yards away.

Because wild rams live in such open country, you sometimes find situations where it's impossible to plan a typical stalk. Perhaps the distance is too great to go around and get above and behind your chosen ram. Other times, he may lay in such a position that any stalk is impossible.

This near record book Stone ram, taken by Don Harrell, shows a light to average coloration. Harrell, from Arlington, Texas, bagged the ram in 1978 while hunting in British Columbia.

In that case you must wait until another day. Occasionally the only possible stalk route will take you in below a ram. If so, you must use it or wait for tomorrow.

I planned such a stalk on a British Columbia hunt. I did not bag the ram but poor shooting rather than a badly planned stalk caused the miss. After crawling out of a warm bag at our spike camp at sunrise, I waited until 9 a.m. for the guide to find the horses. They had climbed above treeline that night even though they wore hobbles. Later we dismounted and climbed on foot from the same spot where Dale had found the horses.

After sitting and glassing for a half hour, we found three rams. Naturally, they were on the opposite side of the canyon. We sat shivering in the light snow and wind until the rams laid down. After descending to the creek and climbing up the other side, the shivers were replaced with sweat. Unless we stayed in the creek to the very top of the mountain, we could not get above the rams. We had no time for that.

As it was, we crawled out of the canyon and up behind some rocks nearly 350 yards from the sheep. When I missed, I wasn't surprised. I'm really only a 200- to 250-yard shooter and the wind blew quite strong. I learned another lesson that day: Sheep often react more to where the bullet strikes than they do the sound of the shot. Perhaps mountain winds do tricky things with rifle sounds.

When the slug slapped rocks above the ram, he leaped up and trotted right toward our hideout behind the rocks. All three rams pranced past our rock at no more than 100 yards. Three shots all went over the ram's back. This time I was not only surprised by the miss but bitterly disappointed and more than a little disgusted with my shooting. I did not have time to cushion my rifle with a coat or vest as I usually do, so perhaps resting the rifle on solid rock caused the shots to go high.

Since that hunt I've heard many hunters tell of sheep running toward them after a shot missed high and it happened to me at least one other time. Once I even shot into rocks across a canyon on purpose, attempting to get rams to move out of the trees and into view.

Any hunter learns new techniques and experiences new phenomenon on nearly every sheep hunt. That first sheep hunt in 1973 naturally taught me more and opened more new experiences than any hunt since.

The day after harvesting a goat, Dale and I rode horseback partway up Spur Creek (actually, Joplin Creek on the maps) along with Patty, our cook. We dismounted and ate sandwiches before hiking farther on foot. Patty would take the horses to the other side for our return to camp.

As we climbed, Dale ambled out of sight. I tried hard to keep up but only wore myself out. Deciding that he couldn't shoot a sheep without me, I dropped back and continued at my own pace. Some guides, especially young men, feel they must prove they can outclimb the hunter. No matter how hard you climb they keep ahead. By the same token if you let them go, they always wait.

My old friend and bighorn outfitter deluxe, Dewey Browning,

This Stone ram sports heavy bases and long horns. David Fox, from Stroudsburg, Pennsylvania, took the 42½-inch ram while hunting with Dalziel Hunting Ltd. in northern British Columbia.

tells a story of himself as a young and energetic sheep guide. "I was working for my dad and apparently the hunter complained to Dad about my fast pace. Dad, in no uncertain terms, told me that you can't kill a sheep if you kill the hunter first."

Farther up the canyon, we found a large basin full of huge boulders. Rather than solid rock, small rocks fused together formed the boulders. At some time it must have been volcanic there. At one spot I watched small clouds puff off the mountain peak. No clouds came in from the other side so the peak must have formed the clouds.

Normally, sheep hunters climb up and down high ridges and in and around different peaks, but seldom do they reach the actual head of a creek. That day we did, and walked around it just under vertical cliffs soaring 100 feet above us to the very top peak. Walking down the other side proved as uneventful as the walk up. In fact, we saw no game all day. When we reached Patty and the horses, she said she could see the bright sun reflect off my rifle and watch like mirrors all day. No doubt sheep and goats can see the same thing. Now I make a point to remove my wrist watch and tape the shiny parts of my rifle, including the polished wood.

Some Stone sheep guides and sportsmen like to hunt from creek and canyon bottoms. Others would rather hunt from the ridge tops. Both techniques offer advantages and disadvantages. Smart hunters trust their guide and follow his or her lead.

Those who hunt from the bottom need not waste energy climbing to the high country if it is void of rams or holds only small rams. When you spot something from below you can check the horns with a spotting scope. Then only if the trophy looks good do you make the climb. You also need not climb one side, spot a ram on the other, drop back down and climb the other side.

On the other hand sometimes you may find a ram on your side of the canyon while hunting from the high ridges. In that case you need not descend and climb up the other side. You will not be out of breath when you stalk the final few yards to shooting position. On some mountains you can actually see more from above than below due to hidden ridges and outcroppings. The fact that you can search down both sides of the ridge offers another advantage to hunting high. Don't, however, walk along the ridge top so you become skylined. Sheep anywhere in the area will spot your movement along the skyline.

Whether you hunt from the creek or from the high ridges, Stone sheep hunting requires much more work with binoculars than Dall hunting. Nearly every variation in Stone coloration blends in with the natural habitat much better than pure white sheep on green grass or dark rock. You can sit for hours without spotting anything when suddenly a ram appears in your binoculars. He may have been laying down and you only spot him when he stands or moves.

Early in my sheep hunting career I learned to search a basin or mountainside systematically. Normally, I look over the entire area with the naked eye. That way you won't waste time if the sheep are moving or on the skyline. Moving sheep, like all moving animals are easy to spot.

Since British Columbia outfitters each control a certain area, the Stone sheep hunter in the province will most likely stay in sturdy cabins and spike camps.

Next scan the entire area in a similar manner with your binoculars. Again, you're looking for something fairly obvious. At last you must search every inch of the basin or mountainside. Do this in little sections like a checkerboard. I start near the top at one end and look for a rock or other landmark to use as a guide. Look over one small area completely and then move on to the next square. If you complete the entire basin without luck, start over. You'll find that sheep hunting requires much more binocular work than leg work. Stone sheep hunters who give any basin only one look and then move on, miss a lot of sheep.

Unlike the backpack and Super Cub hunts of Dall country,

most Stone sheep outfitters use horses. Some hunt from sturdy cabin or tent base camps while others make extensive use of spike camps. Most use a combination of several camps depending on where the sheep are and they move from camp to camp so they distribute hunting pressure. Perhaps unfortunately, long gone are the days of pack trail rides into sheep country. Practically all outfitters use planes to get the hunter into base camp. Fortunately, most outfitters do use one- or two-day packtrains to move the hunter from base camp up to sheep country.

Reno, Nevada's foremost sheep hunter, Dr. Bob Broadbent, hunted with outfitter Don Peck some ten years before I did. When I first showed up at Peck's, Broadbent's words to me came rushing back. Peck never changed. Fortunately neither has his beautiful Tuchodi country. Before I booked with Peck, Dr. Bob told me of his hunt and especially his pack trip from base up to Jim River.

"Moving day on the trail with Don Peck has to be just one step down the ladder from sheer pandemonium," Bob told me. "There is no helping him and the air would be blue with recriminations for first a recalcitrant horse, then a broken piece of harness, then the weather, then all of my allegedly unnecessary equipment. But miraculously the confusion would transform itself suddenly into an orderly, well-packed string of horses, headed by Don himself, shirttail flying, mounted on a wild-eyed horse moving at a fast trot. And his companions, be they dude, cook or horse wrangler had to mount up in a hurry and lay the leather on to avoid being left behind," Broadbent reported.

On my first day, we didn't take a pack string but the three guides and three hunters all met their horses. We would ride out together up the river before splitting up and hunting one on one. After mounting up, the other five horses and riders all headed out. My horse just stood there despite my best efforts with my heels in his ribs and hearty giddy-ups. Peck ambled over with a branch as big around as my wrist and handed it to me. "Got to get his attention first, son."

Dr. Bob soon learned that bone-shattering pace could wreck both body and spirit. He even suggested to Peck that they walk the horses for a brief respite. "Gotta keep moving; long ways to go before dark," was Peck's response. Toward the end of a long day Broadbent tried the tactic of appealing to Peck to have compassion for the poor horse who carried Broadbent's 190 pounds in addition to his assortment of hunting gear. "Wear that one out and we'll get you another," Peck said.

Stone sheep outfitters use pack horses more often than those outfitting for Dall sheep. Just a day's ride away from airplanes and camps gets you into prime sheep country.

The next day Broadbent took a beautiful 12-year-old ram with horns measuring 41 inches on one side and 37 on the other. A few years ago Don Peck passed into the country where all rams wear 40-inch plus headgear, but his son, Ross, carries on the family tradition of deluxe hunts. I think Ross also learned to hustle cribbage games from his dad.

Packing horses for the trail is another of the outfitter's arts. It must be done just right or you'll spend most of your trail time repacking. Horses allow you to hunt far away from base camp with comfortable tents, solid food and extra gear.

From spike camps most outfitters ride horseback from camp each day, either farther up a canyon or up the mountainside to the edge of tree line before starting on foot. As you climb on horseback, remember the horse needs rest just as you would. In extremely steep places hang on to the horse's mane rather than the saddle horn. In other places you may have to lead or follow the horse over rough places. Many hunters hang on to the tail going up steep inclines.

Pack trains need not go far from main camp to be effective. Often, just a half day or day's ride from base camp gets you far enough away from air and camp activity to locate excellent rams. Then after campfire chatter dies down at a spike camp, that wonderful silence, broken only by the wolf's howl or the coyote's yelp, overtakes the camp. As you sit in peace, the bubbling mountain stream with its braided copper reflection of the day's sunset mesmerizes you.

Even though some Stone sheep reside in the Yukon and a very few in the Northwest Territories, serious Stone sheep hunters must turn to British Columbia. Wildlife experts say that at the very least 10,000 Stone sheep make their home in British Columbia. Hunters harvest only 250 to 300 each year.

Overall, biologists report Stone sheep populations in British Columbia are declining due to habitat deterioration (civilization) and wolf predation. Fortunately, a wolf control program now in effect and range burning brings back some fragile ecosystems for better winter feed.

Sheep numbers west of the Dease and in mountains that drain to the Pacific remain stable at 4,000. Experts report some 6,000 to 7,000 sheep in the eastern part of British Columbia. This total population of 11,000 shows a decline from the population in the 1970s of 17,000. All outfitters work under a quota system.

The Muskwa and Kechika drainages in the northeast contain

Serious Stone sheep hunters must turn their sights to British Columbia. Wildlife experts say that, at the very least, 10,000 Stone sheep make their home in that province. Only 250 to 300 of the rams are harvested each year.

the densest sheep populations. Other well-populated areas in the east include the Toad River, Muncho Lake, Tuchodi, Gataga and Sikanni drainages. In the west the area between the Stikine River and Iskut River, east of Telegraph Creek is well-populated with Stone sheep. The Spatsizi area also supports excellent numbers of Stone sheep.

Depending on the hunt area, you'll probably fly commercial into Fort St. John or Fort Nelson, British Columbia, or Watson Lake, Yukon, to meet your outfitter. Then you'll fly bush plane, either pontoon or wheels, into your hunt area. Many hunters drive up the beautiful Alaska highway to the jump-off points.

Practically all Stone sheep areas teem with other wildlife. If you can only afford a dream sheep hunt once, or must save for years between hunts, you may want to add another species to the hunt. The added cost is much less than planning a separate hunt for other species. But many sheep hunters prefer to concentrate only on rams when hunting the high country.

Regardless of whether or not you hunt species other than sheep, you have an excellent chance of seeing goats, moose, caribou, bears and wolves. In a few select areas you may spot majestic elk in the lower country near sheep mountains.

Fishing in high mountain streams rates excellent in Stone sheep country. Take along a rod and small selection of spoons, spinners or jigs. Most streams contain both Dolly Varden and arctic grayling. Both make excellent table fare and a grayling right out of the water is perhaps the most beautiful fish in the world with its sail-like dorsal fin. If you forget your tackle try cheese or meat on a bare hook and use a willow stick. Of course, check state or provincial regulations well before the hunt begins.

All sheep country from the desert south to the alpine north is exceptionally beautiful. However, if one were to name the most stunning sheep country of all, many would choose Stone country.

Many dedicated sheep hunters prefer Stone rams because of their great headgear. Although bighorns to the south grow more massive horns, there is something magical about the possibility of matching the great Chadwick ram and its 50-inch plus horns. Also, Stones with the argali or wide spread type horns may measure 31 inches from tip to tip—nearly three feet!

For whatever reason, the great horns, the beautiful country or the abundance of other wildlife in the area, every sheep hunter should hunt Stone sheep at one time or another.

6

Hunting Bighorn Sheep

After catching a wonderful case of sheep fever on my first Stone hunt, I knew I had to hunt other sheep. Following many letters and phone calls researching bighorn outfitters in Alberta and southern British Columbia I selected Alberta outfitter Dewey Browning.

Now, many hunting years later I've had the opportunity through my work to meet many fine sheep outfitters and guides. Never once have I regretted my decision to hunt with Dewey. He's not only a most knowledgeable outfitter but he became a close friend over the years.

On returning home after my Stone sheep hunt in 1973, I located the few sheep hunters available in my home state of Iowa. Needless to say, all highly recommended sheep hunting. But they declared Stone hunting was much easier than bighorn hunting and that I wouldn't see nearly as many sheep on a bighorn hunt as I did on a Stone hunt. This made me wonder because I didn't see that many total sheep on the Stone hunt.

On the last Friday of August in 1975 I climbed my first bighorn mountain in Alberta's "Will Not" Canyon. By noon we had not seen a single sheep of any description. However, by the time we started down around 5 p.m. I'd seen 20 head of sheep. Maybe this bighorn hunting wouldn't be as tough as they said.

Unfortunately I didn't harvest my first bighorn until 32 hunting days later, spread over a two-year, three-hunt period. In general, wholesale bad luck caused the delay. I did see a tremendous number of sheep and several fine rams, including one that would rate extremely high in the record book.

After hunting other canyons, we returned to "Will Not" on the fifth day of the hunt. The young guide in camp had to go in to town for two days so the other hunter in camp and I both accompanied Dewey Browning.

We left camp on horseback under a heavy, overcast sky. Light sprinkles fell until we started to climb in sunlight. By 10:30 a.m. the overcast returned. We glassed and climbed until reaching the top about noon. Still no sheep in sight. At 1:30 p.m. a wind and hail storm hit so we snuggled under a fallen spruce for protection. Every few minutes one of us crept out to look for sheep.

By 3 p.m. the sun returned again and we immediately spotted two old ewes. Shortly after, we found eight ewes and lambs. Then on the way down we spotted six rams on the opposite side of the canyon. At least two and maybe three carried exceptional horns.

The next day we rushed back up the same canyon. The sheep didn't disappoint us. We found them before 10 a.m. in the exact same area. Unfortunately, we couldn't stalk them without being seen. Rain, wind and snow alternated with bright sunshine. Again we slid into our sleeping bags and dreamed of huge horns.

Bernie returned that night but we decided all four of us should hunt together since the band contained at least two keeper rams in addition to the huge old ram. I won a coin toss for the big boy and we hoped to both score at the same time.

Dawn arrived clear and cold the next morning. What a relief to ride and climb without rain or snow in our faces. After a late start due to lost horses, we found the rams from our regular glassing spot at 11 a.m. We studied them in the spotting scope while waiting for them to lay down. All agreed that the dark faced old leader of the band would measure at least 37 inches with 16-inch bases. The second best ram looked like a trophy also.

Before noon the rams bedded in an accessible spot so we scampered down the mountain. After a refreshing drink of icy water we started up the other side. A finger of spruce trees going nearly to the top let us stay out of sight of the rams as we struggled up. As we neared the ram's altitude, we slowed and repeatedly checked the wind.

Bernie crawled to the edge of the trees and peeked out. When he gave us the thumbs up, we shed our packs and crept to the edge.

The author (right) and famous Alberta bighorn outfitter Dewey Browning with the author's second Alberta bighorn. Age rings show the old ram to be 11½ years old.

The sheep lay below us and all looked either downward or in the other direction. Rough shale scraped my elbows and knees as we carefully crawled into position behind some low-growing juniper about 75 yards above the rams. What a beautiful sight: 10 rams laying peacefully on a typical shale slide on a brilliant Alberta day. I slid my rifle forward onto the juniper and looked at Dewey.

Dewey motioned us to wait and get our heads together. In soft whispers, he said that since the rams all lay so close together he was afraid that one shot might hit more than one ram. We should wait until they stood and then each shoot on the count of three. My ram lay near the left of the band and the other hunter's at the right. We would have no problem shooting the wrong ram.

Through my rifle scope, my ram's black horns looked huge. When he turned his head sideways, I saw daylight between the bottom of the horn's curl and his jaw. Then the bluntly broomed tip came well above his nose. I kept the cross hairs on the back of his neck and could have shot him several times. My heart beat against my chest and sweat trickled down my back. Never had I seen such a wonderful sight.

A few minutes later, the little sickle-head ram on my end stood up. He sensed no danger but probably just wanted to stretch or eat a bite. I relaxed and lowered my rifle to see what was going on.

A shot shattered the silence. My trophy leaped up and sprinted into the timber before I could react. What had happened? I took a couple of wild shots as my ram raced through the trees but to no avail. The other hunter scampered down the shale.

"Where's he going?" I asked after swallowing my disappointment.

"Down to look at his ram."

His ram measured 33 inches on the curl with nearly 16-inch bases. With an exact comparison, we realized that the black-faced ram measured at least 5 inches longer and an inch bigger around at the base. What a trophy.

Later Dewey and I pondered the day's events and cussed ourselves for trying for two rams at once. However, most often the plan would have worked. The other man had hunted with a different outfitter the year before and did not see a legal ram in 14 days. He also missed an easy shot at a ram on the second day of this hunt. No doubt something in the back of his mind told him he might not have another chance and so he pulled the trigger as soon as the little ram stood.

Disappointed at the time, I came to realize that I would have missed out on many wonderful hunting days in the next year and a half if I had bagged that particular ram. And I did have the distinct privilege of watching such a great trophy from only 75 yards. Not many hunters can say the same. Yet I wake up at night, even today, dreaming of that magnificent ram.

That band of rams and the stalk proved fairly typical of bighorn hunting in Alberta. We rode horseback into a canyon, climbed and glassed to the top, spotted the rams, waited for them to lay down and then went down one side and stalked back up the other to come out above and behind the rams. Everything except the final result occurred in textbook fashion. That's not always the case.

Too often neophyte sheep hunters exhibit a great lack of patience. Hunting nearly every other game you must get right on with a stalk or the shot or he may leave the country. Not so with sheep hunting.

First of all, if at all possible wait until your ram lays down late in the morning before you start a stalk. Otherwise he may wander

Bighorn hunters spend much more time glassing the high country than they do walking or climbing.

off feeding for quite a distance. If that happens you may run into him in an unexpected place and spook the ram or you may not even find him again. But if you wait until he lays down, you can be well assured he'll be in the immediate area until late afternoon when he feeds again. Bighorns, even more than Dall or Stone rams, will stay in or around a given basin all day or for several days. You'll also experience a situation where the ram lies in such a position that you can't stalk him without being seen. Again you must wait.

On the first day of my second Alberta bighorn hunt we saw nothing until mid-afternoon. Using binoculars both Dewey and I searched every inch of open ground on the far side of "Will Not" Canyon several times. Suddenly I noticed a "rock" which looked like it had four legs and a head.

"Gimme the spotting scope. I think this rock's a ram," I whispered to Dewey.

"Wait a minute. I want to check two rocks at the head of the canyon."

When I looked back at my rock the head appeared on the other end—the ram turned around. Dewey didn't hesitate getting the scope to me when I mentioned the different head position. Sure enough, a beautiful, old ram stood there like the king of the mountain in a little boulder-strewn meadow. We decided the ram must have been there all day but had been bedded down.

Then the ram wandered about feeding a little and strolled to a long flat shale slide just under the rim. Where he then lay, any stalk would be impossible without the ram seeing us. The day was too far gone to hike out of the canyon, go around to the back side and climb over the top. So we merely watched through the scope, made notes on what we thought he measured and waited to be certain he didn't move out before dark. To save effort climbing back up to the same spot the next morning we left our packs and even my rifle covered with rain gear in a spruce tree.

What a wonderful hike up the next morning with no pack and rifle to carry. Alas, we glassed and scouted both sides of the ridge all day without finding the ram.

Rather than go back the third day, Dewey and I took pack horses for a two-day spike camp up Washout Creek. I still carried memories of the huge black-faced ram from the year before and really hoped to find him. If Washout proved fruitless we'd go back to "Will Not" and look again for the nice ram we'd by now named "Doughnut Ram." His horns carried their weight well out and the perfect circle they formed looked like a doughnut.

I never did see that ram alive again but LeRoy Forrester, the other hunter in camp, did. In fact, he and Bernie climbed up the backside and found the ram within 100 feet of where we last saw him four days before. The old ram sported 35-inch horns with 15½-inch bases and scored nearly 175 points. If we had attempted a stalk the first day, I'm sure the ram would have taken off and none of us would have seen him again.

Waiting instead of stalking also really paid off for Dr. Roy Schultz on his 1968 Alberta sheep hunt. Unlike my hunt, Schultz didn't see a legal ram for the first 11 days of his hunt. In fact, he hadn't seen any legal rams on a 14-day hunt the year before either. On the 12th day they spotted a band of five rams heading for a pass at least 1,000 yards away. All they could do was watch. Harry McKenzie, Schultze's outfitter, said they'd let them go over the pass and then chase after them.

After the rams disappeared from sight, they climbed to the ridge. They found the rams bedded down a half mile away. "There was no way we could stalk them, without being seen long before we were in rifle range," he told me. "Harry said we should wait them out and they'd come back to feed toward evening."

It must have been tough for Schultz to sit and wait, especially

Most bighorn sheep outfitters use horses to reach camp. During the hunt, horses are used to reach the hunting area each day.

since this was the first legal bighorn he'd seen in 26 hunting days. But wait they did, alternately dozing and glassing for four hours. Finally, at 4:30 p.m., the rams rose and fed slowly toward the hunters. Schultz laid his .300 Wthby Mag. over his folded jacket and settled the cross hairs on the heavy-horned ram. When the ram came within range, a gentle trigger squeeze did the job. Darkness overtook the hunters before they reached timberline. Fortunately McKenzie's horse heard them and whinnied. Two tired but elated hunters let their horses follow their trail to camp in the dark.

In general, wild sheep act predictably. They feed in the open in the morning, lay down in the open at midday and then feed again in the evening. However, rams can sometimes break all the rules and disappear for long periods.

One day on an Alberta hunt, Dewey and I found six rams high above on an open shale slide. Since they were laying down, we headed up at once. Twisted, crisscrossed deadfalls made climbing tough but we reached the ram's altitude in little more than an hour. Alas, no rams were in sight. We walked out and found their beds. Several tiny springs seeped forth cool water from the shale. Above one bed we saw where a ram laid his head in the sand. The rams had to be close since we found sand, still wet with urine.

After carefully picking our way across the shale slide we lunched and glassed from the next basin. Surely the rams would show up someplace. Dewey felt the rams went into the timber. At 6 p.m. we continued on to the top and looked down the other side. We never found the rams all day and yet we knew they had not left the canyon. Fortunately we did find them the next day and I took my first bighorn then.

On another two-day spike trip up Washout Creek we found fresh, huge ram tracks and fresh droppings leading into a large timber area near the top. Eventually we circled the entire timber but never found tracks coming out. In two days we never did see any rams. At the time I felt positive the tracks belonged to my record book, black-faced ram.

Such events frustrate even veteran hunters, especially when most sheep hunters believe sheep don't like the timber. I'm certain frustration plays a part in most every sheep hunt, but dedicated sheep hunters just try again the next day.

Frustration, however, can make you do some strange things. For instance, we spent one beautiful day in Alberta up a side canyon off Timber Creek. From the top we could see miles in all directions. No sheep, not even ewes and lambs showed themselves all day until about 4 p.m. when we found one scruffy old ewe by herself. Besides not seeing any sheep all day, we'd started late because the hobbled horses wandered off during the night. It was 10 a.m. before Dewey finally located them. The day before we found only three sheep all day. In frustration we even pushed boulders and shot the rifle into rocks to make a racket on the shale. Perhaps doing everything wrong would help. It didn't.

Communication between guide and hunter rates very important on a bighorn hunt. Sometimes you must split. When you do, be certain you understand *exactly* where you are to go, where you will meet your guide and when. Nothing makes you quite as nervous as

Bighorn country is no doubt the most stunning in the world. While it may be difficult to define a sheep mountain, any sheep hunter can easily recognize one.

waiting for a guide or companion and wondering if you're at the right place or at the right time.

Also be certain you and the guide are discussing the same ram when you're selecting one ram from several. The day I downed my first bighorn, I almost passed him because Dewey and I were talking about two different rams and didn't realize it.

The day after we searched all day for the lost rams, Dewey and I went up the same canyon. After again finding no rams, Dewey suggested we split up. He'd hike farther up Lucky while I returned to a good lookout spot in case the rams emerged from the trees. An hour later a single ram wandered out of the trees and shuffled up a shale slide. Ten minutes later eight additional rams came out and fed their way up the slope. Just before noon the rams lay down. I drew a hasty map and headed upstream to find Dewey. He'd seen only five small rams so after looking at my map we made plans for a stalk.

We went upstream and then climbed to come out behind and above the rams. Perhaps a steeper ridge exists but I have yet to find it. My hands nearly drug the ground inching up the slope. Later we kidded that we wore the knuckles out of our gloves going up.

After a two-hour climb I found the large boulder I picked as a

This is an extremely dark Rocky Mountain bighorn. Don Harrel, from Arlington, Texas, took the ram while hunting in Wyoming's Area #2 during the 1980 season.

landmark. Rough shale made crawling to the edge difficult, but at last I peered over and saw six buckskin and three dark rams, all laying down. After only a few minutes Dewey announced that none of the rams were legal. I always trusted Dewey but I really thought two of the rams, while not great trophies, were legal. After 32 days I would take any legal ram.

Soon, however, I decided that we weren't talking about the same sheep. From his position slightly above me, Dewey could see only the top five rams. The larger rams lay below the others. With only one safe spot to set the spotting scope we rolled over each other to take turns using the scope.

Sliding my down coat under my .300 Win. Mag. Browning I took a deep breath and fired. Since the ram lay facing me I kept the crosshairs at the junction of his neck and shoulder. The ram rolled over twice and lay still. The other sheep didn't seem to know what

This is the third largest bighorn ram killed since 1924. David Onerheim, above, took the record book ram while hunting in British Columbia. The ram scored 201$^1/_8$ Boone & Crockett points.

to do and actually walked toward us until I stood up.

A lack of communication nearly cost me that ram. Dewey didn't see all the sheep and I didn't realize that. I could have easily left the mountain without my first bighorn ram.

Although the ram lay less than 200 yards away, we had to slip and slide down for 30 minutes before we could find a way to cross the narrow but steep canyon. Then another hour back up to the ram. Later we broke our little spike camp and rode in the mist back to base camp. Darkness enveloped us so bad that I couldn't see the horse in front of me so I let my horse follow the best he could.

Outfitters in Alberta and British Columbia are issued permits and a designated guide area. Therefore, most Canadian bighorn outfitters work out of base camps. These normally offer wonderful wall tents and plentiful food. Some outfitters hunt only from base camps, riding out to the ridges each day. Others make use of spike camps to enlarge the hunt area. On my last Alberta hunt rather than hunt from the regular base camp, we set up large, comfortable tents at the headwaters of Forbidden Creek. From there we hunted both on foot and on horseback. I was actually hunting the minute I set foot out of the tent.

Like Stone sheep outfitters in northern British Columbia, both Alberta and B.C. outfitters use pack horses to change camps or take spike trips.

Rather than control the permits, outfitters in the U.S. rely on hunters obtaining the permits through a drawing. Because of this many American bighorn outfitters never know exactly what area they will hunt. Therefore they usually hunt from spike camps.

Actually American bighorn outfitters use a great variety of hunt and camp techniques and it's hard to write about them in general terms. Some even use town as a base and hunt from horses or on foot each day from the end of the road. I know of few, if any, bighorn outfitters in either southern Canada or the U.S. who use bush planes to reach the hunting area as northern outfitters do for the thinhorn species. Roads or at least four-wheel trails reach into even remote areas so you don't need planes.

For your best chance at taking a representative bighorn, you should go wherever you can obtain a permit. Because the outfitters are allotted so many permits in Alberta and British Columbia the price of the hunts run at least twice as high as similar hunts south of the border. But if you want a bighorn hunt and can afford the price, by all means sign up with a Canadian outfitter.

All Canadian outfitters in both British Columbia and Alberta hunt the area immediately surrounding the great Banff and Jasper parks. You not only have an excellent chance of scoring, but you may find one of the old park rams who wanders into the legal hunting area. According to outfitter Dewey Browning, the area near the headwaters of the Clearwater and North and South Ram rivers contains the most sheep of any Alberta area.

You'll find both true Rocky Mountain bighorns and California bighorns in British Columbia, so if you prefer to hunt one or the other make certain what subspecies the outfitter hunts before you sign a contract.

The massive horns on Onerheim's sheep measured 49⅜ and 44⅝ inches. Shown with the ram in this photo is Lance McLean, Onerheim's guide.

In the United States, apply for permits in each and every possible state for your best chance of winning a drawing. In no state are the odds of winning very good, but you definitely can not win if you don't apply. In all cases you get your application money back if you don't draw a permit.

At the present, Colorado with 368 bighorn permits probably offers the hunter the best chance in the drawing. On a statewide basis about one in 14 hunters draws a permit. However, since you must apply by area in Colorado, your actual odds may vary. Occasionally they even offer an area which is undersubscribed. The Rocky Mountain Bighorn Society put out an excellent guide to sheep hunting in Colorado which included drawing odds for various units. The guide is currently out of print and is not available. The Colorado Division of Wildlife hopes to reprint the book.

To further increase your chance of success, Colorado works on a preference system whereas unsuccessful applicants receive preference in the drawing for up to three years. According to wildlife officials, around 4,000 bighorns make their home in Colorado.

Although Idaho only offers 105 resident and 11 nonresident permits, they receive about 7,000 applications so you have about one chance in 60 in the drawing. In Idaho you may apply for either Rocky Mountain or California bighorns. Rocky Mountain bighorns occupy the central mountains of Idaho, with most located in the Salmon River drainage. You'll find the California subspecies in the southwest part of the state.

Wyoming offers the most nonresident permits of any state. Out of nearly 300 total permits, nonresidents may draw for 70 to 75 each year. Some 6,500 residents normally apply so residents have a one in 33 chance while about one out of every 23 nonresidents draws. Experts say Wyoming holds between 6,000 and 7,000 bighorns. Wyoming hunt areas 1, 2, 3, 4, 5, 7 and 10 probably contain the largest herds but these units also receive the most applications. Drawing odds vary greatly, with some going as high as 70:1 while others drop to 6:1.

Montana offers the most bighorn licenses each year but they also receive the most applications. Only about five percent of the hopeful applicants statewide receive one of the 500 licenses. According to wildlife officials, Montana's sheep herd totals more than 5,000 animals.

Montana also offers an unlimited number of permits in six hunt units bordering Yellowstone. Hunter success runs very low (around three percent) in these units. However, if you want to hunt sheep in an extremely beautiful but rugged area and taking a ram is not the most important reason for the hunt, these units offer the only opportunity in the United States without winning a drawing. You must be in top shape to hunt here. Montana sets a harvest quota for each of the six units and the hunter must stop hunting within 48 hours after the quota is reached. It is the hunter's responsibility to keep informed about the harvest quota. Most guides carry a radio with them on the hunt so they stay up-to-date when harvest quotas are broadcast on Montana AM stations.

Washington, Oregon, New Mexico, Nevada and South Dakota all offer a few bighorn permits each year. Nevada's and South Dakota's go only to residents. Nevada is the only state to offer separate licenses for desert, California and Rocky Mountain

Arnie Johns is shown here with his Idaho, California bighorn. Arnie's ram shows the typical California thin horn. It also sports a very wide spread.

bighorn sheep. For detailed information on regulations and applications for all states see Appendix 1.

Trying to hunt other game on a bighorn hunt in either Canada or the U.S. is rather tough. In some cases permits won't allow it and in others you don't want to lose hunting time concentrating on other game. However, you may well see other exciting big game on any bighorn hunt. In the U.S. look for elk (especially on early hunts), goat, bear and sometimes mule deer. In Canada you may spot elk, goat, caribou and grizzly.

A grizzly provided almost too much excitement on one memorable Alberta hunt. Dewey and I stopped for one more glassing on the way down the mountain late that afternoon. After 20 minutes or so we rose to continue down when I heard a snort. A grizzly sow and two roly-poly cubs stood not 50 yards away.

She barred her teeth and swung her great paws a couple of times. Her claws gleamed like huge knives in the late afternoon sun. Fortunately she swatted a cub and headed down the ridge away from us. We watched as she lead the cubs down the ridge, across the creek and up the other side. With each step, fat bounced from side to side on the silver tipped cubs. Out of pure coincidence, the next day in a completely different canyon, we heard her snort again and found one large and two small beds in the snow but never saw her again.

Most Alberta or British Columbia hunters either drive or fly to Calgary, Kamloops or Prince George to meet their outfitters. Then they drive to the end of the road and hunt from there or take a packtrain into more remote areas. Your U.S. outfitter will tell you where to meet him but in any event, if at all possible, I like to drive rather than fly. You can include more gear and don't need to pack it nearly so well. You experience far fewer problems with your rifle going by car than by plane.

You'll find that any sheep hunting literature you read or any big game hunters you talk to, all rank a mature bighorn ram at the very top of the trophy ideal. I must agree that no trophy in the world is quite as stunning as an old battered bighorn with massive horns that carry their weight all the way out and has broomed tips that look as big around as your wrist. He is indeed the king of the mountain.

7

Hunting Desert Sheep

June 16, 1980. That date forever remains etched in my memory. At 9 a.m. my office phone rang. "Dick Mandeville calling from Nevada."

"I'm sorry I don't know any Dick Mandeville from Nevada," I answered and started to hang up.

When he told me I'd drawn a permit to hunt desert sheep in Nevada I thought he was one of my sheep hunting friends kidding me. When he said, "Yes, really you won the drawing," my knees shook and I nearly collapsed. After taking my first ram in 1973 I applied in Nevada, Arizona and with the Haulapai Indian tribe each and every year but with little hope.

Soon after I hung up, the phone rang again with Nevada outfitter Jerry Hughes relating the same message. By noon two more outfitters called.

For any sheep hunter and especially one who has three of the four North American species, drawing a desert permit rates almost as exciting as the actual hunt. I'd already scheduled an elk hunt for about the same time. If I couldn't work both hunts into my time, I'd have to drop the Teton elk hunt.

Needless to say, I didn't get much work done that day. I called all my sheep hunting friends and asked advice. Most were as excited as I was. Even my wife shared the joy.

On June 18, I received an official-looking envelope with

"Nevada License Refund" marked in the corner. My heart skipped more than a few beats until I realized it was a phony letter from one of my best friends.

Within a couple of weeks, I heard from several outfitters and one hunter in Nevada. He also drew a permit and would hunt the adjoining area. He offered to help me hunt and I could use his camp in exchange for a whitetail hunt in Iowa, my home state. Unfortunately Iowa didn't allow nonresident deer hunters into the state in 1980.

According to my notes of June 28, I started jogging, exercising and dieting. I never seem to get into top shape for sheep hunts but this would be different. I'd hate to have a tag and not be able to climb.

Desert sheep country, at least in Nevada, looks much different than other sheep country. Rather than hunt above timberline, much desert sheep habitat lies below tree line. Everything looks backwards to a veteran sheep hunter. At the bottom, where up north the largest trees stand, you see only small desert plants, yucca and Joshua. As you climb higher into desert country juniper and pinyon trees become evident. Then higher the spruce and pine show up, even huge ponderosa pine. On the wind-swept mountain tops, centuries old bristle cone pine hang on to life with little visible support. Much Arizona and Mexican sheep country contains very few, if any, real trees.

However, desert sheep country, like all other sheep country, rates a 10 on the stunning beauty scale. Golden sunrises and purple sunsets coat the mountainsides and desert ridges each day. Bright colored desert flowers paint the desert floor. But above all, the magnificent desert ram stands guard over his domain.

Desert sheep hunting may prove the most varied of all sheep hunting. The general sheep hunting methods still hold true, but depending on the particular terrain, you may hunt using a variety of techniques. For example, the first few days of my Nevada hunt we got off the horses only to glass. I always thought sheep hunting meant climbing every day, then glassing.

My first actual stalk on the Nevada hunt did follow typical sheep hunt rules, however. After leaving our comfortable camp sitting at about 5,000 feet in the Desert National Wildlife Range, we rode horseback toward Hayford Peak. We passed several snow patches on the way and an honest, spring-fed creek. Riding through an old ponderosa timber stand we found a good opening. We stopped and glassed the peaks ahead.

Outfitter Jerry Hughes, the author and friend David Welch admire the author's record book desert ram taken in Nevada. Unlike northern species, desert bighorn rams prefer rolling hills, low ridges, the desert floor and high peaks.

Jerry Hughes, my outfitter, soon spotted eight head of rams near the very top of Hayford. Through the scope we picked out one trophy ram and three smaller rams along with a few yearlings or half curls. Because of the distance and the fact that the largest ram lay behind the others, we really couldn't tell much about his size.

I've never ridden a horse in such rough or steep country but I never complained. Jerry's fine horses could stand the climb better than I. After clearing the thick timber we saw several ewes and lambs. By noon we had ridden within 200 or 300 feet of the top of the 10,000-foot peak. We could have ridden to the very top but caution put us on foot for the final ascent.

We rode around to the backside of the peak and felt the wind brush our faces. One foot in front of the other, always with eyes focused ahead. We crept upward with me in front.

On reaching the top, we slowed even more, taking only one or two cautious steps before stopping. Due to the slope of the mountaintop, we couldn't see over 40 or 50 yards. The rams should be just below us.

Suddenly two small rams and nine ewes and lambs jumped up and ran in front of us. We couldn't find the big ram or any of his companions. Tracks told the story. The sheep had lain just a little below us, but spooked when we ran into the ewes and lambs.

On northern sheep hunts you really don't worry about ewes and lambs spoiling a stalk. During the hunting season, with few exceptions, they stay far away from rams. However, in desert sheep country you may find ewes with rams or at least in the same general area because of the limited amount of forage.

Because of available forage, you don't always find desert sheep high in the peaks or high basins. In fact, in many areas you'll find no such thing as high basins. Often, desert sheep feed at lower elevations in dry washes and rolling foothills where they find more and better forage. They do, however, stay near rough, rocky, mountainous terrain for escape. Low ridges and hills radiate off the main mountains. We often rode from ridge to ridge around the peak, stopping just below the ridge and crawling up to glass the little valleys and the next ridge.

After receiving the elusive desert sheep permit, I researched the sheep and the hunting daily. From all I could read and from what sheep hunting friends told me, the hard part was over. Hunting sheep was easier than getting a permit.

After hunting five or six days I began to wonder how easy it was. Oh, I saw plenty of sheep but with the exception of the big ram we spooked, I'd seen only ewes, lambs and young rams. Maybe it wasn't as easy as they said. Spotting the light brown critters in their world of brown and gray requires much more patience than the white sheep of the north.

My sheep hunting friend Dr. Robert Broadbent warned me before the hunt, "The first afternoon of my desert hunt my wife Kay and I headed up a gulch to scout. Kay kept dragging her heels. Instead of keeping up with my pace she'd be 50 yards back glassing. She finally told me that she didn't want to miss anything and reminded me that the biologist said that hunters usually walk by more sheep than they see."

Broadbent told me that it was Kay who first spotted his ram. After excellent directions from his wife, Broadbent finally located

Desert sheep can survive without open water for long periods of time, so hunting water holes is not always effective. Perhaps the best method to hunt desert sheep is to find a good vantage point and glass an entire ridge or mountainside.

the lone ram standing broadside and immobile, blending perfectly with his surroundings of Joshua and black brush.

Since the ram looked directly at them Broadbent decided to have Kay stay out in plain sight while he made a stalk. When Broadbent got to within 150 yards of where the ram should be he crawled up the slope with his jacket under his rifle ahead of him. The ram was nowhere in sight. Using his binoculars, Broadbent scanned the mountain, bush by bush. He finally spotted the ram laying beneath a Joshua tree. A trigger squeeze and Broadbent had his ram, actually the day before he planned to start hunting. He told me he didn't know sheep hunting could be so easy.

Patience rates high on the importance list for any sheep hunt but especially so on desert sheep hunts. More than any other sheep, desert rams blend in with their habitat. I found this true on photographic hunts in Arizona as well as my actual sheep hunt in Nevada.

Covering a little ground completely rates much more important than covering a lot of ground. Find a good vantage point and glass, glass, glass. Always start by looking over the entire ridge or mountainside without your binoculars in case rams might be moving or standing on the skyline. Look for trails or beds. Then go over the same area with your binoculars. Most neophytes, if they spot nothing with the binoculars, get up and move on. This can be a fatal mistake.

If you don't spot anything with a sweep or two of the binoculars then divide the area into checkerboard squares and search each one in turn. Inspect each and every bush, rock or other suspicious object. Could that dead limb be a horn? Could that pale rock be a rump patch?

Using a steady position to glass for sheep is every bit as important as using a steady shooting position. If you can't lay down then brace your arms on your knees to use your glasses. In some cases you might lean across a boulder and steady your arms on the rock. Anything, but stay steady as possible. Hour upon hour using your binoculars causes eye strain and headaches even with the best glass if you're quivering or shaking all the time.

Whenever I see anything suspicious which I can't identify, I go back to it again every few minutes until I figure it out. Often what first looks like a rock may look like a ram after it turns a different direction or moves just a step or two.

Sheep hunters and guides kid each other about looking at stone sheep (on anything but a Stone sheep hunt). The expression, of

Spotting scopes save the desert sheep hunter much needless walking and climbing. With a good scope you can decide whether or not the ram deserves a closer look.

course, refers to looking at rocks that appear like sheep. I'd much rather waste time setting up my spotting scope to check out "stone" sheep than miss a ram by thinking it was only a rock.

I can't count the number of times I failed to spot sheep even after two sets of eyes went over the particular area many times for an hour or more. When we did spot the sheep we knew they didn't drop in out of the sky or come over the ridge. No, the rams had been there all the time but they were laying down, behind a rock or otherwise hidden or camouflaged.

As almost anybody who spends much time in sheep country can tell you, the actual terrain that you look at across a canyon or on the next mountain is not as flat and unbroken as it looks. Ridges, boulders, little draws and other natural formations can hide a ram or even a band of rams from sight. Before you give up on any area, look at it from as many different angles as you can. Go higher, lower, right or left but get several angles.

Immediately after you spot a ram, mark the spot exactly so you don't lose the ram. Look for a distinctive boulder, tree, wash or even the skyline above him. After you complete your stalk, the terrain will look much different from the other side of the canyon. If you haven't marked the spot well, you may stumble on your ram before you're ready. Remember, you may be out of sight of the ram for several hours. Most often, the ram will be right where you left him or at least nearby.

Not marking the ram exactly almost cost me my beautiful Boone & Crockett desert ram. We rode out of camp early that morning under a partly cloudy sky. My down jacket felt good but I knew the day would warm up later. We rode along the base of the hills stopping to glass at each ridge. We headed up Wagon Canyon and rode to the ridges in the pinyon, juniper range.

Shortly after 10 o'clock we tied the horses and crept up one more ridge. Laying his hat beside him, Jerry pushed his binoculars over the edge.

"I see a ram. Think it might be a good one but can't tell for sure. I'd better get the scope," Jerry said.

Before he backed down to get the scope, Jerry pointed the ram out to me so I could take a look. After a quick look confirmed the fact that the ram did indeed deserve a better look I turned my binoculars on the surrounding territory. I didn't want to spook the ram by running into other sheep we didn't know were in the area as we did on Hayford Peak.

While I looked for other sheep, Dave Welch, our friend and helpful observer, crawled up and asked where the ram was.

"Over there," I pointed, without looking up from my binoculars.

Just as I spoke a small ram moved into my view about 100 yards above the old ram.

"I don't see anything. Are you sure you saw something?" Dave asked.

About then Jerry returned with the scope. But as Dave said, the big ram was nowhere to be found. After a little discussion we decided the old boy must have laid down, but exactly where we didn't know. In the excitement neither Jerry nor I had pinpointed the ram's exact position.

"Did you ever see the ram Lloyd? How big do you think he was?" Jerry asked.

"Only for a minute. Then I started looking for other sheep. But he'll go at least 150 points. He's big enough for another look."

Jerry studied the young ram in the scope and soon announced that the young ram was only four years old but he'd definitely make the legal limit of 144 points.

Because desert rams blend in with their surroundings so well, you must spend many hours with binoculars. Binocular work is much more important than leg work.

"Boy if that's the case, then the big ram will go at least 160 or better. Even if that little ram is legal I don't want him. What do we do now?" I asked.

"Since we don't know where he is I hate to make a stalk," Jerry said. "And we can't go at him from above because of that little ram. Could you hit him from here when he stands up again?" Jerry asked.

With a stiff and changing wind and the distance being at least 400 yards, I decided it was foolish to attempt a shot from our present position. Jerry said we could leave Dave behind to give directions and try a stalk from below.

We started down a deep coulee, angling away from the place we thought the ram should be. Each time we looked back Dave just shrugged. He still hadn't seen the ram. After a half hour, we crawled on hands and knees out of the coulee. Still no ram. We crawled down the next little wash and up the other side. Sharp rocks tore at the skin on my palms and knees. Once a cactus drilled its spine into my leg. Everything in the desert wears horns or thorns.

"The ram should be within 75 yards or so," Jerry whispered.

As we slithered forward like snakes I noticed the little ram above us. He stared right at us. I tugged Jerry's pant leg and pointed at the little ram.

"Lloyd," he said, "we gotta do something and do it now. That little ram will spook in a minute and take the big one with him. Your ram must be right in front of us. You stand up and the ram will stand, but you should have time to take a look, decide and shoot him."

Seemingly with a will of their own, my legs launched my shaky body upward. Before I pushed halfway up, the ram stood. I didn't need a second look. His horns dwarfed his body. Before I knew what happened a shot shattered the stillness. Echoes bounced off the canyon walls. The beautiful ram lurched and fell back into his bed. I honestly didn't even remember pulling the trigger. When I looked again I realized that the ram had stood so close I could have hit him with a rock.

A loud rebel yell from far behind us joined our two yells as one. I knew the ram was large and beautiful but his actual size fooled me until we started taping. Numbers whirled in my head and came out well above the Boone & Crockett minimum. On paper they totaled over 177 points. After drying, they officially scored 175⅛.

But we nearly lost a wonderful record book Desert ram because no one had pinpointed his position exactly. Also, the small ram no doubt saw us crawling. Why he didn't spook avoids my understanding even today. Also, I don't recommend stalking so close to the ram (we were within 25 yards) unless you bowhunt.

Once on an Alberta bighorn hunt, I nearly lost a ram because he moved and we also ran into ewes and lambs. (I relate this tale of a bighorn hunt in this chapter on desert hunting only to point out the importance of keeping careful track, not only of the target sheep but of other sheep in the area. Very often you'll find other sheep near or with your target ram in desert country.)

After spotting two majestic old rams late one afternoon, Dewey and I put them to bed and returned the next day. Unfortunately a day-long snowstorm prevented us from making a stalk. The snow did break long enough to confirm the rams were still there. The next morning we found the rams on the same large open basin. We

Because of easy access to desert sheep habitat, elaborate base camps can be easily established. The guide and hunter will ride horseback from this camp into the most promising sheep habitat.

left Gladys, the camp cook, with the horses and started up a drywash full of knee-deep snow. When we started, the two old rams along with a few others were laying beside a patch of low-growing willow. The drywash would bring us out just above and a couple of hundred yards west of the sheep.

Even after climbing in and around the peaks for two weeks, the climb through the snow exhausted me before I was halfway up. Dewey impatiently motioned me upward whenever I stopped to gasp for breath. About halfway up, two ewes and a lamb crossed the wash, heading for the rams. They must have seen us but we continued on.

When we at last struggled over the edge, the rams had disappeared. Downcast, we sat and nibbled on a sandwich. After sweating profusely in my denim jacket and down vest, I now shivered uncontrollably in the cold wind. Dewey looked back at the cook with his binoculars. She pointed left and made a curling motion with her hands. We crawled that direction.

After crawling perhaps 150 yards over sharp shale, we found the rams peacefully grazing away from us. From a prone position I shot the larger ram at about 150 yards. While the ram didn't measure quite what I'd hoped (165, he had not grown much during the important fourth and fifth years), he was 11½ years old and his teeth were bad. He would not have lived through another winter. Later, Gladys told us that after the ewes passed us they went to the old rams and one even pushed at my ram and made him get up. We were lucky they didn't leave the area.

When hunting desert sheep remember the fact that sheep can't count. Also like most wildlife, sheep often don't run off if they can keep track of possible danger at a good distance. But if you drop out of sight rams spook because they can't see the possible danger. Dr. Broadbent used the fact that rams can't count to make his stalk when he left his wife in plain sight. The ram felt safe when he could keep his eyes on Kay. The companion or guide left in sight can also keep track of the ram while you make a stalk.

On a photo trip to the Kofa Range in Arizona we used the fact that rams can't count to excellent advantage. After spotting six rams from the pickup, we watched them with the spotting scope for several minutes. The rams had seen us so rather than lose them by all going after the rams, one man stayed in plain sight while two of us dropped out of sight and stalked the sheep around behind the ridge and above. Unfortunately by the time we arrived in position the rams quit sparring but we got some excellent ram photos. Later, our partner said the rams kept their eye on him the entire time and never knew we were around.

By the way, desert sheep are undoubtedly the easiest of all wild sheep to photograph. During the hot summer months they go to water holes often. Northern sheep don't need standing water nearly as much as desert sheep. In both Arizona and Nevada, local sheep conservation organizations such as the Arizona Desert Bighorn Sheep Society and the Fraternity of the Desert Bighorn in Nevada, build many water holes for the sheep. Contact these organizations for locations of water holes where you might photograph rams during the summer months (see Appendix 2). If you can't hunt desert sheep at least you can enjoy the marvelous country and magnificent sheep with photographs.

In general, desert sheep camps are more deluxe than camps in northern sheep country. Roads make the difference. Because of the terrain and lack of large timber tracks, roads crisscross most desert sheep country. In most good hunting areas, you must stay on the roads but at least they lead right to the campsites. Outfitters carry in any and all equipment to your hunt area. Since they can travel by truck, they can set up as large or as elaborate camps as they want.

Nights around a desert campfire offer an opportunity to talk of past hunts, today's mistakes and tomorrow's plans.

Outfitters can also carry in all the fresh food they want. In Hughes' Desert National Wildlife Range camp, we fed on steak and potatoes every night. I find in my log book a note for the sixth day of the hunt: "Darn we had steak and fried potatoes again for supper." Being only 40 miles from Jerry's home in Las Vegas and having a truck in camp, we also went to his home for a wonderful Thanksgiving supper.

In the desert, dead, dry, Joshua and ironwood make wonderful firewood. After they burn down to embers, the coals stay extremely hot, not only to cook your supper but also to start your morning fire. Dutch ovens and grates allow you to cook most anything you want. The campfires also help take the evening chill

One problem with Mexican hunts is the fact that you must take along so many extra people. Make them stay back when you make a stalk.

off as you sit and tell tales of past hunts. Desert nights do get cold.

Backpacking represents an alternative to fixed camps in desert sheep country. With a lightweight, backpacker's sleeping bag, some dried food and a water supply you can move from area to area as the hunting dictates and not worry about going back to camp each day.

If you do backpack, be certain you carry enough water or know exactly where to find dependable water holes. A desert hunter, more so than northern hunters, must have water.

The ecology of desert sheep country is fragile at best. Anything left by a careless hunter or camper stays in place forever. Backpackers should be certain that they take out anything they take in. This goes for food containers, candy wrappers or anything else that could lay on the ground and spoil the scenery for future hunters or other desert visitors. Even orange peels and other organic matter takes years to decompose in the desert. Please respect the desert and leave it the way you find it.

With roads or trails giving easy access to most of the best desert sheep country, if you have no luck at one camp, you can easily move camp by truck to another spot. In the north country

*This beautiful Mexican desert ram scored only 156 Boone & Crockett points.
However, it was discovered to be between 12 and 15 years old.*

you must move camp by horseback and put up with the restrictions this method of travel incur.

Since I first applied for desert sheep permits in Nevada, they have issued more permits almost each year. At the present, Nevada issues 109 resident desert sheep permits each year along with 12 nonresident permits. Around one in 17 residents who apply draw a permit while only one in 100 nonresidents draw out. Best estimate of the total desert sheep population in Nevada is around 4,945.

Arizona wildlife personnel estimate they have approximately 6,500 desert sheep. In 1995, Arizona offered 112 permits of which 11 went to nonresidents. Over the past 15 years, Arizona has offered more permits each year.

In the past New Mexico offered several desert licenses in the San Andies Mountains. But an outbreak of scabies back in 1978 decimated the herd. Hopefully, their population will continue to rebuild. Since then New Mexico has established a huntable herd in the Paloncillo Mountains. Licenses are issued by a drawing.

Utah offers around 25 resident permits each year along with two nonresident permits. Some 1,750 desert sheep make their home in Utah.

Colorado offers five resident desert permits.

California contains an excellent desert sheep population but they only recently opened a hunting season and to date only offer eight permits.

In northwest Arizona, the Hualapai Indian tribe offers six desert bighorn permits on a draw basis. You need an Arizona permit but you do not need to draw in Arizona if you win one of the Hualapai hunts. According to a good friend who hunted with the Hualapai, they put on a deluxe hunt and the guides are most knowledgeable. Since they hunt the Grand Canyon area, most of the hunting is down rather than up. It must be a strange feeling to hunt sheep from the top without first climbing for hours to reach the top. Sheep hunts are also available on the San Carlos Indian Reservation.

Mexico, without a doubt, produces the most and the largest desert rams. At last report, the Mexicans hunt Baja California Norte (northern section), Baja California Sur (southern section) and Sonora. For the most part, you'll find the *weemsi* subspecies in the southern Baja. These sheep grow smaller horns than the *cremnobates* and *mexicana* subspecies in the north and in Sonora.

According to Mexican officials they allocate their permits in a drawing similar to drawings conducted by state fish and game departments. However, in many cases, they give preference to hunters who need only the desert ram to complete their slam. At

This fine desert ram shows the typical Mexican wide flaring horns. Leland Speakes took the ram in Arizona's Kofa Range during the 1986 season.

this time the price for a Mexican hunt lists at $12,000. It's no real secret that you'll spend much more before the hunt's over. Everyone involved with the hunts has their hand out. The total may well exceed $15,000.

If you do hunt Mexico, be certain you contact a consulate office near your home to obtain the proper rifle permits. To the best of my knowledge you still may not take any "military" size rifle into Mexico. In general, this means any .30 caliber rifle. Most hunters take a .270 Win. or .243 Win. The Foundation for North American Wild Sheep (see Appendix 2) can help you with details on setting up a Mexican hunt.

A hunter would be rather foolish to plan to hunt anything other than sheep on a desert sheep hunt. The permits are too hard to obtain to take a chance of not getting a ram by concentrating on other game.

However, in most desert sheep country you can enjoy watching other wildlife. On my Nevada hunt we saw numerous mule deer. In Arizona you may see deer or javelina. You may also see the scourge of the desert, the wild burro. These once domestic, gone wild, animals do more damage to wild sheep and desert habitat than all the hunters in the world could do with unlimited permits.

Yes, you need luck to win a desert sheep permit drawing. But remember someone must win and you can't win if you don't apply. I applied for seven years before I drew, but I know sportsmen who drew out the first year and others who have never won after 20 years.

While desert sheep hunting in many respects doesn't seem quite like real sheep hunting, it offers a fascination of its own. You don't smell the bracing odor of spruce or drink from cold mountain streams. You don't watch wild sheep graze without a care across grassy meadows high in the peaks.

But you do watch magenta sunsets paint a spectacular rose hue across the mountaintops at twilight. You ride or walk under the dark green arms of the Joshua and gaze at sparkling white yucca blooms. You admire tiny bright yellow, red and pink desert flowers. You curse the horns and thorns but you notice a distinct absence of mosquitoes and other flying pests.

Above all, you stare with awe and wonderment at the huge curling horns that crown a small sheep king of the mountain.

8

Trophy Rams

L ooking at my trophy room wall, two rams stand out. The desert ram stands out partly because of the massive horns. They rate in the top portion of Boone & Crockett. One bighorn ram doesn't come within 15 points of making the record book. But it stands out in my memory. Both rate true trophy rams in my mind.

What makes a real trophy ram? In fact, what makes a true trophy of any species? Many sportsmen consider only the size of the horn or antler in the definition of a trophy. In fact, many even think the specimen must qualify for the record book to be considered a trophy.

Although some sportsmen will argue the case, I believe that three things determine trophy quality: a memorable experience, the animal's age and the actual horn or antler size.

Memories Of The Trophy Hunt

A memorable experience, regardless of the trophy horn size, rates highest with me. The head on your wall should bring back memories of the hunt, the magnificent country, adventure, lung-busting work, companionship on the hunt, etc. When I say regardless of horn size I don't want to infer you should shoot any size ram just because he leads you on a merry chase. Young and undersized rams should be left for another day even if legal. In fact, I once shot a ram that I should have left to grow. Perhaps I should say a memorable experience with any mature ram, regardless of the trophy horn size, rates highest with me.

In the chapter on desert sheep, I related part of an Alberta bighorn stalk. That's the smallish ram hanging on my wall which ranks right beside the huge desert ram in my mind. That year we camped at the very headwaters of Alberta's Forbidden Creek. We hunted in beautiful sunshine and we hunted in bitter cold. We hunted on dry ground and in deep snow. I sat on the boundary of Banff Park and watched a large band of bighorns feed and rest inside the park. At least three of the rams would score high in the record book.

On that hunt we watched sheep from the cook tent. Some days we walked, hunting from the first step out of the tent. Other days we rode to ridges an hour or two away. After carefully creeping up to check a large band of rams which proved to be all youngsters, we rode past them within a stone's throw without spooking them in the least.

Dewey and I spotted my ram late one afternoon on a sunny day with no snow on the ground. After putting him to bed we returned the next day. As we approached the little ridge, snow fell in large flakes completely obliterating our view of the mountainside where we'd seen the ram. While waiting for the weather to break we built a small fire. As the snow increased, we gradually built up the fire until a roaring blaze kept us warm. As we waited, the talk turned to sheep hunts of the past and rams of the future. The weather broke only long enough for us to confirm the ram indeed stayed on the same mountainside.

The next day we rode out under a bright sun in the blue Alberta sky. Bitter cold tore at my lungs with every breath but we found the ram again. After caping my ram Dewey decided it was foolish for both of us to go back to the horses which waited in the opposite direction from camp. He took the horns and cape to the horses while I headed for a little pass toward camp with the meat.

Knowing that even with a cold morning, the sun would warm the thin air before midday and that I would climb for at least two hours, I had left my down coat with the horses that morning. Even with only a denim jacket and down vest, I soaked my clothes with sweat while climbing the ridge. I stayed warm from the excitement of the stalk and shooting but began to cool as I hiked down the mountain toward the pass.

As I waited for Dewey and the horses, the sun disappeared behind the mountain and I began to shake uncontrollably. Deep

Although this ram is not a record book animal, it is a trophy in the author's eyes. By counting annual rings on the horn, we know this ram lived for 11½ years. Often, a trophy is defined by the hunter, not the score.

snow covered any wood in the area but I knew I had to start a fire. Getting weaker and colder with each minute, I finally managed to find a little semi-dry kindling and a little wood. Unfortunately I couldn't stop shaking long enough to light it. Twenty minutes later I tired again but fortunately Dewey rode up with my warm coat at the same time. I stripped off my wet upper clothes and donned the down coat. Every bone in my body jarred as Dewey set a tough pace back to camp. He, too, was wet through.

By the time we reached camp I felt what can only be described as completely exhausted from the cold, exertion and the hard ride. We saved the first sheep meat for the next day when we'd both feel more like savoring the delicious backstraps.

Add those events to the more normal marmot, eagle, moose and sheep sightings, purple sunsets on snow covered peaks and a bed of spruce boughs. How can I look at that "average" ram on the wall and not have wonderful memories rush back? Memories not only of the agonizing climb, losing the rams, the terrible cold and exhaustion but also of my heart pounding as I squeezed the trigger and the wonderful sense of accomplishment when we counted 11 annual rings on the ram's horns. Yes, to me, that average ram rates a tremendous trophy.

Age Of The Trophy Ram

A ram's age is the second consideration when determining trophy quality. O'Connor often wrote, "Any old ram (10 years or more), whether it measures 35 inches or 45 inches, is a trophy to be proud of." These rams have finished the chore they were put on earth for, to breed new generations of rams.

My good friend and past president of the Foundation for North American Wild Sheep, Jerry Christian, once took a not particularly long or heavy Dall. However, the ram proved to be nearly 15 years old. Jerry is as proud of that ram as he is his Boone & Crockett bighorn. Another friend took only an average size desert ram but he couldn't be prouder of the 13-year-old ram if it broke the world record.

Unlike the deer family, elk, moose, deer, caribou, which shed their antlers, a ram wears horns which he keeps and continues to grow until his death. On these horns, we can read a story of his life, his good times and bad, his battles and his loves. Only on an old ram can we read the entire story.

Unlike the rings on a tree, aging a ram by his annual rings is not an exact science. As well as annual rings, seasonal rings form on all sheep. Horns of a desert ram especially, may be tough to age. Annual rings form at a time of slight hormonal change along with the time of little food in the winter. Since the diet of desert sheep remains rather constant, they may not form as distinct a ring as the northern species. The annual rings near the base of an old ram may be difficult to distinguish from seasonal rings.

Unless you find a ram with perfect tips, you can not start counting rings at the tip because of brooming. Many rams broom off all their lamb year and I've seen rams who broomed off most of their yearling year as well. The third or fourth annual ring represents a better starting point. Normally the third ring is made of two or three light rings close together and the fourth ring cuts the deepest on the horn.

Aging a ram on the hoof is not as difficult as it might seem. Normally you have plenty of time to study your quarry with a spotting scope before you start a stalk. States such as Nevada insist each hunter attend an indoctrination course before they issue the permit. At these courses, state wildlife biologists teach you to both

The longest horned ram ever taken in North America, the Chadwick ram, represents the dream of all trophy hunters. This fabulous ram scored 196⅛ Boone & Crockett points and sports typical argali horns.

age the ram and determine how big he is from a distance.

Dewey Browning and I once sat across the canyon from an old ram for a couple of hours. With the scope we not only figured within one point his total score but estimated his age exactly. The other hunter in camp took the ram several days later. His measurements verified our calculations.

Another time in Alberta, we watched a huge old ram across the canyon for three days in a row before we made the stalk. I'm certain the ram was at least 10 or 11 years of age and he scored between 190 and 195. Unfortunately I can't prove either figure because I never got a shot at the ram.

As well as annual rings to count, an old ram somehow looks old. My 11½-year-old ram shows gray hairs on his neck and chest and around his eyes. Old rams also act old. While younger rams spar with each other or walk around trying to look important, an old ram will lay and watch the proceedings or just chew his cud.

When you estimate a ram's age or count the rings, don't forget that lambs are born in the spring and you see them or shoot them in the fall. Many sportsmen say a ram is seven years old or eight or nine or whatever. Actually the ram you harvest in the fall is 8½, 9½, etc. Annual rings are laid down in mid-winter. On a ram with perfect tips, the three inches or so of lamb growth is actually a half year of growth. Likewise, the horn between the last ring and the skull is just over a half year of growth when you shoot the ram in the fall.

Horn Size

The third and certainly not least important quality to consider for a trophy ram is size. Most sportsmen talk about the ram's horn length. Measure from the lowest point on the front of the base around the outer curve to a point in line with the tip. For years, 40 inches represented the magic number. However, you can hunt for years without ever seeing a 40-inch ram. I've seen only one ram on the hoof which I knew passed the magic 40-mark.

Since few Dall rams broom their horns, 40 inches still represents a good yardstick of exceptional trophy quality. The Boone & Crockett minimum for Dalls is 170 points but I think any Dall 40 inches or over makes a wonderful trophy. Since many Dalls carry light, thin horns, you may need 42- to 43-inch horns to score 170. A broomed Dall with 14½- or 15-inch bases should score near 170.

Since the "typical" Dall ram shows wide flaring or argali

Although this ram looks heavy, the horn doesn't curl far enough down before turning up to score in the record class. This ram is probably 6½ to 7½ years old.

configuration, I'd rather shoot a ram with either of these type of horns than a tight curl ram. With good length, horn mass or heaviness is a bonus. Any extremely old ram, especially a broomed one, should make a real trophy since brooming is unusual in Dalls.

The minimum Boone & Crockett score for Stone sheep is also 170. Moreover you need a ram scoring closer to the 170 in a Stone than in a Dall to be considered a fine trophy. Any Stone measuring from 39 to 40 inches represents an outstanding trophy and if you find heavy bases or massive horns you have an exceptional trophy.

You'll find more broomed Stone rams than Dalls. Most hunters would much rather take an old broomed Stone with massive horns than one with 40-inch plus horns that are thin or still wear perfect points.

Since you must draw a permit in the United States (other than in the unlimited areas of Montana) I believe that any legal bighorn in the United States is a fine trophy. Colorado sheep might offer the exception to this rule. What constitutes a legal Colorado ram differs by area, but most require only a one-half curl. Most sportsmen can't really justify calling a one-half curl ram a trophy. Actually legal definitions by one-half curl, three-quarter curl, etc. are a poor description but I'll refer to that later.

Alberta and British Columbia bighorns need another yardstick however. Although they require 180 points to make the record book, I think 170 to 175 makes a wonderful trophy. This translates to about 35 inches by 15½-inch bases. Of course any old ram (10 years or older) with heavy, broomed horns gets the respect of most sheep hunters.

Although you must also win a drawing to hunt desert rams, the ram should measure nearly the 168 points required to make the record book. Desert sheep are really in good supply compared to the number of permits issued. Hunting weather is much more apt to be good on a desert hunt and you should find a ram at least over 160 on most desert hunts. Any bighorn or desert ram carrying 15-inch bases and 35-inch horn length will make the book. In fact, any broomed ram with 36- to 38-inch horns is excellent and any desert or bighorn over 40 inches broomed is the greatest.

Most game departments use some sort of curl fraction to define a legal ram. In the judgment of most biologists and veteran hunters this is the poorest way to rate a ram. In fact, by looking at various regulations, different states even have different standards as to what constitutes a three-quarter ram. Other states, notably Nevada, require the ram to measure so many points (145) or have obtained

This fine Stone ram, taken by Charlie Gephart in 1974, sports 42½-inch horns. Notice that this ram did not broom his horns, which resulted in the 40-inch plus measurement.

a certain age (7 years). This system is much more realistic.

The first ram I shot sported what's known as a full curl. However, because the ram had a small head and tight curl, the young ram measured only 32 inches. Although more than legal, I should never have shot that ram.

On other rams, especially bighorns and desert sheep, the horns grow far back with a shallow curve. These horns may measure 40 inches or better and never go near a full curl or even three-quarter curl. Many old rams broom enough horn to not qualify as three-quarter curl.

The old "doughnut" bighorn ram I wrote about in Chapter 6 barely qualified for Alberta's four-fifths curl but scored near the record book and produced a fine trophy. Although three-quarter curl rams qualify in most states, the rule results in many three- and four-year-old rams being shot. We should naturally leave these to breed and grow. According to several reports, many states are now considering going to some age or total measurement requirements as Nevada has done.

Ram horns are about the easiest to score officially of any horn or antler in the book. The score sheets spell out exactly how to measure the horns. First measure the total length of the horn from the lowest point on the front of the base around the outer curve to a point in line with the tip.

Next measure the circumference of the base at right angles to axis of horn. Do not follow the irregular edge of the horn. Divide the total length of the longest horn by four and mark both horns at these quarters starting at the base. Then measure the circumference at the first, second and third quarters.

Although you will not deduct any score for difference in horn length, you do deduct differences in the base and quarter circumferences. When measuring total length, don't run the tape down into any chips or broken spots. However, when measuring circumferences, you must pull the tape tight into such depressions. A large chip out of my desert horns cost me an inch or two on the total score.

Over the years, sheep horns do shrink. The Stone ram my dad shot in 1973 measured just under the book minimum 170. Today, it measures only 165. For some reason, one set of horns may shrink quite a bit while another will shrink hardly at all over the years. Some experts theorize that desert horns shrink less because they are quite dry to begin with compared to the more northern horns. Both Boone & Crockett and Pope & Young require any horns to dry for 60 days before they can be officially measured. Although this does not represent the actual ram on the mountain it does give every sportsman the same starting point.

Unfortunately you can't take a tape measure into the mountains and get the ram to stand still while you measure his trophy qualities. Fortunately, you can learn to judge with fairly great accuracy how big a head is in the field. A few heads may fool even experts but most run to form.

First, in order to judge sheep horns you must look at as many horns as possible. On my first sheep hunt, I'd never seen a live sheep and only a few mounted heads. With more experience I would have passed the ram. Go to museums. Go to a large taxidermy studio. Go to hunter conventions and sports shows.

You can also go to several wintering grounds in both the U.S. and Canada to study live sheep. December usually offers the best

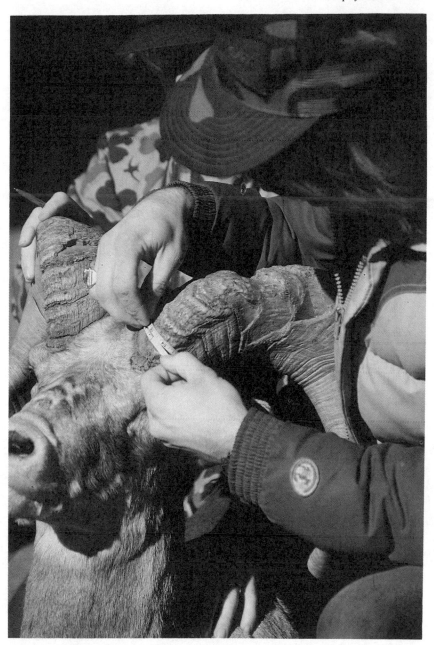

When scoring a ram, measure the horn base perpendicular to the center of the skull, as shown above.

viewing, before the rams leave the ewes. In the Whiskey Mountain area near Dubois, Wyoming, you can view rams from your car every winter. Rams normally come down during the winter near Corwin Springs, Montana. Depending on the winter you can often find rams close to town at Ouray, Colorado. Banff and Jasper parks in Canada also offer excellent wintertime viewing. If you know where to look, you can find rams in Yellowstone during the summer and fall months but you have to climb to them.

I have never met a sheep guide who wasn't an excellent judge of sheep horns. However, occasionally a guide might be in a hurry to finish the hunt and suggest you take the first legal sheep. Also I enjoy judging myself and comparing notes with my guide. After all, you are the one who must look at the trophy on the wall.

In judging sheep, first look for mass. Top trophy rams appear all horns. You wonder how they can carry such a weight. This is true regardless of the species or the curl type. Real trophies have large bases and carry the weight well out on the horn. Remember, an inch more around the bases will add many more points to the total score than an inch greater length.

To approach the magic 40 inches, a ram's horn should curl well back, go below the line of the jaw and then come above the bridge of the nose. If the ram is well-broomed and qualifies with the above guidelines, he is a monster you should celebrate in song and story.

I once saw a 4-year-old ram high above Lucky Canyon in Alberta showing the potential to score high in the record book. He needed only another five or six years. We'd looked at a different ram for several minutes with the spotting scope. As it turned out, this ram had broken one horn off near the base, ruining the trophy value. With nothing better to do we turned the scope on younger rams.

As we watched, the rams obliged us by walking up to the skyline and posing like sentinels in the sky. With blue sky as a backdrop, we soon noticed the young, half-curl ram. His horns went well back but more importantly, they curled so far down that we saw sky between the horn and the rams lower jaw. His bases appeared to be at least 15 inches at the time. Given a few years he must have scored well into the 190s. I've never seen a young ram with bigger horns nor have I ever seen so much space between a ram's jaw and horn.

On argali-type horns with Stone and Dall sheep, try to view the ram head-on as well as from the side. The tips should run well out

When measuring horn length, don't dip the tape into any missing chinks. However, when measuring circumference, the tape must be pulled tight into such holes.

beyond the outside of the curl. Wide-flaring horns should look massive before they turn out.

If the horns look light (not massive or heavy), curve above the point of the jaw and have perfect points, the ram is young. Even unbroomed rams which have their points come above the nose are probably young.

On the other hand, real trophy horns look huge. They show both mass and length. Heavily broomed bighorns and desert rams will always score well. Even a neophyte can recognize a book ram. Unfortunately, few hunters ever see a book ram. Perhaps the best guideline is your own opinion. If you can't decide if the ram rates a real trophy, he is not.

Some rams fool even experts. Droopy horns, especially in bighorns and desert rams, go well back on the curve but never come near the bridge of the nose. These horns look more oval than round viewed from the side and if they are heavy they can score high. Well-broomed horns also may never go near full curl, but remember mass scores more than length.

You'll see a few horns that appear to carry the mass well out on the horn but these won't score well if you start with small bases. They just appear big. Small rams or those with miniature heads appear to wear larger horns than they actually measure. Compare the ram's size with others in the band.

My desert ram fooled me in the opposite direction. Although I knew he would score well, I didn't realize he made the book until we started taping. His horns carried the weight so well and in such perfect proportion that they didn't look like record book material.

Actually, finding record book or at least bragging-size rams is mostly a matter of luck. You can hunt areas known for big rams for years and never see a record book ram. And in the true spirit of sheep hunting, record book rams really are only the icing on the cake. By the same token you may stumble on that book ram anywhere or even find several huge trophies at the same time.

That was the case of David Onerheim when he found and bagged what is now the third largest bighorn since 1924. Before Onerheim booked his British Columbia hunt, his outfitter, Lance McLean, told him that if he could climb a bit, he could get him on a nice ram. McLean also mentioned a big ram he had spotted for two years in a row but could never find during the hunting season.

McLean and Onerheim drove and climbed into the hunt area two days before the season opened. After setting up camp, they climbed and glassed the day before the season opened. They found

T.S. Marcum's ram, at first glance, looks larger than it actually measures because the ram carries horn weight well. However, the bases and corresponding quarters come up an inch short of what they should. Even so, this ram, taken near Timber Creek, Alberta, scored 184³/₈ B&C points.

a huge mountain goat. As darkness crept into the valley below, the weather turned cold.

"Suddenly," Onerheim said, "Lance laid down his binoculars and got behind the spotting scope. 'Rams!' he exclaimed. 'There in the brush. All I can see is a glimpse of their horns now and then when they move.' "

"Finally the rams climbed up a small cliff and out into the open. Lance said they were both heavy rams but there would be no way to stalk them where they are. The slide area they were in could only be seen from our location. You could be 100 yards from them and never know they were there in the steep, rocky little chute. We also spotted more trouble, a large grizzly moving in the direction of the rams,'' Onerheim reported.

At dawn opening day, Onerheim and McLean were again climbing the mountain. At one point, a nice six-point bull elk stepped out on a rock ledge and looked at the hunters broadside from about 60 yards. Onerheim had an elk tag. When McLean asked if he wanted to hunt elk or rams that day, Onerheim shook his head and watched the bull turn into the brush.

"When we reached yesterday's observation point Lance quickly set up the scope and announced the rams were still there. With no course of action available, we sat and watched as the rams fed and sparred with each other. Soon the rams started down the chute,'' Onerheim said.

"Lance was worried. If the rams moved down, crossed the creek and continued into the heavy timber, we would lose them for good. Lance said we should try to head them off at the creek. We shouldered our packs and slipped and slid downhill as fast as our legs could handle the snowslide. An hour later we reached the bottom. After crossing the creek several times we reached an opening in the brush almost directly below the spot where we had last seen the rams. From separate vantage points, we sat quietly watching for 30 minutes. The rams might have beaten us, as it had taken us much longer to reach the spot where they could have been in 15 or 20 minutes.

"We could find no tracks anywhere, but that didn't mean much. They could have moved in one direction or the other and crossed. Maybe they were still up there. Maybe they turned and went through timber to another snowslide. Maybe they went up the mountain. One thing for sure, we couldn't see much from where we were. We stared up, looking for the rams.

"Initially it felt good to climb, after going downhill for so long. The goodness quickly wore off, however, as my legs became fatigued. The timber was much thinner on this slope, but the brush was thicker and tugged at us as we groped our way upward. We reached an area we thought must be close to where we last saw the rams. Lance dropped his pack and said he would move up closer to glass and that I should stay and rest.

"I looked up to see Lance on a ledge, a couple of hundred yards above me. He motioned for me to leave my pack and get up there, quickly,'' Onerheim said.

David Onerheim's trophy ram scored 201¹/₈ B&C points. It is now the third largest bighorn ram harvested in North America since 1924. Note how massive trophy horns look even from the underside.

After hauling himself up to McLean, the hunter and guide crawled silently over rocks and around brush to a place where they could inch over the top.

Finally Onerheim spotted movement behind the trees only 50 yards away. He placed his rifle over the ledge and looked at a huge, heavy-horned ram with more than a full curl. Before he could fire, McLean stopped him.

"Lance motioned that the other ram was better. How could it be, I thought. As my eyes scanned the brush and rocks through the tree branches in front of us, I saw the second ram put his head down to feed," Onerheim said. "All I could see clearly was his massive horns and head. I slowly moved the rifle scope on him, and watched, my heart pounding in my throat. I did not want to shoot him in the head, and his body was completely blocked by trees."

The ram finally took a half-step forward and Onerheim's .30-06 broke the ram's neck. The other ram nearly ran over the hunters in its confusion. It would have scored 195 or better. Onerheim's ram scored 203⅞ in the field and officially scored 201⅛ Boone & Crockett points. The longer horn measures 49⅜ inches and the shorter 44⅝ inches.

Not only did Lady Luck bring the hunters within shooting distance of a record book ram but two record book rams on the first day of the hunt.

We can help Lady Luck by hunting in areas with the best chance of taking a real trophy ram. In some cases, the trophy hunter must hunt an area with fewer rams than others to find his trophy. Often the area with the most rams doesn't hold many or any record book rams. The best genetics, the right mineral content of the soil and nutritious forage all go toward producing top rams.

According to Boone & Crockett records, five record book desert rams came from Baja California and one from Sonora, Mexico, between 1990 and 1994. In the states, Arizona produced 32 record book desert rams, Nevada produced 13, California produced three and Texas produced one.

Nevada's Clark and Lincoln counties produced 12 of the state's 13 record book desert rams between 1990 and 1994. Of Arizona's 32 record book desert rams, eight came from Mohave County, seven from Yuma County and four from Coconimo County.

California might loom as a dark horse area for big desert rams. A very limited hunting season offered the first nonresident permits

*Note how this Colorado ram carries his weight all the way around his
heavily-broomed horns. Bowhunter Ray Alt bagged this ram later in the year. It
scored 185 Pope & Young points.*

in 1988. Since no hunting has been allowed in modern California history, you might find some super rams there.

Alberta and Montana produce by far the most record book big-horns. During the 1990 to 1994 period, Albert recorded 20 heads in the book and Montana 97. According to outfitter Dewey Browning, the headwaters of the Gregg, McLeod and Cardinal rivers annually produce the largest rams in Alberta but not as many rams as other areas. All three rivers are located between the larger Brazeau and Athabasca rivers.

In Montana, the three-county area of Granite, Deer Lodge and Missoula accounted for 43 of the record book heads from 1990 through 1994. Farther north and west, Sanders county produced 21 record rams during the same period. The following hunt districts correspond to the counties in 1988; Sanders County—district 121, Granite County—district 216, Deer Lodge County—district 213 and Missoula County—district 203.

Colorado may offer more and more trophy rams in the future and should be considered a good dark horse state. Only recently has Colorado allowed nonresidents to hunt bighorns. Normally nonresidents hold out for better trophies than do residents. The state certainly produces young rams with impressive statistics. For example, in one three year period unit S7 (Freemont County) pro-duced a 2-year-old ram with 14-inch bases, a 5-year-old with 16-inch bases and a 6-year-old with 16⅜-inch bases. Unit S6 (Parts of Saguache and Chaffee counties) produced a 3-year-old with 16-inch bases and two, 3-year-old rams with 15-inch plus bases. However, these rams must be allowed to grow into mature rams and Colorado allows hunters to shoot half curl rams. Colorado's 3-year prefer-ence system will also make it a bit easier to get drawn for a permit there than in other states.

Stone sheep ranges don't change much over the years. Prior to 1980 most of the record book rams came from the Muskwa-Prophet, Dease and Cassiar areas in British Columbia. Between 1990 and 1994, British Columbia produced 19 book rams and the Yukon Ter-ritory produced two book rams. In 1986, the Muskwa-Prophet ranges produced all four of the Foundation for North American Wild Sheep competition winners. In 1987, the Stone Mountain area produced three of the top five awards.

According to outfitter Ross Peck, the eastern range from the Muskwa-Prophet to the Toad produces the largest rams. The famous Chadwick ram genes are still around. This fact, combined with efforts on range enhancement and wolf control, makes for

This excellent ram will score near the book, and will eventually grow into a real trophy. Note how far the horn curls down before going up.

excellent rams. However, since these eastern areas are accessible to resident hunters, they receive heavy hunting pressure. Rams need the chance to grow to 10 or 12 years of age to make the book. Peck also credits the new bridge of the nose, full curl regulations for allowing some deep curl, young rams to grow to trophy age. Patience in Stone country produces the best trophies. You must pass those young, just legal rams, until you find a trophy that fits your qualifications. Because of the outfitter's quota system, based partially on harvested ram age, and the full curl requirement, hunters should find more and more good Stone sheep in the future.

Prior to 1980, nearly all Boone & Crockett Dall rams came from Alaska's Wrangell and Chugach ranges. A few came from the Yukon but seldom any from the Northwest Territories. Between 1990 and 1994, nine book heads came from Alaska, one from the Yukon and two from the Northwest Territories. Nearly all the

Alaska rams came from the Wrangell, Chugach area. At the present time Alaska allows what they call a seven-eighths curl ram to be harvested in most units. However, in parts of units 12, 13 and 20, you must find a full curl ram and the state limits the number of permits issued in these units to promote larger rams.

All the Dall rams winning the Foundation for North American Sheep competition in 1986 and 1987 came from the Northwest Territories. Most came from the central two hunt units and one from the southernmost unit of the Mackenzie Mountains. The Northwest Territories have to rate about the best chance for a book ram today. Most experts agree that big rams were probably always in this province but not many sportsmen hunted them until the new, young breed of outfitters came along in the early 1980s.

Remember, you alone determine whether a ram measures up. Think about size, age, overall attractiveness and the memories the ram will bring back. That's your trophy ram. If it makes the book, you have a bonus.

9

Bowhunting
Sheep And Goats

For many bowhunters, the possibility of roaming high places and stalking wild sheep or mountain goats seems an unattainable goal. Something like climbing Mt. Everest or dating a beautiful celebrity. Somewhere, in some long-forgotten time, someone started the rumor that sheep and goat hunting included very long-range propositions. Since then, outdoor writers and hunters around campfires propagated the myth. They tell with glowing words and flowing phrases of the 400-yard shots required to bring down these beautiful mountain animals.

But pay attention. Actually more sheep and goats are shot with a rifle at under 150 yards than over that figure. In fact, I took my desert ram under 40 yards, well within bow range. The rifleman doesn't stalk closer simply because he doesn't need to and he is afraid he might spook the game.

NAHC Bowhunting Advisory Council Member Chuck Adams, one of the many dedicated sheep and goat bowhunters, reports, "The mountain animals are highly visible on the slopes and crags they call home, making them ideal for any one who enjoys spot and stalk techniques."

Actually, veteran sheep and goat hunters can't come up with any reason for not hunting them with bows, presuming you're able to climb and shoot. Why shouldn't bowhunters enjoy the high country as much as riflemen?

Without a doubt, more bowhunters hunt whitetails than any other game. But the vast majority of whitetail bowhunters stay on a stand either in a tree or on the ground. Other than scouting, the bowhunter must take only a passive role and let the deer come near the stand.

In contrast, the sheep and goat hunter with a bow plays an active role. Other than special circumstances, the ram or goat won't come to you. Rather, you must spot and stalk the quarry in the high country. Nothing in nature offers more excitement than stalking in the high country.

Neither sheep nor goats are particularly hard to find, stalk or harvest. In fact, the same equipment you use on whitetails works well on high country animals. Sheep and goats neither represent the most wary nor the most intelligent of wild game. No, the thrill of hunting the high country comes with the awe-inspiring scenery, the eerie silence of the high basins, the majesty of the animals and the other aspects we discussed in the opening chapter. Stalking the beautiful creatures can sometimes present difficult situations, especially in wide open basins, but normally you can find something to stalk behind, around or in to sneak within bow distance of a ram or goat.

Since the early 1980s, many bowhunters have taken to the field in search of high country game. Also, many sheep and goat hunters took up the bow as a new challenge in the high country. At this time several outstanding bowhunters have the grand slam.

Men no longer run an exclusive sheep and goat hunting club. Furthermore, men no longer run an exclusive bowhunting club. Many women now hunt the high country with a bow. And they do so with outstanding results. In many cases, I believe the female personality is more suited to hunting the high country than the male. They exhibit much more patience and determination.

Due to special regulations in some areas, bowhunters actually gain a big advantage over rifle hunters. Many areas in both the United States and Canada offer either bow only areas or bow only seasons. In these areas you may hunt sheep or goats which have not been spooked by rifle hunters. In some cases, the animals never hear a rifle.

Alberta offers perhaps the best and most well known bow only sheep area. Unit 410 (BG15), located outside the town of Banff lies just outside the southeast corner of Banff Park. Not only do they prohibit all rifle hunting in this unit but the hunting season extends well into the annual rut. In fact I know of no other sheep

Linda Strong proves that bowhunters can get close to sheep for an accurate shot. Above, Linda stalks to within range of a Dall ram in the Northwest Territories.

hunting area in North America that offers hunting during the rut.

Wild sheep, like all wild game, become much less wary during the rut. Sheep can't count and neither can they seem to pay attention to more than one thing at a time. During the rut, that one thing is sex. I won't say sheep do outright dumb things during the rut like caribou, but they pay little attention to anything other than their favorite ewe or ewes. By the way, wild rams don't gather a harem like elk nor do they stake out a territory like deer. Completely promiscuous best describes a ram's rut behavior. They move from ewe to ewe as they find interest.

You need only travel to the Whiskey Mountain wintering area outside Dubois, Wyoming, in November or December to witness ram behavior during rut. The same animals hunters sought only a month or two before now let you approach in your car while they court their ewes or put on sparring contests.

As good as hunting rams during the rut may be, the rut offers one distinct disadvantage. Because the sheep are grouped together, you find many, even dozens of rams watching your every move. And, you can easily run onto ewes and lambs in the middle of a stalk and ruin the whole thing.

Not only does the Alberta bow only season offer the archer an opportunity to hunt an area where a rifle is never fired, but by

Bowhunter Linda Strong is shown here with her trophy Dall ram.

November many monster rams come out of the park for the rut. Normally, the rams migrate to areas lower than their summer range. However, hunting this area during November can be tough. Deep snow and cold forces the hunter to be in top physical shape.

In the end, the many advantages of hunting sheep during the rut in a bow only area more than outweigh any disadvantages. All licensed Alberta sheep outfitters receive one or two archery permits for this area.

Colorado offers around 80 resident and 10 nonresident archery bighorn permits each year. The state reserves six units for archery only. In addition, the archery season opens before the rifle season in two good units. In only a few Colorado areas must the archer compete with rifle hunters during the same season.

The archery season in units S-12 and S-20 now opens two or three weeks prior to the rifle season. Both units hold excellent sheep populations. Unit S-12, including portions of Lake, Chaffee and Park counties, sits between Leadville and Fairplay. Even though S-12 offers good access, the area is so large that most rams stay back in remote areas. The northern portion contains mostly alpine tundra while the southern end is timbered ridges with open parks.

You'll find unit S-20 west of Salida and Poncha Springs.

Vehicle access is quite limited but you can reach most of the sheep terrain in a day or less. Most of the area lies above timberline.

Colorado units S-32, north of Georgetown, and S-34, northwest of Colorado Springs, probably hold more rams than any other bow only area. Access into area S-32 is fairly easy. Most of the sheep range is timber with rock outcroppings. In the last year or two bowhunters took several huge rams in this area so the drawing odds will not be good for a few years.

Although unit S-34 offers easy access, sheep are often difficult to locate because of the many steep canyons, heavy brush and timbered cover. However, you'll find the sheep range at much lower elevation here than most other units.

Units S-35 southwest of Pueblo, and S-46 north of Cripple Creek, represent the big and little of Colorado's archery only areas. Many roads crisscross the huge unit S-35, but vehicle access to the real heart of the sheep range is limited. Bowhunters who will backpack or ride horses in will experience a real quality hunt.

On the other hand, little unit S-46 offers fairly good access but spotting the sheep can be difficult due to heavy timber and rocky terrain. However, once you locate a sheep, the same terrain makes stalking simple.

Units S-44 south of Eagle and S-57 east of Estes Park represent the last two archery only units in Colorado. Access to S-44 is not considered difficult. The northern boundary follows a long ridge that is often above timberline. The ridge is rounded but generally rocky with less vegetation than other areas. The larger unit S-57 offers good access and contains a good number of sheep.

The long narrow unit S-9 offers the most archery permits of any area but you must compete at the same time with rifle hunters.

The state of Washington contains one unit for archers only. The Department of Wildlife offers four special permits for this area which makes up part of Yakima and Kittitas counties near the city of Ellensburg. Like other archery only areas around the country, this area offers bowhunters the chance to hunt sheep never spooked by rifles.

Bowhunters in Wyoming must draw a regular rifle bighorn permit and then purchase a special archery license. Although Wyoming does not offer any archery only areas, they often allow bowhunters to take the field two weeks prior to the rifle opening.

Dall sheep hunters can select from two bow only areas to avoid rifle hunters. In the Yukon, apply for unit GMS9-03 south of Whitehorse. Unlike rifle permits in the Yukon, the special bow only permits are issued through a drawing. Alaska also offers one bow only area. The 25 permits for the Eklutna Management Area near Anchorage are issued through a drawing.

Although British Columbia doesn't officially offer any archery only Stone sheep areas, the Todagin Mountain section of unit 6-20 is listed as a no shooting area. It is not listed as a no hunting area, so you may hunt Stone sheep with a bow there.

No other states offer bow only sheep areas or special early or late bow only seasons. However, in most good sheep country even rifle hunters seldom see another hunter. If you can draw a permit and want to bowhunt, give it a try even if you must hunt with rifle hunters.

For the archery goat hunter, Colorado offers three bow only areas. Bowhunters may choose the southern portion of unit G-2 southwest of Buena Vista, unit G-5 between Durango and Silverton and unit G-8 northeast of Gunnison. Nonresidents may apply for unit G-2 or G-5

Mountain goat populations have declined in Washington. In the mid-1990s only 14 permits were available to bowhunters. Two bow units—Corral Pass and Smith Creek—are in the Cascades; the Hamma Hamma unit is in the Olympics.

As with sheep hunting, goat hunters in other states and provinces should consider a bow due to the limited number of rifle permits available in any one area.

If patience rates high on a sheep or goat hunters successful techniques list, it must rate at the very top of a bowhunting sheep or goat hunter's list. If you find your quarry in a spot where you can't stalk within bow range, you must wait for the animal to move or come back the next day and try again. Some bowhunters consider 60 yards the limit of their effective range. Most experts however, consider 40 yards and under a much better situation. Take a shot at over 40 yards only if you have practiced and know what your arrow will do at that distance.

Hunting sheep or goats with a bow starts the same as rifle hunting. You climb, glass, climb and glass. However, after you locate your quarry you must find a route which will lead you to within bow range without being seen. As with the rifle hunter, the bowhunter should, if at all possible, come out above and behind the ram or goat. But since you must stalk closer, you may have to

NAHC Bowhunting Advisory Council Member Chuck Adams has successfully hunted mountain goats with a bow. Hunting goats with a bow requires more patience than hunting with a rifle. However, because of their calm, phlegmatic attitude, goats may be easier to approach with a bow than sheep.

end up below or to the side of the quarry if that's where you find available cover.

From a distance, many sheep basins look wide open and flat or bowl shaped. Most often you can find something to stalk behind, around or through. The desert ram that I stalked to within 30 or 40 yards is a case in point.

Although I didn't need to stalk that close with my rifle and certainly didn't want to, the fact that I did proves a bowhunter could have easily shot the same ram. In my case two deep coulees provided excellent cover for the stalk.

Looking back on the terrain, I'm certain I also could have stalked within bow range of at least one bighorn and a Dall ram. Most good Stone sheep country is broken enough or contains enough boulders to stalk within bow range. As you plan a stalk, remember you must not approach with the wind at your back and you must not let the ram see you. The sound of moving rocks normally won't bother a ram.

Rain, snow or fog can provide excellent cover if you must move a distance across open ground before you can get behind a ridge or boulder or in a ravine to make the final stalk. Normally even fog won't help you stalk those final yards to get within bow range, but it will make the initial stalk easier and quicker.

If you find nothing to offer cover for the final approach, you must wait. The ram or goat may move into an area that offers good cover or even move toward you. The wait can seem like the toughest minutes or hours of your life but wait you must. Don't lose a good trophy because you lose your patience.

In certain areas, your ram may appear every day in a place where you simply can't stalk him. But by observing his habits for several days you can learn if he always moves into a basin from a certain area, over a certain saddle or from a certain timber. If you do, then set up an ambush at that point and wait for the ram. Normally you'll find goats in rugged areas where you can easily find a route to make a stalk.

Wild sheep and goats are not particularly hard to take. Even so they may stumble quite a distance before falling dead. Like the whitetail hunter, you should wait as long as possible before following the critically wounded animal. Let him go off, lay down and die. If you push the ram or goat they may travel much farther. Because of the open terrain sheep and goats call home, you can usually watch them without actually following. However, some-

Like rifle hunters, high country bowhunters make good use of horses. NAHC Bowhunting Advisory Council Members Jim Dougherty (above) and Chuck Adams used horses on a mountain goat hunt that was plagued by snowstorms.

times even the best shot and best plans can go astray.

This happened to Colorado bowhunter Linda Strong on her Dall sheep hunt in the Northwest Territories. Only by determination and heroic effort did Linda find and finish off her ram after making an excellent chest shot. Linda caught a bad case of sheep fever when she hunted and bagged a bighorn with a rifle in 1980. She started bowhunting two years later and now hunts with either bow or rifle depending on the season.

Linda and her husband, Bob, hunted with outfitter Greg Williams of Nahanni Butte Outfitters. They backpacked with the help of Greg's pack dogs. During two long days walking into the best sheep country, the Strongs and their guide Shane, spotted several sheep including two full curl rams. They decided to pass the rams because the sheep carried extremely tight curls that wouldn't measure up to real trophy standards. Other than one 36-hour period of rain and fog, the trio set up camp at a different spot each night, wherever they ended the day's hunt.

Midway through the hunt, Shane spotted a beautiful full curl ram with flaring horns. Unfortunately the ram stood in a wide, flat, open basin. They counted 100 other sheep in the basin including ewes and lambs. While Bob stayed with the dogs, Linda and Shane tried a stalk. By moving slowly, the hunters got between the ram and the other sheep without spooking them.

Eventually, Linda crawled out on a rim above the ram. She wanted to stalk closer but she could find no place to move out of sight. She tried a shot downhill at an extremely steep angle. The arrow flew over the ram's back. The ram didn't know what was going on and didn't spook. They decided to wait until morning to try again. In the meantime Bob set up camp below the rams.

The next morning Bob joined Linda and Shane looking for the ram. After searching for several hours, they found the ram a short distance from where they left him the night before. Unfortunately they couldn't stalk into good position for a shot because of the wide-open basin. But while trying to get close they spooked the ram.

"The ram started out of the basin back in the direction we originally came from," Linda told me. "Fortunately he only walked and he stayed below the ridge. We dropped our packs and tried to get ahead of the ram. We'd go to the ridge and peek over, then back out of sight and hurry on. After several peeks, the ram remained ahead. By this time my breath came in short gasps and my legs ached like someone had hit them with hammers."

To be certain your archery tackle is kept in top shape at all times, bring a sharpening stone with you on the high country hunt. Broadheads must have a razor edge to penetrate the heavy muscles of a ram or goat.

Finally between 2 and 3 p.m., Shane peeked over the ridge and found the ram bedded in the rocks. Shane thought the ram would stay down long enough to stalk within range. Linda started the 200-yard stalk.

"We picked out a large boulder we estimated was within 35 yards of the ram. Other rocks and a little ridge would cover me to the boulder," she said. "A little breeze flowed up the mountain so he wouldn't catch my scent. I moved pretty fast about halfway. I couldn't resist a peek and saw the ram get up and shift a bit. Fortunately he lay down again and I vowed not to peek again.

"Crawling downhill proved impossible so I turned over and sort of slid down on my back as slowly as possible. At the time I felt nothing but later found out the rocks had bruised my hips and shoulders. When the big boulder came into sight, I crouched and crept down behind it. Pain shot through my cramped legs but my breathing steadied by this time.

"After taking a deep breath I started to draw and stand up. The ram must have heard something because he jumped up just as I drew. There he stood at 35 yards so I stepped out and shot. Thud, the arrow hit him square in the chest. I made a perfect shot. My throat tightened and my heart beat in my chest. I felt no pain in my legs, only elation. I wanted to scream with joy."

As the ram jumped, whirled and ran, Linda slunked back behind the rock to give the ram time. She thought he'd go no more than 30 or 40 yards and lie down and die. Instead, the ram ran along the hillside and then up through a saddle and down into a huge basin. Bob and Shane saw the arrow protruding from the ram's chest and blood as he ran across the saddle, but then they lost sight of him. They were all astonished that the ram ran that far, but they started the search. The ram had run into a huge basin made up of rock slides with boulders the size of a house. He could be anywhere.

"We crawled up, across and down the rock slide. Shane even crossed the basin to the next ridge to get a different angle of view or to see if the ram crossed over that far," she said. "No luck. When darkness overtook the basin late that night we gave up and returned to camp. After being on such a high after the shot, my spirits dove to deep despair back at camp. I felt terrible about the wounded ram, just sick at the thought we couldn't find him. I never spent a longer night."

Before they quit that night, Bob found a faint blood trail. He also saw where the ram's hooves dug into the tundra and where he

Several bowhunters have taken the grand slam, including NAHC Bowhunting Advisory Council Member Chuck Adams. Chuck bagged this Dall sheep in the Northwest Territories.

veered off toward a massive rock slide. However, the trail didn't last long.

The next day with no other clues, the trio worked the basin in a huge grid. They worked across, dropped down and across again. A day-long drizzle slickened the moss on the rocks.

"After we completed about half the grid, I fell on a wet rock and cut my leg. As Bob patched the leg, I sat dejected but determined. While he waited for us, Shane happened to look up across the valley and spotted my ram laying on the next ridge. He held his head up but we could see blood on his white side. What a huge stoke of luck. We'd have never noticed him while working our grid,'' Linda said.

Bob stayed put to keep track of the ram. They didn't want to lose him again. Linda and Shane climbed over the top and around to the back side of the ridge. On the way, they stumbled into sheep on top including one real nice ram. Shane hoped they could get Bob back on that ram later. Linda and Shane carefully avoided spooking any of the sheep on top. Heavier drizzle and fog forced the pair to stop several times to wait for the fog to lift. When they reached a spot directly above where the ram should be, Shane stayed back while Linda crawled and slid down the side.

"Everything looked different from this side of the basin and above the ram. I worked my way down through rock, sparse timber and more tundra. Suddenly my ram jumped up about 3 yards away. Talk about scared. I expected him down farther. I hadn't seen him because he lay in sort of a little divot. Anyway, he took off into the rock slide. I released a shot but not a good one. I was really spooked myself. My wits were shot.''

The ram crossed another large area but Linda didn't know exactly where. By this time, the woman was absolutely determined to find her wounded ram. She glared in his direction and glared at her guide. Linda headed across the slide with Shane in the rear. They looked at Bob across the canyon for signals.

About halfway across the slide, Linda and Shane had to wait for the fog again. Then they saw Bob signal. They trekked on across the slide to a ledge. Linda crept to the edge and peeked over. Her ram lay 15 feet straight down.

"I've got him now, I thought as I drew the string back to my cheek. Just as I released the ram jumped and ran again,'' she told me. "The arrow missed. By this time it was a marathon but my ram was getting weaker. I saw him stumble as he ran into the timber.

"When he didn't come out of the little timber patch, I headed down and found him in a little draw. When I moved another step the ram saw me and ran off 75 yards but then stopped and looked back at me. I thought, this is it. He's a long way but I couldn't cross another rock slide. My legs felt like spaghetti but I concentrated as hard as I could and let fly. I thought the arrow would never reach him. It arched and hit the ram in the hind quarter. The ram took two wobbly steps and fell, blood gushing from an artery hit.

"I felt like I had climbed Mt. Everest, won the Miss America

Chuck Adams' Stone sheep would make any rifle hunter proud. Chuck bagged this ram in British Columbia one month after his successful Dall sheep hunt.

contest, won the lottery. I don't know, but it was the most exhilarating feeling ever, so tremendous. It was the perfect climax to a perfect hunt," Linda concluded.

By this time it was 10:30 p.m. on a beautiful August night in the Northwest Territories. Bob watched the entire final stalk. Shane yelled for Bob to come over. They all fell into sleeping bags, exhausted at 4 a.m. What started as a fairly typical stalk and good shot turned into a 36-hour test of conditioning, determination and skill. Almost a nightmare.

Linda offered a few tips for bowhunters, but especially women bowhunters. "Practice every day with your bow. Shoot standing, crouching, uphill, downhill, through brush. Practice stalking marmots, rabbits, squirrels, deer, anything, but practice. You also must learn to judge distance and be in top condition. I felt very at home on the hunt. A woman must relax and let herself get dirty. If you try to look like you're going to the club, you won't have any fun at all. Enjoy the beautiful sheep country. Above all develop confidence in yourself and your ability. And stick to it."

Linda's story points out perhaps the most important strategy for a bowhunter, male or female. She selected a particular boulder within bow range of the ram before she ever started the stalk. Most rifle hunters have a general idea where they will end up but within 100 yards or so it doesn't really matter.

On the other hand, bowhunters must know exactly where the stalk will end. Pick out a tree, rock, bush, anything that brings you within range. Then avoid any temptation to peek at your ram. Stay out of sight until you reach the target mark. When you select the rock, tree, etc., be certain you can reach that marker out of sight of the ram. If you can't find a reliable route, wait.

Always leave your guide behind for the final stalk. Two people are twice as easy for the ram to see or hear than one. Also, if he stays behind, your guide can watch the sheep in case it moves. Glance back at him once in a while.

If for some reason you don't get a shot or miss badly, don't give up. Often if the ram is not badly spooked, he may just walk off a short way and stop. In more remote areas, even the sight of a hunter won't spook a ram too badly. Even rifle shots don't mean much to rams in some areas. They may be confused for a time but usually settle down unless they connect the shot with the sight of a hunter.

Bowhunters accustomed to sitting in a stand don't worry too much about range. They know before they climb the stand exactly how far away each bush or tree is and therefore know the exact range when their deer steps up beside the marker.

Sheep and goat hunters, however, must estimate the range each and every time they see their quarry. Neophyte mountain hunters tend to overestimate the range in the big, open country. I once went through three rifle clips on a goat and sheep hunt before I figured out I was shooting over the back of everything.

Practice your range-finding technique every time you're outside. How far is that car? How far to the lamp post? In the field, how far to that tree? How far to that tall cornstalk? Check your estimates. Step them off. If you're fortunate enough to live in

Chuck Adams bagged this bighorn ram in Alberta.

mountainous country, head up on weekends. Learn to figure distances from a certain rock to another from across the canyon or downrange a couple of hundred yards. Don't just guess. Step them off to be sure. If you have time, you may even be able to mentally mark off five- or ten-yard increments as you could on a football field.

With most bows, if you aim for the center of the chest you will still hit a vital area nearly five yards on either side of your sight pin. For that reason, I like to set my pins more than five yards apart. With the pins set for eight or ten yards apart, you'll still slip the arrow into a fatal spot. At the same time, the setup offers a greater spread of shootable range.

Any sheep or goat hunter must know where his ram or billy might end up before shooting. You must be able to get at the animal after he falls. Once in Alaska, I passed up a nice goat. If he dropped in his tracks, I could never climb down to the tiny ledge on which he stood. If he fell over the ledge, he would tumble 5,000 feet down to the creek ending up with broken horns.

The bowhunter must use even more caution since his quarry will seldom if ever fall where it stands. If you have any doubt at all you must wait. No true sportsman wants to let any animal go off and die without being retrieved. After you do shoot, watch the animal but don't push him.

Colorado bowhunter Tom Tietz completed his grand slam of North American rams and guided many hunters as well. According to Tietz, patience is the bowhunters best friend on sheep hunts. "You must be patient and wait for the right opportunity and right spot before you stalk a ram with your bow. Some places are just not right for a stalk. Other places are. Bide your time and wait. My own Dall is a prime example. We spotted the ram almost immediately the first day, but I didn't shoot until the next night. We kept the ram in sight almost the entire time but never found an opportunity to put on a good stalk."

Tietz offers a different opinion of goat hunting however: "In my experience goats are different. They are not particularly hard to stalk. The normally rougher, more broken goat habitat is made for stalking. And then a goat's personality is more easygoing than a ram's. They seldom spook badly if you make a mistake."

Chuck Adams, who we talked about at the beginning of this chapter, has taken his grand slam of North American wild sheep and goats with his bow. His list of equipment for the high country hunter makes sense without overloading a hunter with useless gear.

"The mountain hunter needs only basic equipment, not every modern gadget in archery catalogues," he said. "A compound bow works best for the hunter who wants to consistently and efficiently put meat on the table. Long bows and recurves are fun to shoot but unless you have an overpowering yen for tradition, stick with a compound."

According to Adams, compound bows are easier to shoot without regular muscle-building exercises. They let off 50 percent in draw weight at full draw. "Compounds using the older round wheels work better for me than bows using the newer cam. The cam shoots an arrow faster but is less accurate, more difficult to draw, nosier and more prone to breakage," he said.

With this desert bighorn ram, bowhunter Chuck Adams completed his grand slam of North American wild sheep. Chuck took the ram with a Hoyt/Easton Gamegetter bow and Easton XX75 arrows while hunting the Hualapi Reservation in Arizona.

"A stabilizer is important to help eliminate bow torque and movement during a shot, giving better accuracy. For sights, I use a four or five pin sight that adjusts for whatever distance you want. They work better and are more practical than newer gadget type sights. I also recommend that you replace your factory installed arrow rest with an adjustable arrow rest. The flipper/plunger or coil spring rest works best," Adams reports.

As well as the basic archery equipment listed above, you should use a clamp-on nock locator, a bowstring silencer and a quiver that fits on the bow. Be certain you camouflage your bow with dull spray paint or tape.

Adams says 90 percent of the best bowhunters use aluminum arrows with plastic vanes (feathers are no good wet). Fit the arrow to your bow and your draw length and use camo shafts. Adams uses broadheads with three to five cutting edges. Be sure you use broadheads the same weight as your practice blunts.

According to Tom Tietz, camouflage is in the eye of the beholder. "Most bowhunters carry a certain stigma—you must wear complete camouflage," he said. "You really don't. You should wear dull cloth made of the softest and therefore quietest material. For sheep and goats I recommend blotchy grays or other dull colors. Regular green camo stands out in sheep country as bad as bright orange."

Linda Strong agrees about camouflage: "I really don't think regular camouflage clothing is necessary. With the proper stalk, you stay out of sight of the ram. I do think you should wear dull, soft clothing however. No sense taking a chance. Also, if you hunt in wet or snowy weather, and don't we all, I find wool pants work great. They keep you warm and dry in any weather."

If you bowhunt deer or elk but never thought you could take on the magnificent ram or goat in the high country, by all means change your thinking. You can go from being a passive hunter to an active hunter on a high country hunt.

If you've always hunted rams and goats with a rifle, you might consider stalking the creatures of the high country with a bow for a new challenge. Stalking a ram or goat to within 20 or 30 yards instead of 100 or 200 yards offers an excitement hard to match in the great outdoors.

10

Rocky Mountain Goats

One black hoof casually stepped ahead, then another. Exactly what supported the hooves escaped my detection. The blocky, pure white animal seemed to stroll on the side of the sheer Alaskan cliff. A fall meant a several thousand-foot tumble down the cliff. A look of amazement must have shown on my face as I watched the animal traverse the cliff without a care.

With no goat permit in hand, I set up my camera. Then the beautiful animal spotted me. He reversed direction without missing a step and strolled away. Even with the powerful telephoto lens I could see no means of support for the animal.

Suddenly the cliff face took a right angle turn. The goat calmly stepped across the chasm and continued. When whatever crack or tiny ledge he walked on ran out, the goat raised his front feet up to another slim foothold and pulled himself up. He disappeared around a corner but in a few minutes the goat spotted my hunting partner and started back in my direction. When he reached a position directly across from me he nibbled on some unseen bit of vegetation on the rock. Never did the animal run or act spooked.

According to biologists North America's Rocky Mountain goat (*Oreamnos Americanus*) probably crossed the Bering Sea land bridge in the middle Pleistocene period. Goats are closely related to the chamois of Europe but not to any species in North America.

Because of its rugged, alpine habitat, few early explorers saw any mountain goats. Lewis and Clark did spot the white animals in what is now Idaho. Alexander Henry saw and described the animals in the Kootenay, British Columbia, region in 1811. However, the animals were the subject of so many myths and legends that early biologists actually doubted their existence. By the late 1800s goats had been studied thoroughly in Montana. Again because of their remote habitat, goats are the least known and least understood by the public of any North American wild game.

For good reason, our native Indians called the mountain goat the white buffalo. Like the buffalo (bison), goats show a hump on the back. Also like buffalo, the animals are rather stocky. Behind the stocky body appears a short tail, in front grows a slender neck and rather smallish head. From the front or rear, goats appear slab-sided, which helps their cliff hugging and ledge walking.

An adult male mountain goat weighs up to 300 pounds, larger than most rams. Except during the early part of the hunting season, goats wear a long, heavy white coat. A five-inch beard hangs below their chin and beautiful thick chaps cover a male's front legs. Mountain goats join Dall sheep and polar bear as North America's only animals to wear a pure white coat year-round.

Both males (billies) and females (nannies) grow black, thin, pointed horns which increase in length each year until they reach eight to twelve inches. Like ram horns, these little daggers lay down an annual ring each year and the horns are never shed.

A goat's skull is extremely fragile. Therefore, unlike rams, goats don't clash head-on. In fact, goats don't spar in fun like rams do. Their dagger sharp horns would kill another goat rather than just cause a headache. Goats seldom, if ever, fight. They only exhibit and false charge with their lethal horns.

Mountain goats are perhaps adapted better to their habitat than other wild game species. Their large, oval hooves include prominent dew claws so they can travel better through snow than sheep can. Their hooves consist of cushion-like pads surrounded by hard shell. The pads form suction cups on smooth rock surfaces giving goats their amazing climbing and ledge-walking ability. These great climbers seldom jump. Rather goats lever or pull themselves slowly up and down sheer cliffs from one foothold to another. In fact, they climb rock much like a man climbs a ladder.

Tracks left by a mature mountain goat are about the size of those left by deer and sheep but they print squarer and wider. They drop deer-sized pellets that appear concave on one end.

Rocky Mountain goats live in the high peaks, usually above sheep country. Because of their remote habitat, goats are arguably the least known and least understood wild game animal. Gary Loghry bagged this goat in Montana's Pintlar Mountains.

Depending on the area, nannies bear their kids in late May or early June. Normally they drop only one kid but occasionally twins are born. Nannies go off alone to a rugged area in the cliffs or occasionally a cave to drop their young. The precocious youngsters can follow their mother shortly after birth. In fact, they can climb anywhere their legs can reach within a few days of birth. Kids normally stay with their mother throughout their first year and into the second. Few, if any, goats live past 11 years.

You'll normally find goats above sheep in the highest, roughest terrain. As I write this, I remember the time I found goat hair on a spruce branch beside a lake at the bottom of the mountain. However, that's an exception. Mountain goats prefer steep slopes or cliffs which offer an untapped food source. No other animal forages in goat habitat. The cliffs also offer protection. No other animal, except man, can get around in goat habitat.

Since north- and east-facing slopes receive the most snow, they hold the most water and succulent forage in summer and fall. However, goats don't need open water because they can find snow year-round in good habitat.

A goat's diet varies from grass and brush to moss and lichens. During the winter months, goats stay on the lowest south-facing cliffs and high ridges where wind removes the snow.

Goats don't adapt nearly as well as sheep. They survive only in true alpine environments. But this same trait means that civilization has little or no effect on goat range, habitat or numbers.

Due to the harsh habitat and single births, mountain goats have never been numerous anywhere. But, neither have their numbers been decimated like most North American species. Once a given habitat reaches its carrying capacity, mountain goat numbers remain fairly stable. Most biologists believe as many goats now live in North America as at any time in the past.

No two animals living in such close proximity to each other exhibit such different personalities as mountain goats and sheep. Wild rams spar with one another. They frolic across their alpine basins. They dash off in the presence of predators, including man. Goats on the other hand seldom run. In fact, they exhibit a noticeable phlegmatic personality. However, they can get around in country that would kill a ram.

Since mountain goats seldom stray far from their rugged habitat, they realize they can walk away from danger. Because they appear so slow and deliberate, many sportsman believe they can't see well. Actually they see as well as sheep but react differently. A goat thinks things out rather than dashing here and there, even after a shot. Because of the rugged terrain, goats, in the presence of danger, must choose an escape route with care and get out of sight the closest way. No animal in nature is more deliberate than our beautiful mountain goat.

On one of my first mountain hunting trips to British Columbia I missed a fine goat with three shots due to some terrible shooting on my part. My guide, Dale Gunn of Don Peck Outfitters, and I sat near the top of a ridge watching the goat in the broken cliffs below. In response to the shots, the goat merely looked all around and then slowly backed away while I tried to reload. He put his front feet up onto a tiny ledge, pulled himself up six feet and disappeared into the cliffs. Never did the billy exhibit any panic or fear.

Dale and I moved lower and waited. Some time later, the goat came back out but didn't see us hiding behind a large boulder. This

Mountain goats join Dall sheep and polar bear as North America's only animals to wear a pure white coat year-round. This goat's summer coat will lengthen and thicken before winter.

time the shot was good. Mountain goats feel so secure in their alpine tors they never panic or move fast.

Although several states offer from a few to many mountain goat permits, only Alaska, British Columbia, Idaho, Montana and Washington hold exceptionally high numbers of these mountain denizens. Due to their remote habitat, fish and game departments can offer no exact figures on goat populations, but fairly reliable estimates put the figure at between 12,000 and 20,000 goats in Alaska, 7,000 in Washington, 4,500 in Montana and over 3,000 in Idaho. British Columbia is home to perhaps 10,000.

Of all trophy headgear, goat horns rate perhaps the most difficult to judge, especially from a distance. Little difference exists between an average, mature goat horn and a record book trophy. Any billy carrying nine- to ten-inch horns is a good trophy and only an inch longer puts the trophy in the record book.

Two physical characteristics help judge the animal in the field. If the horns appear to be three-quarters the length of the head, the horns rate good. Anything over three-quarters and you have a record. Although not a true measurement, a goat's ears in a normal position appear four inches long. Therefore if the horns go twice as high as the ears they should measure eight inches. Also look for heavy bases for an exceptional trophy.

Further complicating trophy judgment is the fact that you have a difficult time determining the sex of a mountain goat until after the shot. Both males and females wear horns of similar length. Therefore you may shoot either sex in most areas. Most sportsmen prefer a billy for both trophy quality and to preserve the species.

Male goats carry heavier horns with larger bases than females, although nannies may grow longer horns. In fact at one time a nannie held the world record. In those days Boone & Crockett considered only horn length.

Although you'll never see goats in large herds, as you might either ewes or rams, normally nannies and kids stay in small herds of five or six animals. Unless a billy happens to wander by a group of females and young, you'll find him alone. Male goats don't herd together with other males as rams do. Keep in mind, however, that you may see an old, dry nanny alone. A nanny's horns bend back more sharply than a billy's which curve evenly back as they grow.

After the shot, measure a goat's horns much like you do a ram's. Measure the length of the horn from the lowest point in front, over the outer curve to a point in line with the tip. Measure the base circumference at a right angle to the axis of horn. Do not follow the irregular edge of the horn. Then divide the length of the longest horn by four and measure the circumference at the first, second and third quarters. The total of the horn lengths and circumferences less any differences must score 50 to make the Boone & Crockett book.

As is the case with trophy sheep, heaviness in a goat horn counts for more score than horn length. In most cases a horn with 10½- to 11-inch length and 5½- to 6-inch bases will score high enough to make the book. The current number one goat wears 12-inch horns with 6½-inch bases. After caping your goat don't

David Fox bagged this 10-inch mountain goat while hunting with Lamoureux Outfitters in British Columbia. Hunters find that goats are more phlegmatic than sheep when danger is present.

forget to remove the rest of the hide for a small but beautiful rug.

According to knowledgeable sportsmen, mountain goats are perhaps our most underrated trophy and in some areas the most underutilized. Goats don't appear such a magnificent trophy as rams. Their little dagger horns don't have the mass or length of the rams. Their deliberate behavior doesn't excite hunters like rams do. But the ebony horns against a snowwhite coat offers a striking trophy.

Actually, mountain goat hunting presents much more demanding physical effort, especially climbing, than sheep hunting. Following a goat also can offer a much more dangerous route than sheep. Unfortunately, the hunting popularity of most North

American wild game is based on peer suggestion rather than actual trophy quality.

The late Grancel Fitz felt much different about the quality of goat hunting than most sportsmen. "The peaceful, placid mountain goat is my personal candidate for the most dangerous game in the world. To those who might nominate the markhor or the ibex, African and Asian mountain game, I'll give respectful attention. Others can hold their peace. Mountain sheep have led me into tricky places where I was frankly scared. But goats, more than once, have had me within a whisker of being killed, so that there is nothing funny even about the memory. No wounded African buffalo can kill you any deader than a thousand-foot involuntary swan dive onto a rock slide," Fitz wrote.

In his marvelous old book, *North American Head Hunting*, Fitz claims that goat hunters, especially neophytes need to have a specially selected guardian angel, one that pays no attention whatever to union hours. During his first goat hunt, Fitz and his guide returned to camp by separate routes. He at last realized that daylight would be gone before he could reach his regular creek crossing.

"So in the gathering dusk I went straight down to the canyon and luckily found a place where it was possible to cross the rushing stream and climb the wall on the other side. My guide had offered to carry my rucksack, containing my coat, a flashlight and spare sandwich. My route lay parallel to the canyon, and when I had covered half a mile I came to a formation of granite that thrust outward from the mountainside until it became a sheer bluff rising from the creek.

"A nice ledge, almost two feet wide, invited me to try to get across the face, and when that ledge pinched out I scrambled up to a narrower one. Before I had gone very far I had been on ledges at half a dozen different levels. And then my troubles began.

"Clouds scudded across the sky, and the starlight was blotted out. Remembering that the creek was a long way straight down, I didn't dare to go on. But I had changed ledges too many times, and in this new darkness I didn't dare go back either. So I sat down on my ledge, and as I rested a little, thinking things over, it began to snow. In just a few minutes the storm had developed into a howling blizzard, and the face of that cliff became a very poor place to spend the night. Somehow, I had to get out of there.

"Feeling for holds that I couldn't see, it was easier and safer to go up, and to feel the way better I took off my gloves. The going

For many people, the peaceful, placid mountain goat is the most dangerous game in the world. "No wounded African buffalo," wrote Grancel Fitz, "can kill you any deader than a thousand-foot involuntary swan dive onto a rock slide." The sheer cliffs behind this bedded goat is typical of prime goat habitat.

was painfully slow. My fingers, soon numb from the cold job of exploring snow-filled crevices, had to be warmed in my mouth. I followed the mountaineer's rule in reaching for a new hold with but one hand or foot at a time, so that I always had three points of support.

"After some three hours of terribly slow but constant climbing I found a rock chimney, and when I had gone up it for about thirty feet I found that the top was blocked. Its walls were icy. I didn't like the thought of going down, and in trying to get out at the top I very nearly fell. There is nothing spectacular about that, is there? Not the same thing as a wounded, charging tiger dropping dead a yard from a hunter with a jammed gun. But, had I slipped just a shade farther, there would not have been many bounces in a dizzy plunge to the creek bed and a tiger couldn't have spoiled my evening more thoroughly."

Fitz finally descended that chimney without accident and after another hour managed to climb over the top. Then after stumbling through a dense jack pine timber, wandering back and forth though a meadow in the dark and the swirling snow and falling in a creek several times, Fitz made it back to camp.

A few days later Fitz and his guide spotted a goat and decided to try for it. The guide suggested he go on ahead and find the best stalk. He told Fitz to climb as fast as he could and when he reached a certain point to come straight toward the bluff to meet him.

"A moment later I started after him, climbing on a slight angle toward the cliffs, and before long I came to a chute, a dry, narrow watercourse grooved into the mountainside by the melting of winter snows. Although it was only about eight feet wide, it was much too steep and smooth, so I went on up beside it until I saw three protruding stones about the size of my head studded across the chute, with the middle one as a sort of apex above the other two," Fitz wrote.

"With my stick I prodded each in turn, testing them, and they seemed solid. The faces of these stones were flat, but the soil had been scoured away from the top edges, leaving an inch or two exposed. With my inside foot I stepped out onto the nearest, worked my hand across the slope until I hooked my fingers over the top of the higher one in the middle, then swung my outside foot across to the far stone, a scant couple of feet from the opposite timber. Not far to go, but spraddled out as I was, facing the chute, I needed one more purchase to balance myself. With the stick in my free hand I drove hard at the gritty earth to plant it firmly.

A guide's pack horse will aid in getting your mountain goat back to camp. No hunter, especially a first-timer in goat country, should go anywhere without his guide.

"On the sunny slope of the opposite mountain I had been doing that all afternoon. On this shadowed northern face, the ground was frozen solid. The point of my stick glanced off.

"I tried again, jabbing harder, and that dead stick broke off an inch below my hand and zoomed 700 feet down the chute to the rim of the canyon, where it leaped out into space for the sheer drop into the rocky creek bed.

"Feeling a little wobbly I attempted to back off, but there wasn't room on the back stone for both feet. Just as I was trying for a solid foothold, my slung rifle had to swing awkwardly and I nearly went sailing down after my stick. It couldn't have been closer, and when, a split second later, I found myself in my original spraddled position, I almost fell off anyhow through sheer trembling. After an instant I steadied. I had to. But I thought no more about backing off.

"There was one other possible way out. If I could get both feet onto the far stone, which had a wider top, I might work my free hand ahead on the earth of the chute, so that it would balance me while I let go the middle stone and made the short step to safety. When I felt cool enough I tried it.

"All went well until I had both feet planted on the farther foothold. Then, under my full weight, the stone under foot made a little crunching sound and began to come loose. How I managed it I don't know yet, but in a flash I was hung up on my three stones just as before. This time, though, I was putting very little weight on the loosened one.

"I was scared stiff—probably more scared than I've ever been before or since—but curiously, there was no trembling. Somehow, subconsciously, that lesson had been learned. I knew that without help I wasn't going to try to get off again, either forward or backward. There was nothing to do but stay there, and even that couldn't be managed indefinitely.

"Ten minutes, ten years, ten centuries later I heard the guide coming back. In another minute I grasped the stout stick that he extended, and my predicament was only a deeply etched memory," Fitz wrote.

I quote these rather lengthy passages from Fitz's book only to point out the danger and excitement inherent in goat hunting. And also to reinforce the suggestion that no hunter, and especially a first timer in goat country, should go anywhere without his guide. In the first chapter I related my terrifying experience on my first goat hunt when I tried to go down the mountain on my own. Don't attempt such folly. Your guide knows the mountain. He knows possible pitfalls and blockages. You don't. Any big game hunter may find himself in a tight spot but I know of no other hunting that offers so many life-taking chances as goat hunting.

Tom Brakefield in his excellent book, *Hunting Big-Game Trophies*, reports his own terrifying experience with goats. He'd made a good lung shot on an old billy but the goat picked his way across the slope and disappeared into a chimney, completely hidden from view. After a lot of hard work, Brakefield and his guide made it to the chimney, but the goat wasn't in sight.

Spike camps high in the mountains make goat hunting much easier. Keep your camp out of sight in the trees if possible.

"We started up the edge of the chimney, staying as much as possible out of the treacherous loose rock and scree that could whisk us right off the steep incline. I led the way so I could shoot without hesitation. Suddenly, almost at the top of the chimney and about 100 feet directly above us, the goat hoisted himself to his feet and lumbered toward the top. There was no time, in three steps he would be over. So it was now or never—more like jump-shooting a cottontail than making the classically deliberate long-range mountain shot.

"I shot, the goat faltered, stumbled and then—almost in slow motion—sailed out into space and hit the loose scree 10 feet below where he had been standing, madly sliding and tumbling our way. We flattened ourselves against the wall of the chimney, fortunately finding a little shelter in a crack there as the goat flew by close enough to touch. His mad, 200 foot slide stopped only against the final rock between him and a 500 foot vertical drop. We shook and

Mountain goats may not possess the majestic headgear of the ram, nor the craftiness of the whitetail, nor the wariness of the elk, but they offer a beautiful, exciting and sometimes dangerous hunt.

puffed, both scared to death and glad to still be alive. My knees wouldn't work right and I had to pause for several minutes to recover enough in order to safely pick my way down to the goat. But, today, each time I look at that head on the wall, I recall that that goat brought us within 18 inches of eternity.''

No, mountain goats may not possess the majestic headgear of the ram, nor the craftiness of the whitetail, nor the wariness of the elk. But they offer a beautiful, exciting and sometimes dangerous hunt in the rugged crags at the top of the world.

11

Hunting
Rocky Mountain Goats

S teady whispers of smoke curled from the stove pipe like ghosts against the steely morning sky as Jerry Owen and his Indian guide, Sam, rode out of camp. Owen's pinto mare snorted impatience and whisked at an imaginary fly with her built-in fly swatter. The hunter and guide silently rode single file, each lost in his own thoughts. The tangy odor of wet spruce soothed their noses as they moved through the heavy timber away from their tent.

Cripple Creek rushed past them, swollen from unseasonable rains but they had to cross. Sam leaned back in his saddle and turned back to Owen. "Hang on and keep the mare's head upstream if she loses her footing," he said. "Looks like the dry socks we brought will come in handy."

Owen slipped his feet from the stirrups and kept them high as possible as he followed Sam into the water. They were nearly across before the water became too deep for the horses. As the animals swam, water rose to Owen's knees. Once safely on the far side, hunter and guide changed into dry socks and continued up the canyon.

"We'd hunted for three days and stayed in camp one day because of rain but we found only a few nannies and kids each day," Owen later remembered. "For the first hour I couldn't see much through the tall spruce. But as we rode higher, the trees thinned and became smaller. Sam pointed and I saw a tremendous bull moose halfway up the slope to the right of the trail. He stared at us a minute and them ambled into the trees.''

By 9 a.m., Sam and Owen cleared tree line. Sam tied the horses to the last scrubby fir and led the way to a small knoll partway up the slope. Both the hunter and guide glassed the large rugged basin surrounding them. Soon Sam pointed toward the high rocks near the head of the creek. Owen swung his glasses in that direction and quickly located the pure white dot against the dark shale. Sam walked back to the horses and returned with a 20x spotting scope. After Sam found the goat in the glass, Owen admired the beautiful animal. Even at the great distance he could distinguish the ebony, dagger-like horns.

"Sam said that since the goat was alone and since we could see his horns so plainly from there, it was no doubt a good billy. But he wanted to move closer for a better look before committing to a stalk," Owen said.

"We returned to the horses and rode up a side canyon out of the goat's vision. A narrow trail wound up the grassy slope on the backside of the big basin, so we rode much higher than I supposed we could. I enjoyed letting the horses do all the work.''

All good things must run out and finally Sam and Jerry tied the horses to boulders and continued the climb on foot. They didn't try to reach the goat but only move close enough for a better look through the spotting scope. As they neared the ridge top, Sam motioned Jerry down. They crawled on their bellies until they could slip the scope over the top.

"Sam looked first and smiled as he rolled away from the scope so I could look. Magnificent, that's the only way I can describe the scene. The pure white goat stood like the old man of the mountain in broken cliffs a couple of hundred feet from the top. The horns glistened in the sun. They appeared nearly as long as the goat's face so I knew we had a good trophy. Long white hairs dropped below his chin and his chaps grew long and heavy,'' Owen said.

According to Owen, his guide said the goat should lay down for a nap soon. Then they would plan a route for the stalk. As it stood now, Sam thought they could climb above the goat. Minutes passed. Owen admired the goat through the scope. Finally the goat wandered toward their position and laid down in the shale just below a large rock formation.

"I think we can climb on up the ridge and come out above the old boy," Sam told Owen.

They dropped back off the ridge and started up the backside.

Goats often live in the roughest, steepest peaks. Use extreme caution when you stalk your goat and when recovering it after the shot.

Old sheep trails provided much better footing than did the slick grass on the steep ridge. For a time, Owen looked ahead every few minutes but soon gave it up. Each time he looked, the distinctive crest they aimed for still seemed hours away. Hearing his hunter gasp and pant behind him, Sam finally stopped for a breath. When Owen's breathing returned to something approaching normal, they continued the steep ascent.

After an hour, Sam motioned Owen to stop. Owen's legs ached and his lungs burned. He wondered how his guide could climb forever without showing any signs of fatigue. While Owen stretched his cramped legs, Sam crawled to the edge of the crest and peered down. There, not 100 yards away, the white buffalo of the north lay watching his alpine kingdom below.

"Sam motioned me up and then turned back to the goat," he said. "When I peeked over the edge, I couldn't believe the sight. How could a job that had been so tough now look so easy? My goat lay on a talus-strewn slope. A few feet to the left and we wouldn't have seen him for a large crag. Fortunately in such an up and down world, the slope below the goat rolled gently down rather than straight down such as the cliffs 100 yards in either direction.

"I slid my Remington 7mm Rem. Mag. over the edge and rested it on my down vest. Just before I settled my cheek to the stalk, a marmot screeched somewhere below. The goat rose slowly and peered in the direction of the sound. I took a deep breath, put the crosshairs just left of the center of his back and squeezed.

"The shaggy animal never moved. How could I miss at such short range? I cranked the bolt and shot again. The goat wobbled a few steps and collapsed. Sam thumped me on the back. My heart beat against my chest. What a tremendous feeling. I'd found and taken the king of the highest mountains."

The first 100 feet or so of the descent presented treacherous cliffs, so Sam carried Owen's rifle to free both hands. Then they picked their way through the broken shale to the trophy.

Jerry Owen took a fine old billy. And he did so in "typical" goat hunting fashion. As with all big game hunting, one should avoid saying always or never or typical because each and every hunt presents a little different condition. However, for lack of a better term, we must talk of *typical* goat hunting techniques.

Owen and his guide rode into good goat country. They spotted his trophy from a mile or two away. They moved closer for a better look, waited for the animal to lay down and then completed a successful stalk.

Very simply put, goat hunting means climbing—sometimes until you are certain that your lungs will burst and your legs turn to jelly. In much of British Columbia and the lower 48 you may use sturdy mountain horses to reach tree line from camp each day. In some areas you may even be able to ride up to high rims.

However, even in areas where you use horses to some extent, in the end, you must put one foot above the other, with an overweight pack on your back. Goat hunters must normally traverse much rougher and sometimes much more dangerous country than sheep hunters. For your safety, arrive at hunting camp in the best physical condition possible. You're much more apt to

Whereas you find sheep in the gentle high basins such as in the foreground, look for goats on the steep cliffs.

stumble or fall if you puff and gasp your way across a cliff or if your legs quiver with every step.

Goat hunters in the coastal mountains on the Alaskan panhandle or across the border in British Columbia and in some areas of mainland Alaska, seldom, if ever, use horses. These beautiful mountains hold some of the best trophies, but the extremely rugged mountains rise sharply from the sea to many thousand feet. Outfitters in these areas use spike camps and backpack camps much more often than those from the more eastern areas of British Columbia.

While sheep hunters may find a decent view of the high basins from either above or below, goat hunters may find their vision obstructed by boulders, tall crags or otherwise cut up rock formations in the cliffs. You may sit and glass an area for hours only to have a goat walk out into plain sight just before quitting time.

In general, goats inhabit the most rugged side of the roughest mountains. Often, one side of alpine areas offers fairly gentle slopes with many grassy basins while the other side looks like something the devil himself constructed. Look for goats on the devil's side. In other areas, you may find goats in the rough peaks above the sheep basins. Because of the broken terrain, you might have to hunt the same mountain from both below and above for a view of everything. Glassing from across a canyon often offers the best view but then you must slip and slide down one mountain and then agonize your way up the other.

The hunter need not arrive in goat country before the sun brings forth the day's first light. Goats feed after dawn and stay in the open all day. Sometime before noon they locate a comfortable bed and nap, chew their cud and watch over their domain until mid-afternoon. Then they rise and feed again until bedding again before sunset. Like sheep, goats may get up and stretch or even feed a little during midday, but they won't move far.

If possible locate your goat out feeding in the morning. Delay your stalk, however, until the goat beds down. Otherwise the trophy may wander quite a distance and you won't find him after you complete the stalk. While you wait, enjoy the animal through your spotting scope. Try to determine to within an inch just how long the horns measure. At the same time you and your guide should study all possible routes for the stalk. Several options may present themselves. Select the one with the best cover and the easiest, if possible, route.

On warm days goats feed and bed on north-facing cliffs in the shade. On cold days, you'll most likely find them out in the sun and out of the wind. However, keep in mind that what seems cold to you may feel rather balmy to the heavy-coated goat. Also, because of his heavy coat, goats, unlike sheep, try to stay out of the rain.

In many areas you'll find both goat and sheep tracks which look very similar. The hoof lobes spread a bit more on goats than sheep, leaving a track that appears squarer than the slightly pointed ram track. Since goats most often walk slowly and deliberately rather than trot or run, they leave a more distinct track without overlapping. Still you may be fooled, but tracking is not as important on a goat hunt as it is while hunting antlered game.

With no snow on the rocks, all guides and most hunters easily spot goats from a great distance. Their fleecy white coats stand out like tiny mirrors. Occasionally you might hunt an area strewn with white or partly white rocks which you must check out, but in general, goats offer easy visibility. Hunting goats in Alaska where you may also find Dall sheep presents another situation, however.

Like sheep hunting, you must spend hours glassing the high peaks when hunting Rocky Mountain goats.

Then you must stop and check each white dot with binoculars or a spotting scope.

However, when you hunt snow-covered peaks, locating a goat can be the toughest spotting of all. Even during warm weather or before the fall's first snows, you often hunt goats where you still see at least patches of last year's snow.

In fact, due to the moisture and the resulting vegetation, you'll often find goats near old snow patches. Study each and every snow patch completely before you decide it's not a goat. As with sheep hunting, you must glass, glass and glass with binoculars before moving on. In the presence of snow, look for trails in the snow and beds. They can lead you right to a billy. If you give up on a certain ridge or cliff too soon, you may miss the goat hidden from view. Sooner or later he'll move enough for you to spot him. By the way, the coat on old, trophy billies normally takes on a slight yellow cast. Of course, old snow patches also appear yellowish or dirty.

Three of a goat's primary senses provide him with excellent protection. In the past many sportsmen felt that a goat's eyesight didn't come close to a sheep's. Biologists, however, now tell us goats possess excellent eyesight. But because of their escape habitat and a goat's natural phlegmatic nature they don't react to sightings as sheep or other wildlife do. They merely stare at the intruder or walk slowly away.

Goats also possess excellent hearing and sense of smell. However, goats, like sheep, live in a world of falling rocks, so they don't react if you loosen a rock while making a stalk. Beware of the wind. Fickle mountain wind can change in an instant. Goats do react to odor.

In the chapters on sheep hunting, I stressed the importance of stalking rams from above. Given a choice, I'd also rather stalk goats from above, but often this is simply not possible. The tops of many goat mountains do not offer safe footing or they may rise too steeply to climb. In other cases, you can't see the goat from above or the billy may reside on the very top.

In these and many other cases, you must stalk the goat from below or from the same altitude. However, the side hill or from below stalk isn't as tough as it sounds. A billy's lack of fear and his passive nature allows liberties on a stalk you couldn't take with sheep or elk. The same broken, rugged terrain which makes spotting goats so difficult offers excellent stalking possibilities. If you can't see the goat, he certainly can't see you. Don't think however, that the stalk will be easy. Few, if any, stalks on the great white buffalo come easy from a physical standpoint.

Before you start on a stalk, pick out some distinctive feature near which you will end the stalk. Believe me, everything appears much different from another angle at the end of the stalk than from where you spotted the goat. In fact, you should pick out two or three markers. Then remember your goat might move a little during the stalk, although he should still be nearby.

The actual stalk may keep you out of sight of the trophy for several hours. Try to start as soon as the goat lies down for his midday nap so you have plenty of time to complete the stalk before he rises for his afternoon meal.

The author, with guide Dale Gunn, spent two hours climbing to reach his British Columbia goat. Make certain you can get to the goat after he falls.

As you close the distance, be more aware of wind direction. You can stalk into the wind or with a quartering wind but if the wind switches to your back, alter the route of your stalk. The closer you get the more alert you must stay. The goat might wander a short distance or may even get up and stretch or eat a few bites before lying down again.

Due to the rugged terrain goat hunters often stumble upon their trophy. They may never see it from a distance and never actually stalk the animal. That happened to me on my first British Columbia hunt.

We were actually hunting sheep that day. After leaving the horses at tree line, Dale, my guide, and I climbed and hunted the gently sloping side of the mountain. The mountainside contained several typical sheep meadows broken only by boulders and a few trickles of water. After deciding we'd find no rams, we climbed onto the top and looked over the edge. The view that met my tired old eyes looked like a scene from another world, a world of broken rock and cliffs.

As we sat down for a sandwich and rest, Dale scanned the rocks below while I loafed and admired the shimmering Spur Creek wind through the canyon below.

"Quick Lloyd, take a look. I see a goat beside that jagged chimney just to our left and below," Dale whispered.

You couldn't miss the shaggy white animal standing against the dark rock no more than 100 yards away. He must have stayed behind the rock when we sat down. By greatly overestimating the distance, I missed three times.

Fortunately we found the goat again after climbing down partway from the crest and this time I dropped the billy.

Although I missed the excitement of spotting and judging the trophy from a distance and missed the thrill of the stalk, I didn't miss the physical exertion normally associated with a long and hurried stalk. We climbed the backside very leisurely. As I related in early chapters, I did have a terrible experience going back down that mountain, but still, all in all, the goat came easy.

That day, I also learned that mountain goats can absorb a lot of punishment without flinching. Goats seldom pump up their adrenaline as rams, deer, elk or about any other wild game does. They normally walk away from danger and therefore don't react noticeably to even a lethal shot. Because of their physical makeup and their thick hair, goats seldom show much blood after a shot.

On my second try at the old billy, I squeezed the trigger.

Wait until the goat lays down for a midday nap before you start your stalk. Then pick out a landmark that is within range to which you will stalk.

Absolutely nothing happened. The goat didn't flinch. He didn't move. He didn't even blink an eye. Had I missed again? A second shot brought exactly the same results. Just as I squeezed the trigger a third time, the goat's knees buckled and he fell to a shale slide below his perch. Upon examination, we found three bullet holes in his lung area which you could cover with a saucer. The goat died with the first shot but because they absorb shock so well, he didn't fall.

Before taking a shot at a mountain goat, and perhaps before you even start a stalk, you must be certain where the goat might end up after a successful shot. A goat's horns, much more brittle than a ram's, can break and you lose a beautiful trophy if he falls a thousand feet off a ledge to the rock below.

Also, be certain before the shot that you can climb to the trophy after the shot. He may fall off or even if he doesn't, the goat may end up in such a position that you can't get to him because of sheer cliffs or other obstacles. I'd bet that more mountain goats are left on the mountain illegally by people because they couldn't get to them than any other big game. We owe it to the wonderful animal to retrieve the trophy.

My good friend B.J. Galvin, once almost experienced such a defeat. Hunting in Alaska, Galvin and Fred, his guide, spotted a fine billy across a wide and especially deep canyon. In fact the canyon fell nearly straight down for 5,000 feet into the Chitina River. The goat knew something or somebody stood across the chasm but apparently didn't care. "The goat looked at us but then went back to nibbling his breakfast," said Galvin.

Since they estimated the distance across the void at over 450 yards, Galvin and his guide hiked around to get above the goat. Unfortunately they couldn't find it again so they walked all the way around to their first vantage point. This time they marked the spot better and again walked around. They found the goat several hundred feet below.

"I started to slide my rifle into position for the nearly straight down shot when Fred stopped me," Galvin said. "He asked just how I figured to climb down to the dead goat. He also pointed out that if the goat lurched or even leaned much after the shot, the trophy would end up in busted pieces on the river far below. Fred suggested we wait. Perhaps the goat would move into a better or safer position. In the end we waited all day but finally gave up. We never saw that goat again but I did score the next day."

After eating a rather bland, freeze-dried breakfast the next morning at their backpack camp, the hunter and guide strolled up a narrow valley. Before they progressed very far from camp, they spotted a band of eight full curl Dall rams feeding near the top of the sloping mountain on their right. While Galvin admired the rams through his spotting scope, Fred located a lone goat about halfway up the rugged cliffs on the left.

"Fred told me he didn't know how we could climb above the goat and if we did we might not be able to spot the billy because of an outcropping," Galvin said. "Since the wind blew down the mountain Fred thought we might stalk to within shooting distance from below and slightly to the left of the animal. My trophy stood at the top of a huge talus slide but the slope was not especially steep. If the goat fell, he wouldn't go far.

"We moved to our left and started up the rock. Almost immediately large boulders, broken crags and chimneys hid our approach. Before we started, Fred noticed a huge scar on the cliff above the goat which resembled a lightening bolt etched at an angle across the cliff. That scar offered us an excellent reference point. Even though I thought I was in fairly decent shape, I soon fell behind Fred. My lungs felt like fire and my knees wobbled with every step. Finally Fred stopped for a rest."

Picking their way up the talus and around broken rock proved tough climbing but not especially dangerous. Fred checked the wind every few minutes and let Galvin rest often as they neared their goal. When Fred felt they'd climbed high enough, they worked their way to the right, keeping behind rocks and rims. They also slowed the pace to almost a crawl. Galvin looked and saw the big scar etched on the cliff almost directly above them. Fred motioned Galvin to stop.

"Fred crept up behind a low boulder, took his cap off and peeked around the rock. He put a finger to his cracked lips and motioned me up. I slipped a shell in the barrel and crawled. With the rifle ahead, I peeked around the corner. The beautiful goat stood about 150 yards away looking down the mountain. After the first shot, the old billy looked around and walked away. I held the crosshairs in the center of his chest as he angled away and squeezed the trigger again. This time, the goat stumbled and fell on the rough rock. Both shots ripped through his lungs."

In this case, the animal's position forced the hunters to stalk from below but because of the rugged terrain and a favorable wind they had no problems. They also could shoot where they knew they could retrieve the trophy in one piece.

Unfortunately, you'll find few camps set up exclusively for goat hunts. Normally, sportsmen hunt goats as a second species or extra species rather than the prime target. Therefore I can't really describe a "typical" goat hunting camp. Most are actually sheep camps, bear camps, caribou camps, etc.

On practically all eastern and central British Columbia hunts, you'll hunt out of regular mountain base camps. If the outfitter has no cabins near goat country, you'll go on spike trips into the best goat country. Either way you spend quite a bit of time on horseback.

In Alaska, you're more apt to hunt out of spike camps. Because of the lack of horses in many Alaskan goat areas, the outfitter may drop you into goat country by plane and then you hunt out of a tent camp on foot or carry your camp via backpack.

On the coastal range hunts, either the Alaska Panhandle or on the British Columbia side, you might hunt partially from horseback or entirely on foot out of tent camps. Because of the extremely rugged terrain, many coastal hunts use backpack camps.

Due to the scarcity of permits, most lower 48 goat hunts are set up after you receive the permit. U.S. outfitters, therefore, use tent camps or perhaps spike camps out of the outfitter's cabin setup.

Surprisingly, considering the number of sheep in the area, neither the Yukon or the Northwest Territories hold many mountain goats. Both offer only a very few goat permits. Likewise eight states offer at least a few goat permits. However, the serious goat hunter should look to British Columbia or Alaska.

According to Donald McKnight of the Alaska Department of Fish & Game, hunters take between 500 and 800 mountain goats each year. McKnight says that Alaska's goat populations remain high or increase each year and represent an underutilized species. For the best chance at a representative goat and an easier hunt (if such a thing exists) try the southeastern part of the mainland, specifically the Wrangell or Chugach ranges.

In British Columbia, you can find a good representative goat, better camps and more use of horses in the northcentral or northeast part of the Rocky Mountains. Until recently, goat populations in the more southern areas of British Columbia went downhill. A number of Kootenay areas were closed to hunting and the goats responded and now produce a huntable population and some big goats. In fact, the Kootenays yield nine-inch goats at three to four years of age compared to five to seven years up north.

According to most experts, your best chance at finding a real

A spotting scope will save a lot of climbing to reach a sub-par trophy. The author recommends a 20x to 25x spotting scope.

trophy goat lies in the coastal range of British Columbia or the Alaska panhandle. Ross Peck reports: "Regarding goats, I think they are one of the most underrated trophies in North America. It may not be too hard to get a goat, but to get a real good goat requires a lot of work and most of the time a lot of luck. If you can get into an area that hasn't been heavily hunted the chances of a trophy goat are much better. Over the years the best goats came out of the wet belts, that is along the coastal range and in areas like the Stikine and Skeane, British Columbia watersheds. Remember, the more mountains you can climb and the more goats you can look over, the better your chance of a trophy goat!"

These coastal mountains rise perpendicular to the sea, soaring to several thousand feet. The country is rough, broken and tough. But it contains some excellent trophy mountain goats along with striking scenery.

In the lower 48, Montana offers no more than over 300 mountain goat licenses through a drawing each year; no more than 10 percent go to nonresidents. Montana also produces some record book goats. Areas in the Bitterroots along the Idaho border produce the most goats.

The state of Washington has reduced goat hunting permits. In the mid-1990s 95 total permits were available, with 14 for bowhunters-only and three for muzzleloaders-only. Mountain goat populations in the Olympics have declined markedly. Now, only five permits are available in the Olympics outside of Olympic National Park.

Approximately 10 percent of Idaho's 59 goat tags go to nonresidents, as do 10 percent of Colorado's 112 permits. Wyoming offers nine resident and three non-resident permits. South Dakota, Nevada and Utah each offer a handful of resident only goat permits. Although Alberta has a rebounding goat herd, there is no open season.

If you want an exciting hunt in a spectacular setting, then try a mountain goat hunt. Most experts shake their heads when they attempt to explain why mountain goat hunting is not more popular. They all agree it should be. Goats may not wear spectacular headgear like the ram. They may not put on a great show banging heads. They may not be the "in" thing. But the slender, ebony horns against their pure white coats make a wonderful addition to any trophy room. Furthermore the hunt may offer more excitement, and possibly danger, than any other big game hunt.

12

Gear And Equipment
For Goat And Sheep Hunting

Hopefully, we all learn from mistakes. The first-time mountain hunter who takes the wrong clothing or gear may learn a painful lesson, one which remains etched in his memory forever. I know I did.

Before my first sheep hunt, I read all I could about the proper clothing and gear. Some advice I trusted and followed. Some I didn't really believe and followed my best instincts. Unfortunately I couldn't find a really good list. For example, how could you experience cold weather on an August hunt? The temperature goes over 90 degrees every August day in my home state of Iowa. I took only a lightweight jacket along. The literature said take strong binoculars. I took 7x15 zooms.

Arriving at camp, the outfitter took one look at my jacket and asked if I'd brought a heavier coat. I assured him I'd be fine. He asked if I planned to look for rams in the next province. No, but I assured him my binoculars were the latest thing. I wouldn't need a spotting scope with those glasses.

The first morning, I shivered as we rode through frost-covered brush and trees. Before we dismounted to climb I trembled so badly I nearly fell off the horse. While climbing, my light jacket felt good. Perhaps I'd made a wise choice. However, after a half hour sitting and glassing on the high ridge, the wind penetrated right though my jacket and I felt like a lump of ice.

Before I'd climbed halfway up the ridge, the binoculars around my neck felt like a ball, as in ball and chain. Once on top, I couldn't focus the darn things properly. After an hour my eyes burned and my forehead felt like someone had stomped on it. Not only did the binoculars weigh far too much for mountain hunting but the glass and prisms were of poor quality.

The list of my other mistakes or omissions on that first trip would only make you wonder why I'm qualified to write this book. Suffice it to say, I learned quickly and learned valuable lessons.

Other than a rifle or bow, optics rate as the mountain hunter's most important gear. We will discuss optics even before clothing in this chapter because you can usually purchase additional clothing but not quality optics near the hunt area.

No sheep or goat hunter should ever step foot on a mountain without a pair of top-quality binoculars. As you no doubt must realize by now, a sheep or goat hunter spends much more time sitting and glassing than he does walking or climbing. That's part of the allure of mountain hunting. Your guide can't do all the glassing. Two sets of eyes spot more game faster than one. Besides, half the enjoyment of a mountain hunt comes in finding game and watching the antics of sheep and goats with your binoculars. Don't plan on sharing your glass.

Before you purchase binoculars for your hunt, consider very carefully both weight and quality. Most books I've read, even Jack O'Connor's, recommend something in an 8X to 10X binocular. They claim lower power binoculars don't produce enough definition for the sheep or goat hunter. I disagree wholeheartedly.

. Weight rates much more important than power for the mountain hunter. You or your guide will carry a spotting scope for the power to actually judge rams and goats from a distance.

Most 7X50 mm binoculars weigh around 30 ounces. Move up to 10X50s and you add another half pound. The popular armored (hard rubber coated) glasses weigh nearly 50 ounces. Even "standard" 7X35 binoculars weigh 20 ounces or more. However, compact binoculars on the market such as Bausch & Lomb's Custom Compacts at 7X26 or Bushnell's Sportview Compact at 8X21, weigh only 11 ounces or less. Even Bushnell's Sportview Compact 10X25 armored glasses weigh less than 10 ounces.

Climbing a mountain toting ten ounces around your neck feels much better than carrying 20, 30 or even 40 ounces. You can tuck these small glasses under your shirt when riding or climbing and never know you have them. Tie a knot in the cord short enough to

No high country hunter's gear is complete without binoculars, spotting scope and pack frame.

just get them over your head so they ride high on your chest. Some hunters stick these small binoculars in a pocket, but I'm afraid they might slip out or I might leave them high on the mountain. Instead, never take them from your neck. Being lightweight, you don't have to.

Purchase the highest quality binoculars you can possibly afford. Scrimp on something else. Top quality lens and prisms let you avoid eye stain and headaches that most often accompany cheap glasses. Zeiss, Bushnell and Bausch & Lomb all offer high quality.

In my experience, outfitters usually own a set of decent binoculars. Most guides, however, do not carry binoculars or if they do they are often inferior. If you don't take along an extra pair of binoculars the guide may borrow yours. Since your guide doesn't carry a rifle, (and because he's in much better shape than you are) he can carry heavier binoculars in a stronger size.

With any binoculars, I strongly suggest they include fold down eye cups. If you wear eye glasses roll the cups down to obtain a larger field of view. In fact, if you don't, any binoculars are hard to use with glasses. However, without glasses use the cups full out. The rubber cups don't scratch your glasses like metal. Even if you don't wear glasses, you may wear sun glasses and find regular binoculars hard to use.

You also need a good quality spotting scope. Most outfitters carry a good scope but some guides do not. I don't feel it's quite as important for both the guide and hunter to carry a scope as it is to both carry binoculars. You can take turns behind the scope, but if you can stand lugging the extra weight up the mountain by all means carry a scope yourself.

When you purchase a scope, don't confuse a hunter's spotting scope with a telescope. Some manufacturers term their spotting scopes telescopes such as Bushnell's Spacemaster and Banner scopes. These, however, use offset prisms. Avoid the long, in-line telescopes used for star-gazing.

Some scope manufacturers offer right angle spotting scopes. They utilize an eye piece set at right angles to the scope alignment. These scopes are very handy in the field since you don't have to lie on your belly to get your eye behind the lens. Rather you can sit and look straight down into the lens. I never became accustomed to these right angle scopes. Since you look down rather than at the same angle as the scope, you have a harder time getting the scope on the target animal. The first day I used Dewey's scope I tried for

Although they may look like toys, the newer lightweight compact binoculars are much better for mountain hunting. You can wear them around your neck all day without even knowing you have them.

10 minutes before I could find the ram in the scope. I really believe, however, that it's only a matter of getting used to the instrument.

In my experience 20X or 25X scopes prove adequate for sheep and goat hunters. I've often tried to use 45X or even 60X but find that the heat waves (mirage) makes these high powers useless in most mountain conditions. You will, however, often be able to use 30X or 35X lens without distortion or heat waves. The stronger power lets you estimate horns at a greater distance.

Most quality spotting scopes offer interchangeable lens. Leave the 20X lens on the scope as you hunt. You'll find the target object much quicker with low power. After you line up the ram or goat, change to a stronger lens to better estimate his horns. A zoom lens on a spotting scope offers versatility that is hard to match with separate interchangeable lens. I've used a 15-45X lens for years to great advantage. I locate the ram with the lower power setting and then zoom up to as high a power as conditions allow.

A good solid tripod is perhaps as important as a quality lens.

Without a solid base, your scope wobbles in the wind so bad you can't use it. I once owned a very solid metal benchrest-type tripod. It definitely held the scope steady but the legs did not adjust. Did you ever try to find a level spot on the side of a mountain?

Look for a solid tripod with adjustable legs. Cheap plastic tripods or even metal pods with plastic adjustments and gears do not offer steady service. You can't imagine how aggravating a trembling scope can be. You don't need a tripod that center elevates. You do need one with sensitive up and down tilt controls. I lost my best mountain tripod. Unfortunately I don't even know the brand. I do know it was lightweight and held my scope steady and adjusted to any mountain tilt.

In my experience and the experience of many mountain hunters, those little, hand held scopes called pocket scopes or monoculars prove worthless for goat and sheep hunting. You can't hold them steady enough to study horns.

I've never seen a spotting scope with fold-up eye cups such as found on binoculars. They should work as well on scopes as binoculars. Without them I must remove my eye glasses to use the scope. It's a wonder I never lost or broke my glasses while using a scope. By the way, bifocals and trifocals often interfere with binocular and scope use. The line on the eye glasses bothers my vision. For that reason, along with many others, I prefer regular non-bifocal lens when hunting.

The only thing certain about mountain weather is it will be unpredictable, especially during hunting season. One day you might experience balmy summer-like weather and the next day you wake up to leaden skies, a roaring gale, falling temperature and snow or rain. You'll also find the temperature and windchill much different riding from camp to the mountain from that high on a ridge overlooking a sheep basin.

You can experience a large temperature or wind variation from hour to hour on the same day. Even on a day with unchanging conditions, you'll need less clothes climbing the ridge than you do sitting and glassing.

As an example of changeable mountain weather, let me relate the notes in my daily log of an Alberta sheep hunt: "Heavy overcast, rained lightly on ride to canyon. 9:15 a.m. rain stopped and sun came out. 10:30 a.m. overcast. 1:30 p.m. hail and wind storm, we stay under trees. 2:30 p.m. sunshine and blue sky. 4:30 p.m. hail storm again. 5 p.m. clear. 6 p.m. hail storm, clothes and boots soaking wet."

Guide John Nelson uses lightweight binoculars to glass a canyon near Colorado's Taylor River. Lightweight binoculars with high quality lenses and prisms rank at the very top of a sheep hunter's gear list. You spend much more time glassing the high basins than you do walking.

At least, you can often see weather coming in the mountains from the high ridges and somewhat prepare for it. That particular day, we saw every weather change coming from the canyon head.

Even desert hunting offers large temperature changes from day to day or within a given day. During winter hunts in Nevada or Arizona, you may need a heavy coat riding out from camp in the early morning. Then by midday, you're more comfortable in only a long sleeve shirt or down vest. However, after the sun slips behind the mountains in the evening the temperature again cools noticeably.

Layered clothing is the answer to most mountain hunting as is an assortment of clothing. You may need your warmest coat and you may not need a coat at all. You can wear a heavy coat out on horseback in the cold mornings and then leave it with the horse when you don a lighter jacket for the climb.

Down-filled, nylon jackets probably save the lives of more deer and elk than all the animal protection groups put together. They create a terrible racket brushing against trees and brush. However, in the fairly or completely open sheep and goat country, you don't experience this problem. And, down-filled, nylon jackets provide more warmth for the weight than any other jacket. With any and all mountain hunting gear, weight is most important.

You can stow your down jacket in your pack and wear only a shirt or shirt and vest while you climb to the high basins and ridges. Then before the winds chill you on top, slip the jacket back on. If you wear the jacket on the climb, you sweat so much you will remain chilled on the high ridge all day. Or on calm, sunny days, you may sit on top with only a shirt.

In the past few years, outdoor clothing manufacturers have entered the world of high technology. Hunters have survived for years wearing cotton long johns. However, the new Thinsulate or Thermolite underwear and outerwear protects the hunter against cold much better.

Many veteran mountain hunters prefer wool shirts but I use flannel. Wool tends to chafe my neck. I also take along a turtleneck shirt or dickey to keep the wind off my neck. Fastening your coat tight enough to keep the wind off restricts movement and feels confining.

To my knowledge, nothing can replace wool pants for keeping you warm and dry. They soak up rain or snow without letting the moisture penetrate to the skin. Many sportsmen wouldn't think of hunting in anything else. Most wool pants, however, are bulkier and heavier than blue jeans.

Before my first big game hunt, I devoured every word such experts as Jack O'Connor wrote about the proper hunting gear. On his advice I wore wool pants the first morning out on horseback. The next day I switched to blue jeans. The bulky wool pantlegs rode up on my leg on horseback and rubbed my knees almost raw. However, now I often don wool pants over my denims for the ride if the brush is wet or full of snow. And I wear wool all day if we hunt in deep snow.

Often you must ride through frost or dew-covered brush and trees in the morning riding out to the particular mountain or canyon you'll hunt that day. Chaps keep the moisture off and also protect your legs from rubbing against trees or brush in tight spots. Leave the chaps with the horse when you climb. Plain, heavy leather chaps work much better than fancy show chaps. Rather than fasten the chaps on, you may want to just slip them over your legs once in the saddle. If you dismount quickly, they stay on the saddle.

Never leave for a mountain hunt without rain gear. Heavy, slicker-type rain ponchos work good on horseback but not on a climb. I tie the heavy duty rain gear behind the saddle and carry

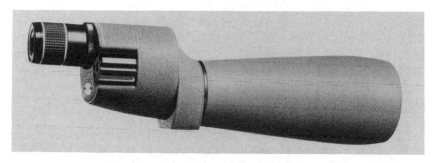

No hunter can operate at full potential without a spotting scope. A 20X to 25X scope works better than a 45X or 60X glass. The higher power scopes become useless in the presence of normal mountain heat waves. A zoom scope, like this Bushnell, probably offers the best package.

lightweight rain gear in my pack for climbing. Lightweight rain suits tear too easily to use on horseback. You might take along the largest size trash or lawn & leaf type bags in a pocket or pack. Cut a hole for you head and arms. I sat beside a fire for three hours one morning in Alberta in a trash bag during a heavy snowstorm and stayed dry. Dewey snickered when he saw the flimsy bag but I stayed as dry as he did in his slicker.

Selecting quality rain gear is much easier today than it was in years past. Today, there are wonderful new materials available in hunting coats and pants. A combination of Gore-Tex and the thin insulating materials offers a water resistant combination.

Many mountain hunters, myself included, prefer a ten-gallon cowboy hat. It keeps rain, snow and sun off better than any other headgear. However, in cold weather, you'll want a warm cap with ear flaps or a stocking cap to keep warm. Large bandana handkerchiefs help keep your neck warm and you can tie them around your mouth and nose if the weather suddenly turns bitterly cold or windy.

Gloves and/or mittens probably represent the most important items of clothing with the possible exception of boots, on a mountain hunt. If your hands or feet become cold, your entire body feels cold. For years I wore fairly thin, very flexible leather gloves with wool liners. These kept my hands warm while being thin enough to slip my finger through the trigger guard. However, they did become wet and cold in the rain.

Newer gloves such as the Gore-Tex, Thermolite insulated gloves by Bob Allen, keep your hands warm and dry under the most severe conditions. Your hands may feel cold the first ten minutes you wear them but then your body heat warms the gloves and your hands stay warm. I wore a pair on a three-day boat ride in northern Quebec when the cold froze even salt water. My hands stayed warm and dry.

In extremely cold weather, I wear a pair of large, bulky, down-filled snowmobile mittens on horseback but then change to gloves to climb and hunt.

Footwear manufacturers have made great strides in the past few years. Yet, veteran hunters probably argue more over the best mountain boots than any other item of clothing. Some like insulated rubber, others swear by leather and still others would hunt in nothing but pacs. At least nobody I know of still wears the old hobnail boots.

For years I've worn leather boots with Vibram soles. Some were lightweight, some heavy, some fairly water resistant, and some took on water like a sponge. But I never could get used to rubber boots. Today I wear Gore-Tex, Thinsulate insulated leather boots by the American Boot company. Lightweight, these boots never take on a drop of water through snow, wet grass or even wading creeks. Many hunters prefer pacs such as L.L. Bean's Maine Hunting boots. These have rubber bottoms and leather uppers. They do keep water out but I've never found a pair sturdy enough for rough mountain use. My ankles turn in them, especially when using the felt innerliners.

This past fall, I tried out a different concept in boot soles. They use air-filled, round cleats or hobs. I've never seen a sole which grips wet grass or snow better. They worked much better than my Vibram soles. You may find them available through other companies but I know L.L. Bean sells one called the Polar Boot and Sorel sells the Maverick with Aero-track. Both are pacs with leather uppers and rubber bottoms. If you wear pacs be certain you take along an extra set of liners.

Whatever boots you wear, break them in before the hunt and wear old boots before the hunt to get your feet used to boots again. Cut your toenails just before the hunt to prevent pinching.

Purchase any boot in a size large enough for heavy wool socks. Wool wicks the moisture and sweat from your feet. I wear a pair of thin socks such as silk under the wool to prevent blistering.

All big game hunters who camp some distance from a town or medical care should take along a medicine and first aid kit. Aspirin, Advil or Tylenol not only cures headaches but relieves other pain such as mild sprains, aching muscles and bruises. For

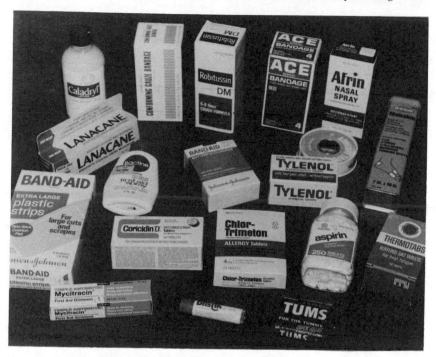

A complete medical and first aid package can save a hunt or at least make it much more enjoyable in the case of illness or accidents.

colds and allergies, include cold medicine, cough medicine and a long-acting nasal spray. An antacid tablet like Tums or Rolaids relieves not only an upset stomach but takes care of that nervous stomach that a hunt often causes. Don't forget lip protection for rough, dry lips and a hydrocortisone cream for insect bites or rashes.

Other medications you should include can be obtained only on your doctor's prescription. Most physicians, if told about your trip, will give you prescriptions. You need an antibiotic for infection, a muscle relaxant and something for diarrhea. Don't forget to include any prescription medication you take every day such as high blood pressure, heart, cholesterol or arthritis pills. Be certain to take along enough for a few days longer than the hunt is scheduled for, in case you get weathered in.

When using any prescription or non-prescription medications, be sure and take only the amount which the directions on the package dictate. Too many people think if one of something is good then two must work better. In the case of medicines, this is usually not true and taking more than the recommended dose may be harmful.

Don't forget simple first aid items such as bandaids, elastic bandage, gauze and tape. Put all your medicines and supplies in a small tightly closed bag or shaving kit and keep it just for use on hunting trips. Check the kit each year for any outdated medicines.

Don't forget personal hygiene items such as toothpaste, toothbrush, soap and toilet paper. Practically all camps have toilet paper but many are rough or hard and slick. I also take my non-trifocal eyeglasses and wear them hunting. With bifocals or trifocals I'm forever jerking my head up and down trying to see through the right part of the lens when climbing. I do keep the trifocals back at camp with which to read, write or play cards.

Canvas duffle bags work the best to carry your clothes and other gear. Many hunters use the old army surplus bags with the fold up, snap tops. I prefer a bag with a zipper on the side. The side zipper saves a lot of digging through the bag or dumping the bag to find one item.

Down-filled sleeping bags work best. If you hunt from a camp I like at least a 5-pound bag. Backpackers may want to use a 2- or 3-pound mummy bag. If your bag has nylon inside, make a liner from flannel. Nothing shocks you quite as bad as slipping into a cold, nylon lined bag. Rather than an air mattress which can nearly throw me off, I use a foam mattress. If you camp in an area with plenty of spruce trees, a mattress made from spruce boughs offers the warmest and easiest pad. If you sleep on the ground, use a ground cloth under your mattress and bag. Always sleep nude or nearly nude. Sleeping with your clothes on brings moisture from sweat that won't dry out in the morning unless you can stand by a fire for some time. You'll actually sleep warmer nude than with all your clothes on.

Most outfitters in sheep and goat country supply all the saddle gear you need. However, I prefer to take my own rifle scabbard and saddle bags. Your own scabbard fits your rifle better than an outfitter's may. After use, a scabbard takes on the shape of the rifle. Because of this your personal scabbard is neither too tight nor too loose. My saddle bags are somewhat larger than outfitter bags to hold my somewhat overloaded camera gear. Be certain, however, that the bags are not too big or too heavy and always balance the load for the horse's comfort.

Your scabbard should be stiff leather and not lined. Sheepskin and other liners tend to hold moisture and form rust on your fine rifle. When you purchase a new scabbard, wet it thoroughly and insert your rifle. After drying, your scabbard fits the rifle perfectly. A flap or hood on your scabbard keeps snow, leaves and twigs out.

After hunting with dozens of outfitters, I've never found a unanimous or even a majority agreement on how to hang a scabbard on a horse. Be certain, however, that you or the outfitter hangs the scabbard so that your rifle's scope rides up. Jolting on a horse can cause your rifle to cram down into the scabbard and can even force the scope out of line if it hangs down with the weight of the rifle on it.

Perhaps the best method of hanging a scabbard is on the left side with the butt to the rear and up at a 45 degree angle. The rifle is handy when you dismount and the scabbard won't fill with leaves and pine needles. But, you can't see and keep track of the rifle easily with the butt to the rear, and hanging it on the left side offers poor weight distribution if you mount from the left. Having the butt forward on the left side fills up with leaves and since the butt is close to the horse's eye, he might spook when you dismount and grab the gun.

If you ride a good distance, such as on a pack trip into the hunting area, you might use the scabbard on the right side, butt forward. This can fill with leaves but you can see the rifle and know it doesn't catch on a limb or slip out of the scabbard. You also have better weight distribution when you mount up. The butt to the rear on the right is perhaps the poorest set up. You can't see the rifle and you can't get at it from the horse unless you use a non-scoped carbine.

Always tighten or remove your rifle sling before putting the rifle in the scabbard. A loose sling catches on branches. Also, always carry extra leather straps to be certain you can attach the scabbard at such an angle so the rifle won't ride too high or too low.

While on the subject of saddle gear, let me offer a few tips on mountain horses and riding. Horses love to roll. Always remove your rifle from the scabbard whenever you dismount even if for only a few minutes. Imagine how much damage a thousand-pound horse can do to a rifle. The same goes for your camera gear.

Unfortunately few hunters have legs the same length as the last rider. Stirrups which are too short cause tremendous strain on your knees. Stirrups too long allow your rear end to take too much punishment. Always adjust your stirrups the first time out. I've found that if you stand in the stirrups and can just put your hand on edge between your rear end and the saddle, the stirrups are about right. On my first big game hunt, I rode all the first day with stirrups adjusted far too short. The next morning, my knees ached so bad I couldn't get onto the saddle. Lengthening them a bit solved the problem.

Outfitters normally expect the majority of hunters to be of the "city slicker" or "dude" type regarding riding ability. Hence, they use docile old mountain horses to prevent any problems. In fact, the horse may be so easy going it doesn't want to move at all. A light switch or willow branch solves this problem nicely.

Before the hunt starts, tell your outfitter your riding history and ability. Don't be afraid to ask for help or admit you've never ridden. On a long ride, keep a straight back and flex your neck and arms occasionally. A horse, like a dog or most other animals, senses a neophyte or someone who is afraid. Don't be timid around your horse but treat it with respect.

If you should ever become separated from your outfitter remember your horse knows his way back to camp. Give him his head and he'll get you back. I once hunted bear in the spring from a slightly different camp than we used the preceding fall. Invariably the horses wanted to turn in where the fall camp stood.

My own hunting list contains many other extra items which make any trip much more enjoyable. You may or may not want to include them.

—A 25- to 30-foot length of synthetic rope often comes in handy around camp or on the trail.

—A length of heavy, monofilament fish line makes excellent emergency ties, shoe laces or something with which to sew your pants up on the trail. I once slipped on a rock and split my pants from crotch to heel. After punching holes with my knife I made a few ties with tough grass. Heavy mono would have worked much better until I returned to camp.

—After a successful hunt, a true hunter can't wait to measure his hard-won trophy. Carry a small tape measure. If you forget it, a dollar bill measures about six inches.

—I include a paperback book for those days the weather forces you to stay in camp.

—A flashlight comes in handy for those emergency trips outside the tent or cabin at night.

—A ski mask keeps your head warm on cold nights and you can carry it in a pocket or your pack in case you experience cold winds on the mountain.

Horses love to roll over, so always remove your rifle from the scabbard whenever you dismount. Imagine how much damage a thousand pound horse could do to your rifle.

—I carry my own knife and pocket steel or stone.

—Nail clippers can clip nails, hangnails, cut fish line or a dozen other uses around camp.

—A cleaning rod is necessary if you drop your rifle or otherwise plug the barrel.

—For some reason I always carry a compass but never use it.

—I carry a Bic lighter for guaranteed fire starting.

—Long ago I learned the value of a pocket notebook and pen. Back home I couldn't remember when anybody shot what or many of the wonderful little things that happen on a mountain hunt. Now

I take notes each day. With the notebook in my pocket, I can make notes each time I stop. Then in the evening at camp, I fill in what I didn't get down and any thoughts on the day as a whole. I note the weather, any game sightings, any funny experience and conversations with my guide. Reading over these notes years later brings back the hunt as if I just came home.

—Items such as candy bars, a deck of cards, maps of the hunt area, tennis shoes or moccasins for camp, extra camera batteries and film all make a hunt more enjoyable. With the guides help, I note on the map where we hunt each day.

—In most areas, you can take along a take-down fishing rod and small reel for sport when you're not hunting.

—Don't forget your hunting license, drivers license, cash, a blank check or two and in some states a copy of your hunters safety card.

You should make a master list of all gear for permanent use. Then check the list as you pack and again as you load your car or get ready to board the plane. Don't forget to include your rifle on the list.

The Mountain Hunter's Rifle

O utfitter Dewey Browning and I first met in the Calgary airport. After catching a wonderful case of "sheep fever" two years before in British Columbia, I selected Dewey for a bighorn hunt in the Alberta Rocky Mountains. On the two-hour ride to his home outside Caroline, Alberta, we visited and got to know each other.

"What kind of rifle you got in that case?" Dewey asked.

"A Browning semi-automatic in a .300 Win. Mag."

"You know, we don't have a fall grizzly season here in Alberta. And you won't see many elk even if you had a license. Kinda overgunned for a poor little sheep aren't ya? And you use a semi-automatic. Don't you know those darn things jam? Bolt works every time."

I should be used to it by now, but every time an outfitter or another hunter questions my sanity at using a semi-automatic or using a magnum caliber for smaller game like antelope, sheep or deer, my fuse shortens. If you want to hear a lot of ribbing, see a lot of head shaking and start a lot of arguments just show up in hunting camp with a semi-automatic in a caliber either too large or too small for the job at hand.

The prized .300 Win. Mag. BAR has accompanied me for over 15 years. Scars show on practically every part. The forend scraped a pack frame going up an Alaskan mountain. The butt broke on a British Columbia hunt. Hundreds of times in and out of a scabbard rubbed the blueing off the muzzle. Salt water in Quebec cut into the finish on both metal and wood. But the rifle has served me faithfully. I've never wounded and then lost game with it. I've never had the thing jam.

In my gun cabinet you'll find one big game rifle (the BAR), one .22, one varmint rifle and one shotgun. In other words, I'm a hunter not a "gun nut" and I say that with the kindest regards to gun experts and aficionados. Some of my best friends own a closet full of guns, one for every purpose.

I don't own a semi-automatic for speed or additional fire power. Rather I selected the BAR because all my life I've shot semi-automatic shotguns, semi-automatic .22s, semi-automatic big game rifles. I'm used to shooting semi-automatics and I don't want to spend months working a bolt to get used to the action. And yes, the only time I used a borrowed bolt action on a mule deer hunt, I hit the buck with the first shot and then numbly tried to pull the trigger again and again without working the bolt. Fortunately, the first shot downed the buck.

Modern semi-automatic rifles work well and don't jam if you give them the same care you give a bolt action or slide action. Perhaps on a benchrest, bolt actions might offer a bit more accuracy but a modern automatic is more accurate than any hunter without a bench. I rant and rave about the semi-automatic not to convince anyone to use one but rather to point out that a choice of a rifle's action belongs to the hunter.

By now you've no doubt figured out that I'm not an authority on rifles, calibers or ballistics, but a mountain hunter need not be. He need only use a rifle capable, within broad limits, of taking sheep and goats. All the information presented in this chapter comes either from personal experience and common sense or from noted gun authorities.

The best rifle for sheep and goat hunting is the one you're comfortable and confident shooting. Use the rifle you're accustomed to as long as it falls within broad limits. I strongly recommend your usual big game rifle rather than purchasing a special rifle for the mountain hunt.

Throughout this book I repeat over and over the fact that sheep and goat hunting normally is not a long range proposition. At least it need not be. However, if you have a choice of rifles or you will purchase a new rifle for your mountain hunt, why not prepare for the possible long shot? I shot a Dall ram in Alaska at between 250 and 300 yards. We lay above the rams and I used a solid rest. We

Keep an eye on your rifle in the scabbard. The author's son, Dave, didn't. A tree slipped between the scabbard and horse and broke the rifle's scope and stock.

might have stalked closer but we also might have spooked the rams or not found another rest that was as good.

Years of personal experience as well as discussions with many hunters and shooters convinced me that you should always trade 50 yards of stalking for a solid rest. If you find a rock pile, tree root, lump of tundra or anything to rest your rifle on or to lean against, and if you can't locate any other such prop closer to your target, at least within reasonable range, stop there and shoot. And always look for such a rest even if you're close to the animal. I've yet to meet the hunter who can shoot as accurately off-hand as he can kneeling, or kneeling as well as sitting, or sitting as well as he can prone.

Because most sheep and goat hunting occurs in broken country, you can always find something to lean against or rest your rifle over. I've shot several rams prone with my rifle cushioned on a down vest or coat leaning over a ridge. I've shot leaning against the underside of a ridge. I've shot leaning over a boulder. I even dropped to one knee to shoot my desert ram which stood within 40 yards.

You should always pad your rifle with a vest, coat or even your hand rather than lay the firearm directly on a rock or boulder. Experts tell me that a rifle laid directly on a hard surface shoots high. I know I did miss high on one such shot in British Columbia. Try it yourself *before* the season begins.

Wild sheep are more high-strung than goats. Their nervous system is much more susceptible to the shock effect of any modern rifle. In other words, you don't need a very large or powerful cartridge to drop a ram. Many Indians in the past harvested sheep with .22s. However, let's select a fairly flat shooting cartridge. Anything from a 6mm or .243 Win. and above does the job nicely. Calibers such as the .25-06, .240 Wthby Mag. or .257 Wthby Mag. exhibit more killing power over 300 yards than the .243 Win. class.

If your hunt includes larger animals such as moose or grizzly, then obviously you'll want a larger caliber. Calibers such as the .270 Win., .30-06, .308 Win., .284 Win., 7mm Rem. Mag. or .300 Win. Mag. still offer a flat shooting rifle but provide more punch for the larger animals. I even know sheep hunters who use a .338 Win. Mag. Within broad limits, therefore, any caliber from .243 Win. up to whatever, as long as the muzzle velocity stays above 2,700 feet per second, works fine on the wild rams.

Goats on the other hand, represent a different theory. I have

Rifle weight and reflectiveness are important. A rifle that sports a synthetic stock, like this Remington Model 700 AS, weighs only a little over six pounds, and the dull finish doesn't reflect sunlight.

never dropped a goat with one shot, although there is little doubt my first shot has killed a goat. Because of a goat's shock absorbing nature, you can kill the animal and not realize it until you've shot a second or third time. Any animal with a reasonable size slug through his lungs dies. Most animals, however, jump or sprint off when hit. Goats often do not. Therefore, the hunter will often think he missed and shoot again.

As I wrote in the goat hunting chapter, I put three, .300 Win. Mag. 180-grain slugs into a goat's chest cavity that you could cover with a saucer. The goat didn't even flinch or blink an eye the first two shots. Many other hunters have experienced the same phenomenon.

On the average, mature mountain goat males weigh more than mature rams. They also wear a thicker coat of hair and their hide is somewhat tougher than a ram's. While you certainly don't need some big bore magnum caliber like you might on grizzly, the sensible hunter might want a slightly larger caliber for goats than for sheep.

For the hunter going after only goats, I'd say the minimum setup should be a .270 Win. with a 130-grain bullet. A .30-06 with a 150- to 180-grain bullet, a .300 Win. Mag. with a 180-grain bullet or a 7mm Rem. Mag. with a 175-grain bullet also do an excellent job in goat country.

I realize I've left out several excellent sheep and goat loads in this discussion of calibers. Again, most hunters do best with their old standby rifle, one they're familiar with and trust. Also, while I've never lost or ran out of rifle shells on a hunting trip, I feel more comfortable with a common caliber readily available almost everywhere.

Bullet construction is important. While a large number of hunters now load their own, many others, myself included, do not. In my experience and in my research I find that you need a bullet with deep penetration and reliable expansion. Remington's Core-Lokt Pointed Soft Points and Winchester's Super-X Power Point Soft Points do an excellent job in the field, as do Nosler handloads.

Weight rates as one of two important considerations in a mountain rifle. Every extra pound you carry up a 2,000-foot ridge expends as much energy as lifting a ton. Regardless of how good a flatlander works into shape, he won't keep up with a spry young guide raised in the mountains. Fortunately, you need not look far to find a reliable, lightweight rifle in sheep and goat calibers.

I remember when Jerry Christian first showed off his special-order, lightweight rifle. It used a synthetic, camouflaged stock and weighed less than eight pounds including scope. Everyone praised the rifle and dreamed about carrying such a feather up a sheep mountain.

Unfortunately, I still tote my heavy Browning automatic with its old Redfield variable power scope. I've never actually put the combination on a scale but the weight must go over nine pounds, perhaps ten. You can be sure that when I break down and purchase a new rifle, weight will be an important consideration. Every time I lug that rifle and scope up a ridge, I cuss it. However, once on flat land, I hate to part with an old friend. Remember, you carry a mountain rifle much more than you shoot it. The rifle should be handy, light and portable.

Since the big game rifle's earliest days, hunters as well as shooters, have felt that any respectable rifle must sport a wooden, especially walnut, stock. Anything else didn't look like a quality firearm. At long last hunters and gun men turn to alternatives. According to Jim Carmichel, shooting editor at *Outdoor Life,* wooden stocks can react to changes in the atmosphere and temperature. This, in turn, may cause changes in a rifle's point of impact. "Even a carefully sighted-in rifle can become useless after a day or two of bad weather," he said.

And where do you find more bad weather than on a sheep or goat hunt in the high peaks. The new synthetic stocks don't react whatsoever to temperature or atmospheric changes. As an added advantage, the new stocks also weigh less than wooden stocks. Depending on the model, you can find these wonderful rifles weighing only six to seven pounds. Needless to say, they are also virtually indestructible and resistant to nicks and scrapes. They just don't look pretty.

The second important quality in a mountain rifle is its

Your rifle scope should be lightweight and nonreflective, like this Bushnell Armor-Sight.

reflectiveness or shine. On a British Columbia goat hunt, our cook, Patty, accompanied Dale and I on horseback up the canyon. After we started off on foot, Patty led the horses across the creek and waited for our return.

We climbed and hunted all the way around the head of the canyon but found nothing to look at, let alone stalk. Coming back down the other side, we saw Patty waiting impatiently with the horses.

"Do you guys know you looked like a lit up Christmas tree when you climbed around in those rocks? The sun reflecting off your rifle was the worst, Lloyd, but I could also see reflections off your watch and ring," Patty reported.

I'd never been on the same mountain with other hunters to notice reflection. If Patty could spot the reflection you can be certain that even a myopic ram or billy goat would spot the mirror-like light even quicker. Not only does a rifle's metal parts reflect sunlight but wooden stocks, especially the traditional varnished stock, will reflect light.

For the past few years, several manufacturers have offered synthetic stocks that greatly diminish the possibility of reflection and even camouflage stocks. Back in the spring of 1989, Remington offered hunters a new lightweight, synthetic stock on a Model 700 action. The stock is made of Arylon, a fiberglass-reinforced thermoplastic resin, and retains the inert characteristics of other production grade synthetic stocks with equal strength but offers lighter weight. The Model 700 Arylon Stock weighs only 6½ pounds.

Unlike other rifles with synthetic stocks, the 700 AS offers the nonreflective stock and nonreflective metal surfaces, including the bolt body. Remington offers a broad caliber choice of .22-250 Rem., .243 Win., .270 Win., .280 Rem., .30-06, .308 Win. and 7mm Rem. Mag. All use a 22-inch barrel except the .22-250 Rem. and the 7mm

Rem. Mag. which sport a 24-inch barrel. All in all, the new rifle should prove a top rate mountain rifle.

All mountain rifles should include a quickly adjustable sling. Carrying a rifle in your hands without a sling soon makes your arms feel stretched to near ground length. The adjustable sling lets you carry the rifle over one shoulder, on your back with the sling across your chest or slung on a pack frame. Under normal conditions, I carry my rifle on my shoulder or on a pack frame. But, when you must cross rough or dangerous ground or you must climb a face-hugging cliff, sling the rifle across your back so it won't slip off.

Normally, sheep and goat hunters have the time and opportunity to wiggle into a steady shooting position. An adjustable sling allows you to add the benefits of a sling regardless of shooting position. Why not take advantage of anything which offers a more secure and steady shooting position?

If you take care to camouflage your rifle to stop reflected glare or own one of the newer rifles with synthetic stocks, don't forget the glare caused by a rifle scope. A non-reflective rifle loses its effectiveness if your scope reflects the sun. Several manufacturers offer such scopes, including Bushnell. Bushnell's "Armor-sight" scope is made from a graphite composite material stronger than steel, lighter than aluminum and impervious to moisture and other weather changes. The Armor-sight scope uses a nonreflective black matte finish. Though stronger than conventional aluminum scopes it is 10 percent lighter in weight. Weighing only 12.5 ounces, the 3-9X scope is 12 inches long and uses a 40mm, wide angle, objective lens. With proper selection, you may now set up a rifle and scope which weighs little more than seven pounds.

Because of their versatility, I prefer variable power scopes over fixed power scopes for almost all big game hunting. For the sheep and goat hunter, a 4X or 6X scope gives excellent results in almost all cases. However, for that occasional long shot a higher power comes in handy. Of all the variable scopes offered, the 3-9X probably meets all the sheep and goat hunter's needs better than other combinations.

If you shop for a rifle scope, you'll be amazed at the number of possible reticles and scope refinements. You'll find dot reticles, fine cross hairs, course cross hairs and tapered cross hairs. You can purchase scopes with a prismatic range finder or bullet drop compensation and wide angle viewing.

For the sheep or goat hunter tapered cross hairs, or one with

Never leave for your high country hunt without first sighting in your rifle. Use a benchrest for the final sighting, but then check it from a sitting and kneeling position.

course outer cross hairs connected to thin center cross hairs, works best. The thicker cross hairs on the outside helps locate your target quicker and the thin inner cross hairs allows fine sighting.

While bench shooters and even hunters who know their ballistics completely and can shoot with great accuracy may find a use for such gadgets as bullet drop compensators, range finders and quick adjustment scopes, I can not. Not attempting a shot at any game animal where I needed to hold the cross hairs over its back, has served me well over the years. Before you can hold over the back, you must be able to judge distance in the mountains far better than most hunters. Don't rely on guides for distance estimation. They may give excellent advice on whether or not the ram is in range but most guides have no conception what 100 yards or 300 yards or whatever is. They know only what hunters have estimated in the past.

Rather than try to judge distance, a simple rule works for my shooting. No shooter can hold the cross hairs on one exact spot without at least some wiggle. The trick is squeezing the trigger just before you expect the wiggle to cross the exact target spot. If I can keep the cross hairs from wiggling completely off the animal, either over or under, then I feel I can take the shot with a high percentage rate of success. If the cross hairs wiggle off, then the animal stands too far for me to shoot. Obviously, I can keep the cross hairs on the animal with the rifle rested on a rock or something than I can free-hand. My system takes this fact into account.

"Did you sight that rifle in?" I asked a hunting friend just before we left home.

"No, why should I? It was on last year and I haven't done anything to it."

Not only did he not sight the rifle in but he hadn't taken it out of the gun cabinet since last fall. I know of no golfers or bowlers who feel they can score their best if they only play the game once a year. Rather, they practice and play as much as possible to keep their skills honed. But some sportsmen for some unfathomable reason think they can shoot the eye out of a spider at 250 yards each hunting season with no practice during the off season.

To become proficient with your rifle or to retain your skills, you must practice shooting. Shoot at least once a month after the weather turns decent in the spring. Then work up to once a week the last month before you hunt.

When you practice, you need not use the same load as you hunt with. Using a lighter load for practice saves a lot of recoil and

Don't let poor shooting ruin an otherwise wonderful hunt of a lifetime. Practice from all possible shooting positions, not just from a benchrest.

makes practice time more pleasant and more productive. You also need not worry about centering your shots on the target. It doesn't matter where they hit as along as you produce tight groups. Center the group just before you leave on the hunt.

Practice does not mean shooting from a bench or similar rest all the time. You should shoot standing, kneeling, sitting and prone. Use your sling and keep an elbow on your knee while sitting and kneeling. If at all possible practice on a range or other safe site where you can shoot not only at 100 yards but at distances out to 200 or even 300 yards.

Just before you leave on your hunt do your final sighting in from a solid bench rest. Then after you center your group where you want, recheck the results from a sitting and prone position. Some hunters shoot slightly different on the bench and off. You won't have the bench on the mountainside.

Read hunting or shooting manuals and you will find different advice on sighting in a rifle. The methods vary as much as the authors. Some are complicated, some simple. Some are practical, some are not. To me reading a ballistics chart is something akin to reading Russian. They talk of mid-range trajectory and bullet drop. Years ago I read something by the expert gun writer Warren Page that does make sense and is simple:

"Sensibly, the hunter should set up or zero his rifle and sight in such a fashion that will get the best out of the rifle for full-range operation—at least out to that yardage where bullets begin to run out of effective steam or become unreliable in expansion. For about 90 percent of today's hunting rounds, what I have long termed the Rule of Three is probably the handiest way to operate."

Page's Rule of Three simply states that any modern cartridge in the muzzle velocity range of 2,700 to 3,200 fps with decent game bullets should be sighted in to group three inches high at 100 yards. This system keeps the bullet in a theoretical six- to seven-inch pipe from point blank to well beyond 200 yards and in some cases out to 300 yards. Your bullet will not stray more than three inches over or under your line of sight. On an animal the size of a ram or goat, a drop or rise of three inches will take the animal if you hold dead on the center of the chest.

His "shoot through the pipe" system is a neat way of minimizing range estimation problems. Furthermore, it puts minimum strain on your memory. You need only remember the effective hold dead-on range for your particular load and when to hold on the very top of the animal. With such cartridges as the .243 Win. or 6mm Rem. with 100-grain bullets, the .270 Win. with 130-grain, the 300 Win. Mag. with 180-grain and the 7mm Rem. Mag with 160-grain, you can hold dead on to approximately 310 to 325 yards. Then hold at the animal's backbone at 400 yards.

For slightly slower combinations such as the .270 Win. with 150-grain bullets and the .30-06 with 180-grain bullets, hold dead on to 260 yards and on the back line at 340 yards. To me, this system works much better and easier than any other sighting or ballistics system.

Above all, don't forget to recheck your sights on arrival at your hunting camp. You can always find a cardboard box or something around camp to set up 100 paces away. If nothing else cut a bit of bark off a nearby tree and use that as a target. Remember, transporting rifles in a car or on a plane is not foolproof even in the best hard-sided case. Don't take a chance on missing that ram or

During practice, don't worry about where your shots center. You can move them during the final sighting in. At that time, sight the rifle to shoot three inches high at 100 yards.

goat of a lifetime with a jolted scope. By the way, after tightening scope mount screws, a drop of clear fingernail polish keeps them from loosening.

Never carry your rifle in a soft case or saddle scabbard in a vehicle or on a plane. Most airlines have restrictions on cases. They must be hard-sided and lockable. The same case should be used transporting the rifle in a vehicle or in a bush plane. A sheep or goat hunt is an expensive proposition. Don't scrimp on the quality of your hard gun case.

I separately insure my rifle on the plane. Airlines tell you it's not necessary because your gear is insured to $500 or some such figure. I'm not particularly worried about losing the rifle forever and collecting the insurance, but that separate insurance tag on the gun case seems to guarantee better handling by airline employees.

Airlines often handle rifles apart from the rest of the baggage. I once waited nearly an hour for my rifle to come down with the luggage in the Calgary airport only to discover it had been there all the time but in a different, special handling area. If you don't see your rifle case right away, ask for help.

Before leaving the subject of rifles, sighting and shooting, let me offer a tip for mountain hunting. Often you may have to shoot at a steep downhill or uphill angle. I've shot nearly straight up myself and saw the results of other hunters shooting nearly straight down.

Old hunting and shooting literature teems with advice on shooting at a dramatic angle up or down. Something about aiming low when shooting downhill and aiming high shooting up hill. Or is it the other way around? I never could keep it straight. My good friend and hunting partner, Larry Stille, believes you must aim differently uphill than down. The simple fact is both extremes require you aim low because your bullet, apparently, rises.

We all know a bullet doesn't rise. In fact, from the moment a bullet leaves the barrel, gravity pulls it down. To compensate for this we adjust the scope so that the rifle barrel actually points upward in relation to the sight line in the scope. That's the only way in which we can hit a target at any distance much over point blank.

Now, if you shoot at the complete extreme of straight down or straight up, the barrel will actually point higher than the sight line of the scope. Therefore to hit your target at either extreme you must aim low. Shooting on the level, at right angles to either straight up or straight down, you must aim at the center of the

On most high country hunts you will find a good, solid rest for your rifle. It's best to pad the contact point between rifle and rest with a vest, coat or glove.

target. As you hold your rifle farther away from the 90 degree level you must aim lower and lower as you approach straight up or straight down. A little up or down won't make much difference but extreme angles can and do.

Larry Stille knows ballistics and shoots much better than I do. I've explained the theory and he still doesn't believe. If you can't make sense out of my explanation, please believe anyway. I've seen it in action and I know the facts are correct.

My dad once shot almost straight down at a Dall ram in Alaska. With the ram laying away from him, he aimed at the junction of the neck and shoulders. The slug kicked up shale just over the ram's nose. Before I learned my lessons, I once was forced to shoot at a ram almost straight above me standing on the skyline. After aiming slightly above the center of his chest, nothing happened after I squeezed the trigger. My outfitter, watching with binoculars saw no shale fly. No doubt the slug flew above the ram into space. I used a steady rifle rest and my aim was good. I simply didn't know the bullet would, apparently, rise.

14

High Country
Outfitters And Guides

Since I first met Alberta sheep outfitter Dewey Browning 15 years ago, I've hunted with him only four times. But a better friend I could never hope to find. Although we live over 1,000 miles apart he and his wife, Niva, visit our home in Iowa.

We regularly call each other and confide our most personal thoughts to each other. Our family joined his for a wonderful vacation in the mountains. We thrill along with the Brownings whenever their talented son, Kurt, wins medals in international ice skating competition. We met the Brownings in Calgary and cheered with them when Kurt skated for Canada in the winter Olympics. In short, we became fast friends.

You won't become lifelong friends with every outfitter you hunt with. However, with careful selection, you have every reason to expect your outfitter to be a decent and hardworking man. And you may develop close friendships. Over the years I've hunted with many top flight individuals, outfitters who I respect for their knowledge of the wildlife, the country and for their personality.

Unfortunately, like any other business or profession, you might find an outfitter who doesn't care about his business, uses inferior equipment, doesn't have many good rams or goats in his area or otherwise doesn't provide a quality hunt. A far lower percentage of sheep and goat outfitters fit into this category than in deer, elk or other antlered hunting.

Why does the sheep or goat hunter need the services of an outfitter or guide? The great majority of states and provinces require at least nonresidents to contract with an outfitter or guide. This regulation does not pad the area's economy but rather prevents hunters from becoming lost, starting forest fires or otherwise causing problems. And in some states and provinces even residents must hire a guide.

If you hunt sheep or goats anywhere in the north country, the law requires you hire an outfitter or guide. Alberta outfitters are allotted four sheep permits each. If you don't contract with an outfitter, you don't hunt sheep in Alberta.

To me, the question is not a legal one. Even if not required to have an outfitter or guide, we should. Unless you live near your hunting area and can spend the time scouting and setting up camp well before the season opens, it's folly to attempt a sheep or goat hunt without a guide or outfitter, even in your own state. I know hunters on a tight budget and tight schedule who try to hunt weekends from the road or hastily set up weekend camps.

For the life of me, I can't understand why hunters would apply for a drawing year after year and then attempt to hunt on their own or hunt only weekends. The permits are simply too scarce and the trophy too coveted to waste time and effort. If necessary I would sell my car, my house, at times I've even considered robbing a bank in order to hire an outfitter for such a special, once-in-a-lifetime hunt (my wife claims I would sell her). I know of no one who would consider going into court without an attorney, operating on himself instead of paying a surgeon to do it or even changing motors in his or her own vehicle. But the same sportsman thinks he can hunt sheep on his own.

You hire a guide or outfitter for his knowledge and his ability to act on that knowledge. He knows the animal, its habits and its habitat. The outfitter owns horses, tack, tents, cabins and the other gear and equipment necessary for a successful hunt. Most often your guide or outfitter makes the difference between a wonderful, successful experience and a failure.

I use the terms outfitter and guide almost interchangeably. Technically, however, an outfitter owns and runs a complete hunting setup. A guide leads you on your daily chase. In smaller operations your outfitter may also work as your guide. In larger operations, your outfitter hires guides to lead you each day while he oversees the entire operation.

Since the outfitter can make or break your long-awaited hunt,

"I would sell my car, my house, at times I've considered robbing a bank," the author says, "in order to hire an outfitter for a special, once-in-a-lifetime hunt (my wife claims I would sell her)."

select him with the same care you do your doctor or lawyer. Before he knew better, my dad once selected an outfitter by picking the best looking ad in the back of a hunting magazine. Complete disaster best describes the hunt. Not only did they see no game or even fresh sign, but the food was poor, the accommodations worse and arrangements practically non-existent. You can not determine the quality of an outfitter by the quality of his or her advertisement.

Before you get the impression that all outfitters and guides are only out for a fast buck or are not dependable, let me say that the vast majority are honest, hardworking men and, yes, a few women, especially sheep and goat outfitters. My only advice is to proceed with caution when contracting with any outfitter the first time.

In the U.S. you must select the area you want to hunt before you select an outfitter. You may want to select the area with the best chance for a representative trophy. Or you might want to select an area with the best chance at a record book trophy. Then you need to learn who outfits in that general area. You'll probably find several choices.

Undoubtedly, word of mouth offers the surest method of selecting an outfitter. If a friend recommends a certain outfitter, trust him. He would not recommend an outfitter who didn't run a good operation to his friend. I know many outfitters who never advertise. They rely on word of mouth from happy clients to supply them with a never-ending string of clients and repeat business.

You can write the game department in the state or province of the hunt. They can't recommend one guide or outfitter over another, but they will send you a list of all licensed people in their state. Unfortunately, these lists often include all outfitters not just sheep or goat outfitters, but it does give you a starting point.

The "Hunter's Connection" ads in the back of outdoor publications also give you a good starting point. Many excellent outfitters advertise. Use these advertisements as a good starting point. Later in this chapter I'll explain how to research possible outfitters so you can select one with the greatest chance of success.

You'll also find stories in magazines like *North American Hunter* about sheep and goat hunts. If the story sounds exciting, if the writer had good luck, said the camp was well run, it's worth looking into further. Write the author in care of the magazine for additional information. Better yet, if the outfitter's name and address is given in the story, contact him directly.

You hire a guide or outfitter for his knowledge and his ability to act on that knowledge. Dennis Callison, of Callison Outfitters, and guide Art Johns, know the animal, its habits and its habitat.

Taxidermists offer another good source of information on high country outfitters and guides. No one in the world likes to brag about or complain about a trip more than a hunter. He'll tell the taxidermist about his trip and whether or not the outfitter did a good job.

Since taxidermists work for a large number of clients they know what outfitters or what areas of the country produce the largest animals or a lot of animals. They offer good advice because they don't want unhappy hunters. If they give poor advice, you likely won't take your taxidermy work to them.

Over the past 20 years or so, many of the largest taxidermy studios set up a hunter referral system or set up part of their business as a booking agent. Many other hunters and businessmen set up booking agent companies. These men and women have contacts with a large number of outfitters and guides. In the vast majority of cases, the outfitters pay the booking agent 10 to 15 percent of the price of the hunt to take care of bookings for them.

Many hunters might wonder why a good outfitter would need a booking agent and why he would give up 10 or 15 percent of the fee rather than book hunts himself. The reason is that the booking agent does all the work of the booking process. He collects a deposit and corresponds with both hunter and outfitter. Many outfitters don't like details. Also, many young, new outfitters need exposure. The booking agent can save the hunter a lot of time and trouble.

Booking agents often know of hunts available at the last minute that the hunter could not possibly arrange in a short time. If you use a booking agent, be certain to research him as thoroughly as you would an outfitter. Also, make certain that the booking agent is an active hunter himself and doesn't just sit behind a desk and make phone calls.

Hunting and conservation organizations such as the North American Hunting Club, Foundation for North American Wild Sheep and the various state sheep organizations offer perhaps the best source of reliable information on guides and outfitters.

As a current, paid NAHC member you are entitled to a free copy of the "NAHC Approved Outfitters & Guides" booklet. This book is compiled using official NAHC Hunting Reports submitted by your fellow members. It is revised and updated every year, and specifies which guides and outfitters cater to sheep and goat hunters. Also, for a nominal charge you can receive photocopies of hunting reports completed by fellow members on a specific guide

When an outfitter loads up the pack horses for the ride to spike camp, keep out of the way unless he asks for help. Outfitter Dewey Browning and cook Gladys Wren have lots of experience loading up the horses for the trip to a bighorn camp near Forbidden Creek, Alberta.

or outfitter. Contact the North American Hunting Club for more information.

If you write to one of the sheep organizations (see Appendix 2) they may only send you a list such as is available from the state or province. If at all possible attend their local or national conventions. There you can talk with other hunters and meet a number of outfitters. Nothing replaces personal contact. You and a certain outfitter may hit it off right away. You can also see exactly what various outfitters offer at one time and place. Besides being an excellent place to visit with other hunters and outfitters, the conventions are just plain fun and interesting. Many state organizations put together weekend waterhole building projects.

After gathering a list of several possible outfitters for your sheep or goat hunt, draft a short letter to each. Outfitters in general don't like to answer mail and they will answer short letters much faster than long rambling letters. Remember, they receive many letters from hunters who have no real plans of actually hunting.

Tell them exactly what species you want to hunt and what year you want to hunt. Then ask what success they had on rams or goats the past few years, what they charge for a hunt and for a list of recent references. References from five or ten years ago don't do much good. You can go into detail and ask many other questions after you narrow your list down.

Rather than write to the references, I prefer to call them if at all possible. The outfitter may supply the phone number as well as the address. If not you can call information for the number. Most sheep and goat hunters are busy people and they'd much rather visit about the outfitter on the phone than take time to answer your letter. When you call ask if they have a few minutes to talk. They might suggest you drop them a note. However, most sportsmen would rather help you on the phone. Ask a few pertinent questions but let the reference do most of the talking.

Most hunters find it hard not to ask how big a trophy the reference took, but that is certainly not the most important question. Find out first if the reference enjoyed the hunt. Find out what type of accommodations the outfitter used. Try to learn something about the quality of his gear and equipment.

Perhaps most important is the outfitter's and guide's attitude. Do they enjoy the hunt? Do they grumble about the weather or the stupid dude hunters they had in the past? If the reference hunted with a guide, did the guide grumble about the outfitter? Find out if the outfitter was easy to talk to and did he spend time with the hunter.

When I lined up my first Alberta bighorn hunt, one reference I talked with did not take a ram. However, he quickly pointed out that the outfitter was not at fault. The hunter missed a shot and experienced bad luck on a couple of other rams. He told me that he not only had the best hunt of his life but that he had already booked to return with the same outfitter. The statement that he did or would return and hunt with the same outfitter really carries more weight than the trophies hunters may take with a certain outfitter.

*Help out around camp doing simple chores like chopping and carrying firewood.
However, always ask before you pitch in.*

Yes, we all hunt to harvest trophy animals but to many hunters the
kill does not rate as the most important part of the hunt.

My good friend, Dr. Tom Richmond, hunted bighorns with
Dewey Browning at least three times. Richmond must be the
unluckiest hunter ever to set foot on a sheep mountain. For one
reason or another he never did shoot an Alberta bighorn. He did hit
one on the horn, which knocked the ram out cold, then the trophy
jumped up and scampered to safety while Richmond and Browning
stood congratulating each other. But nobody would give Browning
a higher recommendation than Richmond.

A number of years before I drew my desert permit to hunt in

Nevada, I researched the local outfitters and settled on one of Nevada's foremost outfitters. Fortunately, when I drew my permit I checked again. Over the years, the outfitter had a few problems I didn't know about. When rechecking him I learned of another outfitter who in the end provided a marvelous hunt.

Needless to say, no outfitter includes disgruntled hunters on his reference list. However, after you narrow your list to one or two outfitters, you should check them further. If you call, rather than write, someone in the game and fish department of the state you may learn something of the outfitter's reputation. State personnel would never put anything in writing but they might give you a good indication on the phone.

Before you reach a final decision, consider contacting people in the outfitter's area. Such people as bankers, lawyers, etc. may know nothing about an outfitter's hunting ability but they may know something about his general reputation or business ability. If your outfitter lives in a large city, you won't have much luck, but in small towns everybody knows everybody else. Before I signed with Browning in Alberta I contacted a banker and a local pharmacist. To locate these people in a small town, just call for information and ask for the name and phone number of the local bank or whatever. None of the people I talked with in Dewey's hometown knew anything about Dewey's hunting but all knew him to be an honorable and reliable man. Don't worry about insulting an outfitter by checking on him. He'll appreciate your taking the time to research your options before you spend your hard earned money. In some cases, outfitters would do well to check out prospective hunters.

After you select your outfitter, ask him all the questions you have before the hunt. Find out exactly what's included in the price of the hunt. Find out if the price includes such items as transportation to the hunt site (by bush plane, truck, horse), food, trophy preparation and trophy shipping. Don't worry if he or she doesn't include all these items but be certain you know what is included.

Different outfitters figure a 14-day hunt differently. Some count the day into the hunt area but not the day out. Some count both the day in and the day out. Some don't count either. Again, it doesn't really matter but you should know. Ask him precisely when and where to arrive. Ask if someone will meet you at the airport. Find out exactly what gear you should bring and what the outfitter provides. Ask for all these things in writing.

Keep your enthusiasm on a guided hunt. It's not the guide's fault when you get snowed or rained on. Guides will do everything they can to get you a shot at a sheep or goat.

For good reason, all responsible outfitters ask for a deposit ahead of time. This may run from 25 to 50 percent of the total price of the hunt and they may want it up to a year before the hunt. Be certain you get a receipt and that you understand how much you will owe on arrival at camp. Some outfitters hesitate to take personal checks when you get to camp. They've been stiffed before. Just ask the outfitter prior to your departure from home how he wants the final payment.

After you contract for the hunt, your excitement level rises with each passing week. During this time, keep in touch with the outfitter. Above all, be honest with the man. Let him know something of your hunting experience, ability, age, physical condition. With good information your outfitter can personalize the hunt for you. Don't be afraid to tell him you've never hunted sheep before or that you can keep going all day but not at a fast pace.

Depending on your ability and physical condition, your outfitter may assign you a certain guide, a certain horse or a certain area to hunt. If you have any dietary restrictions, be certain to tell the outfitter ahead of time. Don't tell the outfitter you're a good rider if you've never been on a horse. Although I ride almost every year hunting, I'll never become an expert rider. With this knowledge, my outfitters never assign me a high spirited horse.

Be certain both you and your outfitter or guide know what type of trophy you want. Everybody wants a record book head but we can't all find one. If you will *only* settle for a 40-inch ram or a 10-inch goat, tell the outfitter. You might say, "I'll pass everything less until the last three days of the hunt, then I'll take any respectable ram." However, if you do hold out and then don't score after passing decent rams, don't blame the outfitter or guide.

But if you want only a good representative trophy let the outfitter and guide know. They can plan your hunt much better and they know what to look for. Above all, be honest with yourself as well as with the outfitter.

When you show up for a first hunt with an outfitter or guide, you can do many things to make the hunt more successful and enjoyable. Don't push the outfitter or guide to become fast friends. Don't be too talkative, or overly friendly. Most guides and outfitters are basically mountain men and therefore, to some extent, loners. On the other hand don't be too aloof or distant. Perhaps the best advice is to be yourself.

Everybody in sheep camp likes to talk about past hunts. Don't, however, monopolize the conversation about your past hunts or the

Don't push the outfitter or guide to become fast friends. Most guides and outfitters are mountain men and therefore, to some extent, loners. Be sincere and honest, and you could develop a lifelong friendship.

wonderful trophies you collected with other outfitters unless your companions ask. Do listen to the outfitter's and guide's stories. Besides being interesting, you might learn something.

Do keep your enthusiasm high. Don't forget, it's not the guide's or outfitter's fault when you get snowed, rained or fogged in. It's not their fault if you can't climb or can't shoot. Don't become so engrossed with the trophy that you miss out on the many wonderful events or sightings on a mountain hunt. Admire the eagle soaring high above. Enjoy the marmot chattering and scolding. Enjoy ewes and lambs romping in a sheep pasture. Try to watch and learn about horses, camp duties, sheep habits and habitat. In other words, enjoy life.

I mentioned before that you probably should not trust your guide's ability to judge distance in yardage terms. However, unless the first day or two prove the guide incompetent, trust him completely in all other matters. Follow his lead in selecting a route to stalk. Follow his lead going up a ridge or down a canyon. He knows the area and you don't. Trust his judgment on trophy size, he's seen more rams than you have.

Ask your guide or outfitter for advice if you don't know what you're doing. Ask about anything you see but don't understand. On the ride back to camp one evening I noticed something that looked like an upside down candlestick holder in a pine tree. Later at camp I described it in those terms. My outfitter thought about it and broke out laughing. I'd seen a mushroom or toadstool which a squirrel had put in the tree to dry out.

When climbing, do your best and even push yourself a bit. If you don't you'll never make the top. But, don't try to keep up with the guide, especially if he's young and has an ego problem. I hunted with a tough young guy like that in British Columbia. The harder I tried to keep up, the harder he worked to keep far ahead. When I finally woke up and slowed a bit, so did Dale. Remember, the guide can't shoot the ram or goat and you can't shoot very well if you can't catch your breath before the shot.

Never try to teach your guide or outfitter about hunting or his countryside. He's the expert. Don't try to tell him how different another outfitter did something. Each has his own methods and his own reasons. Again, you hired him for his expertise, so use it.

Be honest with the outfitter on the hunt itself. If you don't feel you can make a certain shot, tell the guide or outfitter. If you don't feel you can make a certain climb, tell them. When we lost track of my ram on the desert hunt, Jerry asked me if I could shoot from where we sat when the ram finally stood up. The distance was at least 400 yards, but worse, the wind blew at near gale force. I told him I might but hated to take a chance. I might miss and spook the ram or worse I might wound the ram. Later we stalked to within 40 paces.

One year after a period of illness, I hunted with Wynn Condict, of Wyoming Safaris. He thought we could get an elk if I climbed to a certain saddle and then he and a guide pushed the elk out of the timber below. When I asked how I would reach the saddle, he said climb from the creek bed far below. I confessed

Trust your guide and follow his lead. Ed Huxen kept his enthusiasm and bagged this Dall sheep at 8 p.m. on the last day of a 15-day hunt. He was hunting with Johnny Drift Outfitters.

that I would have to start climbing the night before to ever make it by morning because of my poor condition. He said he was sure glad to find that out then rather than the next morning. We changed the plans.

Don't be afraid to ask for help. If your stirrups are too long, ask for your guide to shorten them. If you can't find a box or something to check your rifle sights, ask for help. If your saddle slips or feels loose, ask for help. Accidents can and do happen, especially if you try to ride or climb when everything is not just right.

Sheep and goat camps offer the most wonderful experience in the great outdoors. Most often, however, you camp one on one with a guide or outfitter or at most with only one other hunter, probably a stranger before the hunt. Strangers often become fast friends but this doesn't happen every time. Don't push yourself on the other hunter but remain open. Listen with interest to his stories but don't push your own unless he seems genuinely interested.

Around camp, offer to help with chores you are capable of or have done before but don't push it. The cook, wrangler, guide or other hired hands appreciate help. You can carry water, split, stack or carry wood or take care of other simple camp chores. Ask before you help. Some camp hands have their own way of doing things and don't appreciate outsiders helping. Keep your eyes open for things you can do to help. Even the most inept outdoorsman can help with some camp chores even if it's only peeling spuds or washing dishes.

When it comes to horses, leave the saddling, bridling, care, etc. to the camp help unless you own horses or really know what you're doing. Even then ask before you pitch in. The outfitter is responsible for the well-being of his horses as well as your well-being. He can't take any chance of someone else making a mistake with the horses. The same goes for pack horses. Few hunters know enough about packs and pack horses to help. Even if you do, the outfitter probably uses his own system. Don't help unless asked.

If for any reason you hunt two hunters with one guide on a sheep or goat hunt, be certain to flip a coin or something to determine who has first choice or first refusal if you see one animal. You'll save a lot of arguments and bad feelings. You can't be arguing or even being polite to one another when the ram or goat is within shooting distance. Normally your outfitter will not allow more than one hunter with one guide but occasionally

On high country hunts you will sometimes camp one-on-one with your guide in a cabin or spike camp. Strangers can become fast friends, but this doesn't always happen. Listen with interest to his stories but don't push your own unless he seems genuinely interested.

circumstances dictate otherwise as it did to me in Alberta when the young guide went into town for two days. You may head for the hunting area with both guides and both hunters together for a time. Normally you won't see anything on the way but why take a chance. A simple coin flip or decision beforehand works best.

Alcohol and hunting really don't make good partners. I don't mean you shouldn't take a drink or two before supper or to celebrate a great ram or billy's downfall. In fact, I can think of few things more enjoyable on a mountain hunt than sitting beside a campfire or heat stove in the evening and sipping a bit of bourbon and creek water.

But drinking in camp can easily get out of hand, resulting in hangovers in the morning when you should be out enjoying the mountains. Heavy drinking also leads to arguments or worse in the close confines of a sheep camp. Take along your favorite bottle but set a limit of a drink or two and stick to it. Always ask the outfitter first before offering drinks to your guide or other camp help. And if he says OK, limit them to the same one or two drinks.

One last word about do's and don'ts around camp: Tipping always represents a problem for many hunters. Most sportsmen want to tip their guide or cook or wrangler, especially if they provide excellent service. But often the hunter on limited means fears his tip might not be significant to the help. Actually, whatever you can afford will be appreciated, not only for the actual tip but for the thought. Normally you should tip the guide more than the cook, wrangler or other camp help. But tipping should be based on hard work and enthusiasm not on necessity.

Sometimes a guide will mention or admire a certain piece of your equipment. If he deserves it, you might give him the extra binoculars, coat or whatever rather than a cash tip.

Outfitters, on the other hand, seldom, if ever, expect tips. You've paid them for the hunt and some even become embarrassed if you offer them a tip. I have given an outfitter a special down jacket that I knew I could replace easier than he could buy one. I've also given special trinkets or other items I knew would please an outfitter or his wife after I knew them well and had hunted with them many times.

Outfitters and guides can make your hunt the most wonderful experience of your life or they can make you wonder why you spent all that hard earned cash for a miserable hunt. Select your outfitter with care, be completely honest with him and do your best to make the hunt memorable and camp life pleasant.

15

Meat And Trophy Care

Snow, rain and mist each fell in turn the day I took my first ram, a Stone sheep, high above British Columbia's Tuchodi River. We had planned to camp out that night but we carried no tent, only sleeping bags. After Dale congratulated me he said we should hustle back to main camp or we'd sleep in wet bags that night.

Since Dale could scamper down the mountain much faster than I could, he suggested I head down. He would follow after cleaning and caping the sheep. We reached the lake at dusk, cold, wet and tired. With the help of the cook flashing a light every few minutes, we reached camp before bedtime.

On previous hunts in the same area for elk, moose and caribou, we let the guide worry about taking meat out. Without paying a large fee for an extra plane out, we could not take much meat home. Also, hunting these animals in the rut, we didn't expect the meat to taste very good. We hunted strictly for trophies.

Therefore, I didn't question leaving the meat with the guide and bringing home only the cape and horns. At home, I'm not fond of mutton or lamb chops. In fact, I'd rather eat hot dogs.

The day we flew out, Patty cooked steaks for breakfast. The exquisite flavor caressed my pallet. Saliva ran out of control. You didn't chew the meat, you held it in your mouth and savored every bite until somehow it disappeared down your throat.

"What is this delicious meat?" I asked.

"Why that's a little backstrap left from the last hunter's ram," Patty replied.

I was furious at best, but held my anger. I never did quite forgive Dale for not telling me how wonderful wild sheep meat tastes. You can be sure that I brought home all the meat possible from my second and subsequent rams.

For the benefit of you readers who are slipping into sleep, let me state it once again emphatically: "You'll find no better tasting meat in the world, domestic or wild, than the meat of the wild rams of North America." Loin steaks (backstraps) from a young, pre-rut moose makes you wish you lived on moose meat year-round. American beef rates finest in the world. I've eaten elk steaks that kept you coming back for more. But I have never eaten finer meat than sheep meat.

The texture and taste of most wild game deteriorates as the animal grows old. Not so wild sheep. An old ram is a rather lazy animal. He doesn't do much more than stroll around his alpine kingdom, eat and sleep. In most cases, you harvest a ram before the annual rut, or in the case of desert rams, well after. Also, the poorer cuts of other wild game and beef don't taste nearly as good as the loins. With wild sheep, you can hardly tell from which area the meat came.

On the other hand, the only mountain goat I ever chewed on wasn't fit to eat. Not only did the meat lack flavor but it was tough as a rifle sling. Just why, I'm not sure. Even more so than a ram, goats just stroll around, sleep and eat. I make it a point to try, at least once, everything I shoot. I tried goat once but no more. Other sheep hunters report the same thing.

In certain areas, most notably mainland states, you must take out any wild game you harvest. In the case of goat, pack it out and make summer sausage or jerky from the meat.

I don't know how many times I hear people, even hunters, say they don't like wild meat. Some would refuse to eat the finest beef if you told them it was elk or something else wild. They might even gag on beef if you told them after the fact that the beef was wild game.

When I've served some family members and good friends wild meat and especially sheep meat, they ate it with gusto until I told them what it was. One lady ate half her steak and bragged about it, but after I told her it was sheep meat, she didn't eat another bite. These people will never like wild game no matter how good. But

For the taxidermist to provide you with a life-like mount, you must provide him with photographs, measurements and descriptions of the animal. Close-up photos showing the face, neck and head will assist your taxidermist.

most reasonable people will enjoy wild game and especially sheep meat if you take proper care of it.

At one time, years ago, someone decided that if you hang and age beef, you should hang and age wild game. So today's wily hunter takes a deer, elk, ram or whatever, and hangs it in a tree with the hide left on. The temperature reaches 50 degrees or warmer every day. He then ties the carcass on top of his vehicle and drives 1,000 miles home.

Then he and his family wonder why the meat tastes gamy, wild or just plain terrible. Your local butcher doesn't hang and age beef with the hide on outside under a tree. No, he hangs it in a cooler with the hide off. He certainly doesn't drive your beef around on top a vehicle in the sun for 24 hours. In fact, if he did any of these things, he would not remain in the butcher business long.

Aging breaks down connecting tissue to tenderize the meat, nothing more. Therefore, aging wild meat should be of benefit. Perhaps it does, but the best sheep meat I ever ate was still running around a high basin a few hours before. The meat had not even cooled completely.

Body heat causes meat spoilage. The hide causes the meat to retain heat so remove the hide as soon as possible. To keep your meat clean, you may want to leave the hide on until you reach camp but then get it off right away and keep the meat cool.

After you harvest your ram, you may want to quarter the carcass for return to camp or bone it out first depending on the circumstances. Quartering it saves time on the mountain but boning it saves weight when you carry it out. Most often your guide or outfitter has a set routine. Within reason, let him do it his way. Do make certain, however, that you remove the hide as soon as possible.

Often your best bet is to cut the loins and tenderloins off the ram. Then cut the front and rear off and carry it out in quarters. In some areas you can leave the mid-carcass on the mountain to save weight. Some people, however, feel that the ribs are the best part of the ram.

As I said before, most often your guide takes care of the field dressing chores. However, if you hunt on your own, field dress a ram in the same manner as you field dress any game depending on circumstances. If you can get your horse to the ram, then field dress it by only removing the body cavity organs. Never cut the throat. You need the cape for the taxidermist. Cut down between the leg muscles to the pelvic bone. Turn the knife over and cut through the skin over the abdomen up to the breast bone, taking care not to puncture any organs. In most areas you must keep evidence of sex—either a testicle or half of the mammary gland—with the carcass.

Reach up into the chest as far as possible and cut the esophagus and diaphragm. Cut around the anus and tie it off. Keep the heart and liver and dump the remainder on the ground. Wipe or wash the body cavity and prop it open with sticks. With a horse you can carry the entire carcass out. If not then either quarter or bone the meat and pack it out. If you hunt alone, take the meat out first unless the weather stays well below 50 degrees.

After washing or wiping the carcass out, keep the meat dry. If you have a long drive ahead or a flight of more than a short day, get your meat butchered and frozen for the trip home. Use plenty of dry ice. If you can arrive home the same day, then keep the meat cool with wet or dry ice.

When you butcher and freeze the meat, use quality freezer paper. With anything else, the meat can freezer burn before you eat it. Of course around our house, sheep meat doesn't get a chance to freezer burn.

Before you cook your ram meat, cut off any remaining fat.

Always measure your goat or ram before skinning or caping to make the taxidermist's job easier. When caping your trophy, such as this guide is starting to do with a Dall ram, start well behind the front shoulders and cut along the backbone, not the neck.

While beef fat adds a good deal to the meat's flavor, wild game fat detracts from the natural flavor. Also, before you cut the loin into steaks, cut off the tough tendon material that is actually the backstrap.

Although you can tell little difference in the various cuts of wild sheep meat, the steaks and chops offer the finest eating. Because of their lack of fat, you must cook them fast and hot. Use only tongs or a spatula to turn the steaks, never a fork. A fork punctures the meat allowing the natural juices to escape. Likewise, never poke a hole in or cut the meat while cooking to test for doneness.

Like beef, ram steaks taste best cooked on a charcoal grill. Cut the steaks about an inch thick and cook over a very hot fire for three or four minutes on a side or until medium rare. Because of the lack of fat, sheep meat dries out if cooked slowly or without a hot fire.

You may also obtain excellent results cooking sheep steaks in an iron skillet. Use the old fashioned, black iron skillet or griddle like you see in hunting camps. Rather than cooking oil, use lard or bacon grease in the skillet. We like to dip the steaks into flour seasoned with salt and pepper before cooking, but you can cook them without. Use the medium-hot to hot setting on your stove. Wait until the grease or lard is very hot (water drops bead and bounce off the surface) before adding the steaks. Cook only two or three minutes on each side.

If you particularly enjoy swiss steak, chicken fried steak or roasts, by all means use the sheep meat in place of beef with your favorite recipes. You can also make excellent hamburger if you add about one part pork suet to three parts of ground sheep meat. But unless you have something against steaks, you can utilize practically all the ram as steaks if you cut it right. You don't go out to a fine restaurant and order swiss steak, hamburger or even a roast if steak is the same price.

My family raised their eyebrows a bit when I first brought sheep meat home. Yes, they knew I said it tasted better than beef but after all, old Dad has funny notions about sheep hunting. I sliced an entire tenderloin into steaks and tossed them on the charcoal grill. After a couple of tentative bites, my three sons consumed everything in sight except one skimpy piece left for my wife and one for myself. After that day I cooked sheep meat when the kids were gone.

I cooked ram steaks for Larry Stille and his wife, Yvonne. Larry knows practically all wild game is good but he hesitated on the sheep meat. Like everyone else, he and Yvonne became big supporters of sheep meat. Other friends say the same but I normally don't tell them what they are eating until I get a reaction. Most can't believe it's not beef. Some people will never admit that any wild meat tastes good, but who needs them anyway?

As well as taking proper care of the meat, take special care of the cape (the hide from the head back through the shoulders) or the entire hide. Most often the guide takes care of caping and skinning the trophy but keep an eye on him. If you bone or quarter your trophy, first remove the cape from well behind the front legs up to the base of the head and cut the head off. Finish the job in camp.

Most guides are expert skinners. If so, let him do the intricate work around the eyes, nose, ears and lips. If you hunt without a guide, freeze the head and wait for the taxidermist to finish the caping job unless you can do the job confidently. With the hide removed up to the base of the head, you can wrap the whole thing up and freeze it.

Guide Joe D'Errico with Gary LaRose Outfitters, capes out a beautiful Dall ram. The clothes scattered on nearby bushes is the author's attempt to dry out gear and clothing.

For a shoulder mount leave plenty of hide on the cape. Always start well behind the front legs. Never cut the hide up the bottom of the neck, this part shows on your mount. Rather cut up the back of the neck to the base of the horns. Too much cape is definitely better than too little. If you want a full body mount, get instructions from your taxidermist before the hunt on how he wants the hide removed.

If you or your guide remove the entire cape in camp, make certain the cape is generously salted. You can't use too much salt. Scatter a good layer of salt all over the inside of the cape and rub it in. Take special care around the edges and around the lips, eyes and nose. Turn the ears inside out and salt them well. It doesn't hurt to resalt and rerub after you think you are finished. After salting, roll the cape up, hang it and let it drip. Finally, unroll the cape and let it dry.

I've been in a few camps that don't use salt. If this occurs, freeze the cape as soon as possible, within two or three days at the worst. Many hunters take an added precaution against spoilage and hair slippage by both salting and freezing the cape.

Before you or your guide start caping the animal, wash or wipe off any blood on the head or neck. This is especially important on a white hide like a goat or Dall ram. In fact for white hides a little bottle of alcohol makes the job easier. Don't let the blood set. After caping, cut the horns off with a saw (an axe works in an emergency) leaving plenty of skull plate for the taxidermist to attach to his form. Generally a cut at the line through the eyes works out fine.

Even if you don't plan on mounting the trophy, save the cape. You can freeze it or have it tanned. You might change your mind someday and want a mount of your beautiful trophy.

Don't forget to check in your ram or goat with the local game department. Regulations differ but in practically all cases you must obtain an export permit, have the horns plugged or tagged. The plugging, tagging or branding assures your identification in case the horns are lost.

Many outfitters, especially north country outfitters, will offer to crate and ship your horns and cape to you or your taxidermist. If at all possible, *take them with you.* Sheep horns in particular, are too valuable to trust to airlines or other hired transportation people. If I fly to and from my hunt, I carry the horns with me on the plane. Don't put them on as baggage.

You may receive some funny looks when you sit in an airport waiting room with sheep or goat horns. You may as I have, get a speech from an antihunter while waiting. You can either argue with them or shrug it off to ignorance. Enclosing them in a box is a simple alternative.

After bagging my record book desert ram, I held the horns in the waiting room with a white-knuckle grip. When the time came to enter the plane, the cute little stewardess stopped me and said I couldn't take the horns on the plane. I calmly explained that she could fight me over the horns but that in the end I would indeed carry them on the plane. I would hold them, put them behind the

Unless you're an expert, let your guide skin the intricate parts around the head of the ram or goat. This is much easier to do back at camp rather than in the field.

seat or in the overhead, but I was taking them on the plane. I guess she believed my bluff. Or was I bluffing? Check with the airline before you book your flight. Also ask the check-in people about carrying the horns on the plane. Explain how valuable they are and if you simply can't carry them, insure them for at least the price of the hunt.

After you finish congratulating yourself and before you start caping or field dressing your hard earned trophy of the high country, remember the taxidermist. He can sculpt a much better representation of your live ram if you take measurements and photos from which to work.

For a shoulder mount, take close-up photos of the front of the face, both sides of the face, a shot from the rear of the head and one from the top of the head. In these photos you're not trying to take trophy pictures to show your friends, you're taking photos to show the detail of the head. Don't worry about cutting parts of the ram out of the photo or what the background looks like. For full body mounts, include photos of the entire ram from the sides as well as the head.

You also need detailed measurements. For a shoulder mount record the distance between the eyes and the circumference of the face in front of the eyes. Also, measure from the front corner of the eye to the nose tip and from the front corner of the eye to the corner of the mouth. You need three neck measurements, one just behind the head, one in front of the shoulder and one halfway between those two. Also, record the distance from the tip of the nose, over the head to the first vertebra at the base of the skull. The measurement from the horn base to the tip of the nose completes the job.

If you want a full body mount, take all the shoulder mount measurements plus measure from the tip of the nose to the base of the tail following the curve of the body. You'll also need the body circumference behind the front legs, ahead of the back legs and at the thickest part of the body. Whatever you plan for the mount, contact your taxidermist before you leave to learn exactly which measurements he needs.

Other than your outfitter, your taxidermist is most responsible for your future memories of the hunt. Far too many hunters spend hours selecting an outfitter, thousands of dollars on the hunt and then try to skimp on taxidermy fees or allow a friend to mount the trophy.

Two or three trophies hang on my wall which absolutely haunt me rather than bring back warm memories of the hunt. Done by inept or amateur taxidermists, they look more like barnyard heifers than elk and caribou. The pinched face on my first ram looks more like a whitetail (or perhaps a mouse) than a stone ram.

Why let some neighbor, who learned his taxidermy "skills" through the mail, mount your trophy just to save a few dollars? These part-time taxidermists really do "stuff" a head. But a full-time professional is an artist. He brings the mount to life. The result looks like the animal might jump right off the wall.

Over the past 15 years, I've been fortunate to work with two real pros in the taxidermy field, Dick Barr of Barr Taxidermy in

Savage, Minnesota, and Joe Meder of Kodiak Ltd. in Solon, Iowa. They both charge reasonable fees and yet produce stunning, life-like mounts. Barr not only creates fine taxidermy work but he judges many taxidermist competitions. Meder judges, writes for taxidermy journals and has won "Best of Show" awards at the World of Taxidermy competition.

Both men recommend a full-time taxidermist, rather than one who works only evenings and weekends. "I don't mean to say that an amateur who works only part-time can't be a real artist, but your chances are better with a full-timer," Barr said.

Visit friends who have had quite a bit of taxidermy work done. Look at their mounts and see if the animals look alive or hang forlornly on the wall. Visit several taxidermist shops and study their work. After a while you'll see who makes a mount look alive and who doesn't. Ask the man to show you some repair work, places where he repaired sloppy caping. Look for detail. Anybody can stretch skin on a form. Look for depth in a nostril, cheap work generally shows flat nostrils. Look for detail around the eye and in the depth of tear ducts.

Compare the man's work with photos of live animals. Do the antlers or horns sit on the head at the proper angle? Does the paint on the nose and mouth look real or did the man glob it on like sloppy makeup? Do the ears sit at a natural angle like the animal is alert?

Joe Meder says choosing a taxidermist to mount that trophy ram or goat is as personal as picking that hot spot to hunt. The hunter and taxidermist must work together for best results. "Unfortunately, the two most-asked questions a taxidermist hears are 'How much?' and 'When can I expect to pick it up?' These are important, but should be the last questions. This line of questioning does not address quality, craftsmanship and longevity of the mount," Meder said.

Fortunately for hunters, taxidermy has gone through a renaissance in technology in the past few years. The profession as a whole made vast improvements in quality and education. State and national competitions are responsible for much of the improvement. "If you are not aware of the quality work available today, then you should attend shows in your area and visit several shops," Meder said. "You'll be amazed at the quality work you find. Many times, I hear comments like 'I didn't realize how nice they can look' or 'I didn't know you could do that.' "

Top-rate professionals like Meder and Barr study photos and

animals in the wild. "I feel it is important to capture the animal's feelings and expressions in a mount. Wildlife, like humans, experience different moods and feelings and these should show in a mount. The serious taxidermist produces in-depth pictures and sketches of what he plans to do. Study his final work, especially in the nose and around the eyes, and compare this with the reference pictures. Ask the man what he has in mind for your mount," Meder said.

The fees taxidermists charge varies a great deal. Part of this difference is in the different levels of ability and demand. However, part of the difference is also due to different quality forms and artificial eyes they will use on your mount.

Quality of work should rate much higher than price or speed in taxidermy. To find such quality you may have to travel quite a distance, especially if you live in rural America. Not all top taxidermists work in metropolitan areas but the law of averages says you'll find more in large cities. And remember, in general the old cliche holds true: "You get what you pay for."

With proper planning, you can come home from your hunt with the finest meat in the world. Then after a few months you can gaze at an almost alive trophy on your wall and memories of the hunt will come flooding back.

16

The Future Of
Sheep And Goat Hunting

Years ago, I thought I could predict the stock market. But when I bought, the market went down. When I sold, the market went up. Trying to predict the winning lottery numbers would have been easier. Everyone I know, other than a complete fool, possesses perfect hindsight. Foresight is another matter.

Hopefully, however, we do learn something from hindsight. If so, we can help assure the success of wild sheep and goat herds in the future. I'd hate to think that my grandchildren won't have the opportunity to climb in the high country and hunt magnificent rams and goats.

Due to lack of early scientific counting methods, no one can estimate closely how many wild sheep and goats inhabited North America when the Pilgrims first pulled their boats onto Plymouth Rock. From the writings of the early mountain men and explorers we know that sheep and goats did not outnumber deer or elk. Sheep populations, however, were much higher than they are today. Goat numbers probably are about the same today as in the past.

Ignorance on the part of mankind, coupled with indiscriminate market hunting and diminishing habitat reduced sheep herds throughout the lower 48 states and southern Canada. Fortunately, modern mankind woke up and attempted to change things for the better. When states first wrote game laws, wild sheep and goats were protected. Most states did not allow sheep or goat hunting until the 1950s or 1960s.

Although sheep numbers have not returned to pre-civilization levels, they have recovered to the level that allows hunting in almost all states with historic sheep herds. However, we have not and will not see sheep over the entire historic range. Today, highways, high-rises, lakes and other evidence of civilization occupy a good part of the historic range. Perhaps with intelligent planning, enough money and concerned sportsmen, our future generations will hunt sheep and goats on the mountaintop.

Although mountain goats in some areas decreased in number over the years, in most historic goat ranges numbers remain as high as ever. Fortunately, goats inhabit the roughest possible terrain and poachers seldom expend the energy to kill a goat. Goats don't come into contact with domestic animals as wild sheep do in some areas and therefore don't contract the diseases of domestic species.

Since goat populations remain fairly stable and since I reported on goat numbers and their outlook in Chapter 11, I'll restrict the remainder of this chapter to the future of the great rams from the far north to the Mexican deserts.

According to Lanny Wilson, BLM wildlife biologist, "The truth is, overall, bighorn populations in North America have experienced a dynamic increase for a number of reasons. The future of bighorn hunting has never looked better."

However, Dall and Stone populations have not experienced any major changes in the last 100 years, he said. Wilson, therefore, predicts a decrease in Dall and Stone populations but not a major one. Wilson says habitat loss represents the major factor affecting Dall and Stone populations in the future.

Wilson reports that the year 1974 was crucial in the history of wild sheep management in North America. In that year the Desert Bighorn Council sponsored a paper entitled "Guidelines for Re-establishing and Capturing Desert Bighorns." All federal and state agencies received copies of the document which gave wildlife biologists and managers the tool they needed to initiate re-introduction programs. The document also gave administrators, information they could use to support re-introduction programs.

Also in 1974, the Foundation for North American Wild Sheep was organized. The Foundation's primary function was to provide funds for wild sheep research and management programs. Since 1974, wild sheep managers, researchers and enthusiasts have been most effective in raising funds, undertaking significant research

With hard work, good planning and enforcement by game departments and a public that cares, our future generations will be able to enjoy pack trips into the mountains for sheep and goat for years to come.

and developing comprehensive wild sheep programs. According to Wilson, the intensity of these programs must continue.

The Rocky Mountain Bighorn Society reports an excellent outlook for sheep in Colorado. "With the coming of trappers, miners, herdsmen, farmers and home-builders, the bighorn were harvested indiscriminately for meat, they suffered diseases brought by livestock and they lost habitat to mines, roads, ranches, reservoirs, cities and towns. By 1915 there were only about 7,200 sheep in Colorado. The decline continued to about 3,200 sheep in 1958 and to 2,200 in 1970. However, by 1984, experts counted at least 4,000 bighorn in Colorado. In some areas, sheep numbers have reached the habitat's carrying capacity.''

According to the Society, threats to Colorado's bighorn habitat continue but an educated public and good management practices allow bighorn numbers to continue to increase. Modern management techniques opened up habitat by removing dense trees and brush and by controlled burnings. As some sheep herds became too large for the available habitat, Colorado wildlife managers initiated trapping and transplanting efforts to reestablish herds on other historic and still suitable bighorn ranges. In a few instances, ewe harvests have been necessary to control sheep numbers.

You'll find the Colorado story repeated all over North America. An enlightened public and knowledgeable game departments protected habitat, transplanted sheep herds and provided increasing hunting opportunities.

Predicting the future can never be considered an exact science. In fact, predicting the future is only an educated guess at best. Jack O'Connor, without a doubt, knew wild sheep in North American better than any hunter or outdoor writer. In his wonderful 1974 book, *Sheep and Sheep Hunting*, he wrote, ''I think the prospect for the indefinite continuation of hunting of desert sheep is very bad—even in the limited numbers available today.'' He cites the invasion of habitat by dams, highways, canals, four-wheel drive vehicles and campers. But since O'Connor wrote those words, desert bighorn populations and hunting permits have increased in all areas with the possible exception of Arizona.

In the same book, O'Connor said the picture for the Rocky Mountain bighorn looked brighter, but not much. According to O'Connor, herds in several areas in Idaho and Montana were static or declining through competition with cattle and elk and to some extent with deer. But again, we can now count more bighorns in practically all areas than were present in 1974. He reported that the Stone sheep and Dall sheep were not yet in trouble but they were hunted far harder than in the past. Today, quotas have regulated Stone sheep hunting for several years and Dall hunting has stood up well under somewhat increased hunting pressure.

If someone as knowledgeable as Jack O'Connor has trouble predicting the future of sheep hunting, I would be foolish to attempt my own predictions. I can report what experts in the field predict, what problems the sheep face and what is being done to protect, conserve and increase sheep populations all over the continent.

Although Stone sheep numbers are down from historic highs, their future looks bright, as is testified by H. Grounds' impressive ram.

Starting in the far north, Donald McKnight, acting deputy director, Alaska Department of Fish and Game, reports, "Our sheep populations are in excellent condition and we expect them to stay that way."

In Alaska, civilization has not made many inroads into sheep habitat. Although Federal law allows Alaskan natives a certain amount of subsistence hunting, the greatest share of them hunt easier species such as caribou and moose. Since Dalls live far from large human population centers, civilization has not affected Dall numbers as much as the southern species. In the past few years, the government hindered access to some of Alaska's best sheep hunting ranges. A good portion of the Wrangells, for example, is a part of the huge Alaskan land use package. This bill forbids the use of motorized vehicles, i.e. bush planes, to enter the area. You can't penetrate these vast areas more than a few miles on foot.

At one time hunters and conservationists expressed concern about energy related inroads affecting Alaskan wildlife. To date such things as the Alaskan pipeline have not shown much effect on sheep populations. Because Alaska, as well as the Yukon and the Northwest Territories, represents such a vast and essentially inhospitable environment, it may never become so populous as to harm sheep populations.

Although British Columbia Stone sheep numbers are down a bit from historic highs, the herd remains in good condition. Civilization made more inroads into Stone country than in Dall, but to date no serious problem has developed. A slight overhunting in the past did cause a decline, but like most wildlife populations, sport hunting never caused dramatic population decreases. Moreover, the Provincial government set quotas on Stone sheep and also instituted a full curl regulation on the fabulous Stone rams. These measures will control the harvest and preserve the younger, breeding population. According to most experts in the area, the new British Columbia regulations should result in more large, old trophy rams.

Like the Dall country to the north, most Stone country will never become civilized to the point of roads, homes and towns. But, in some areas certain factions would like to see dams built in Stone country. These dams would have a detrimental effect on the sheep.

Each year more and more British Columbia residents decide they want to hunt sheep. By law they need not hire an outfitter or guide but they may hunt on an outfitter's territory. I'm certainly not saying that residents should not be allowed to hunt. After all, the mountains belong to them. However, in most areas throughout North America, residents are less concerned with trophy quality than are nonresidents who must travel a great distance and spend a large amount of money to hunt Stone sheep.

Bighorns and desert sheep suffered the effects of mankind to a much greater extent than have the thinhorns in the north country. Tom Brakefield, in his book, *Hunting Big Game Trophies*, goes so far as to suggest the rapid decline of the bighorn sheep in the first half of the 19th century, although largely unheralded, is in its own way as dramatic as that of the bison.

Good management over the years produces rams such as this beautiful 200-plus point bighorn taken by David Onerheim.

Since the coming of civilization to the mountains, the range of the bighorn narrowed considerably. In the past, bighorns ranged from the Dakotas and Nebraska in the east to the coastal mountains in the west, and from Alberta and British Columbia in the north into southern Mexico and Texas. Many experts agree that nearly two million bighorns inhabited North America before the first Pilgrim settlement in 1620. Today the number is probably not over 100,000, if that.

On the positive side, bighorn populations almost everywhere are increasing. Modern game management, concern and money from sportsmen and range enhancement all help not only increase sheep populations but increase their range. At the present, you'll find at least some bighorns in all states which had historic populations, even though you won't find them in all historic ranges. And to the best of my knowledge, at least a few permits are issued in all these states except Texas.

Hunters can still hunt bighorns without winning a drawing if they want to hunt Montana's unlimited license areas or come up with the cash to hunt in Alberta or British Columbia. Prospects for success are not as high as in Stone or Dall country, but does one have to bag a ram to have a successful hunt?

Desert sheep have felt the same pressures since the coming of civilization as the bighorns, perhaps to an even greater extent. Desert ecology, fragile at best, with harsh living conditions make desert sheep populations even tougher to bring back. On the other hand, since I started sheep hunting in the early 1970s, both desert sheep numbers and hunting permit numbers increased. With hard work and money, desert populations can further increase over the years.

Nevada is a prime example. Back in the early 1970s Nevada offered only 20 some permits with two going to nonresidents. At last count they offered 109 resident and 12 nonresident desert sheep permits along with 30 resident California bighorn permits and two resident Rocky Mountain bighorn permits. To date, Nevada is the only state offering permits for all three bighorn subspecies. On the other hand, over the same period, the number of Arizona desert permits stayed about the same or went down a bit.

Perhaps even more detrimental to desert sheep survival than civilization is the feral burro and horse problem. Years ago, prospectors brought burros and horses to the desert. Then along came the Model T. Prospectors let the animals go wild in favor of the horseless carriage. Wild burros in particular compete directly with wild sheep for forage and water. And the burros foul water holes so bad that sheep avoid them. Unfortunately, animal rights groups screamed loud enough about the plight of the wild burros and horses that the federal government protected them to the great detriment of natural species such as wild sheep. The extremely fragile desert ecology requires decades if not centuries to recover from the damage caused by feral animals.

As with other species, regulated sport hunting of wild sheep and goats never caused declines in populations. For example, while other states built their sheep herds and offered sport hunting by permits, California banned sheep hunting over 100 years ago and only within the past few years has opened legal hunting on an extremely limited basis. But over that period, the once numerous sheep herd sank to fewer than 2,000 animals.

Civilization in its various manifestations, not sport hunting, caused the decline of the once great sheep populations. Wild sheep over the years competed directly with domestic livestock and other wildlife for forage, especially on winter ranges. Not only did the sheep lose the battle for forage, but they caught diseases. Wild sheep have little or no immune system to fight diseases of domestic sheep. Conditions such as lung worms, scabies pink eye and pneumonia, all contracted from domestic animals, decimate wild sheep numbers.

Dams, highways, towns, fences and other remnants of civilization block migration to sheep wintering grounds or lambing grounds. Fortunately, modern man is aware of wildlife and its problems. Today, a hue and cry goes out when prospective man-made concrete structures are suggested on or near bighorn habitat. Public opinion does carry weight.

In one way, sheep hunting did cause problems with sheep populations. In some cases, the great prestige of sheep hunting and the grand slam in particular, caused some unethical, big-money poachers to illegally take huge rams. In other cases, poachers and slob hunters gave all hunters a bad name by killing sheep out of season or otherwise illegally killing them.

One spring on an Alberta grizzly hunt we parked the camper alongside a dirt road. While Dewey set up camp, I noticed a dead animal laying in a ditch below the road. The two- or three-year-old ram carcass was complete except for the head. I never could figure out why anybody would want the horns from a small ram. I could understand someone wanting the meat but not the head. Later we found where they killed the ram on a wintering ground.

Fortunately, modern reward programs set up by states and various conservation organizations have slowed poaching. With large monetary rewards and guaranteed anonymity, many people now turn in poachers, including their friends. In the past small rewards and the fear of testifying in court kept many otherwise law abiding people from turning in poachers to law enforcement officials.

According to Lanny Wilson, the new horn plugging program should help slow down or stop poaching of sheep for their trophy value. This permanent plugging or otherwise marking and recording legally taken sheep horns prevents poachers from claiming legal kills. It also prevents thefts of sheep horns by having the name of each hunter on record with a match to the plug number. Some states and provinces actually drill a core from the back of the horn and insert a numbered plug. Others brand or otherwise tag the horns in a permanent manner.

As a side benefit, the plugging and recording helps game departments know the size of the sheep being taken and the exact locality of the kill. These tools help biologists and legislators better manage the sheep herds. The actual core sample removed tells biologists much about the mineral content of the habitat as well as the forage. In fact, after enough core samples are tested and recorded, it may someday be possible to pinpoint within a few miles, exactly where a sheep lived.

All states and provinces now work hard to restore and preserve their sheep herds. States such as Wyoming, Nevada, Idaho and Colorado led the way by capturing and transplanting sheep populations to areas of historic habitation.

The Arizona sheep transplant program is working. Due to the state programs, hunters broke both the desert and Rocky Mountain bighorn sheep records. Idaho recently developed a new net gun fired from a low-flying helicopter to capture sheep with much less stress on the sheep than other capture methods.

States also trade or sell sheep from large, healthy herds. Texas recently completed the second desert sheep trapping operation in Nevada, capturing 25 sheep for release in west Texas. The famous Whiskey Mountain herd in Wyoming has long supplied rams, ewes and lambs for transplant projects all over North America.

Utah obtained 36 bighorns from Whiskey Mountain between 1983 and 1984 to transplant in the Flaming Gorge National Recreation Area. By 1988 the herd numbered over 90 head. In 1987, Colorado obtained 20 desert sheep from Arizona for transplant in exchange for 200 pronghorn. The list goes on and on but one thing is certain: Game departments work hard restoring wild sheep populations.

Over the past 10 to 20 years, many private conservation organizations have led the way in conserving and preserving wild sheep all over North America. These organizations are made up of hunters, outfitters, guides, biologists, wildlife managers and other interested individuals who want to help. The organizations raise money to fund research, transplant and management work. They also actively take part in projects to improve habitat and push

While bighorn populations will never recover to historic highs, the future of bighorn hunting looks good. This wonderful old ram taken by T.S. Marcum while hunting with R.W. Turner is testimony to that fact.

legislators to enact laws to the benefit of wildlife in general and wild sheep in particular.

A partial list of such organizations includes the Foundation for North American Wild Sheep (FNAWS), the Arizona Desert Bighorn Sheep Society, the Rocky Mountain Bighorn Society (RMBS), the Rocky Mountain Conservation Fund, The Fraternity of the Desert Bighorn, Nevada Bighorns Unlimited, British Columbia Wildlife Federation, Northwest Territories Wildlife Federation and the Grand Slam Club.

Not the first, but without a doubt the largest such organization is the Foundation for North American Wild Sheep. The Foundation, formally organized in 1977, really started from an informal gathering of 24 Midwest sheep hunters called together by Jim Froelich, a well-known sheep hunter from Sawner, Wisconsin, in 1974. The Foundation had funded well over $3 million in grant-in-aid projects.

Each year, usually in February, FNAWS holds its annual convention. Here, some 2,000 participants raise funds for the following year. Outfitters, artists, state game departments and others donate hunting and fishing trips, sheep permits and works of art for auctions and raffles. The convention is also an excellent place to meet outfitters, guides, biologists, other hunters and in general learn the up-to-date information about sheep and sheep permits all over North America.

In 1988, FNAWS funded a project in Idaho to locate bighorn lambing areas, determine seasonal distribution patterns of ewes and evaluate herd productivity. They also funded a Nevada project that could play a significant part in the survival of a remnant band of desert sheep. They funded a guzzler (water catching and storage device) in Utah as well as a transplant project.

Using FNAWS funding, the state of Montana reintroduced bighorn sheep to the Taylor-Hilgard range. North Dakota received a grant to fund bighorn transplant projects and lungworm treatment efforts. What was once a struggling program in Oregon, now has excellent prospects because of new funding sources such as FNAWS. The Foundation recently funded $1,000 as part of a total reward of $4,550 offered for a specific ram poaching in Wyoming.

The Phoenix-based, Arizona Desert Bighorn Sheep Society also raises funds for sheep projects in Arizona but even more important, they work on habitat improvement projects throughout the year. Twenty or more hardy souls spend weekends in the desert building dams and other water catchment facilities for the desert

David Fox took this 179-point desert bighorn while hunting in Baja Sur, Mexico. For the past 15 to 20 years, game departments have reintroduced sheep herds and restored sheep habitat. Sheep numbers, and the number of permits available to hunters, continue to increase.

sheep and other wildlife. The group usually gets together in the desert on Friday night, eats a large and delicious meal and then works hard on Saturday and Sunday, spending the nights on the desert floor.

Tom Brown, president of the Rocky Mountain Bighorn Society reports, "Cooperation is a theme we will emphasize. We should cooperate with other conservation organizations as well as with state and federal game management professionals. We can accomplish much more together than we can individually."

In 1988, the RMBS voted to join other groups funding habitat improvement and research projects in Wyoming's Encampment Canyon. Like the Arizona Society, the RMBS also participates in weekend habitat restoration projects. One such effort was the Clear Creek, Colorado, winter range project. They improved the local sheep habitat and helped the state fund the project.

Needless to say, these projects benefit all wildlife, not just wild sheep. One could write an entire book on the fund raising, funding and projects the various organizations take on but suffice it to say: They are instrumental to the future of sheep hunting in North America. For a complete list of organizations and their addresses, see Appendix 2.

Indoctrination courses required by many states before you can obtain your sheep hunting permit also help secure the future of quality sheep hunting. In Nevada, one of the first to set up and require such a course, hunters learn to identify trophy rams. They are also shown how the state increased the sheep herd and therefore the number of permits through sound wildlife management practices. Education ranks high on the list of aids to our wild sheep's future.

If hunters stay alert to possible problems, keep their state game departments alert and educate the legislators to the problems of wildlife, the outlook for wild sheep and goat hunting in North America will remain high for our children and grandchildren. But hunters and conservation organization must not relax.

Appendix 1:
State And Provincial
Application Sources

To apply for a sheep or mountain goat hunt, contact the fish and game department in the state or province that you intend to hunt. They can provide you with information about hunting regulations, nonresident licenses, guides, outfitters and licensing or regulation changes. Always contact the state or provincial agency at least one year before your hunt, and then again after the first of January. Your outfitter should be able to keep you apprised of any last-minute licensing or regulation changes. In most Canadian provinces you must submit license fees in Canadian funds. Your outfitter can help, or contact the province for the proper money rates. Practically all states and provinces require a cashier's check or money order and will reject personal checks.

Alaska Department of Fish & Game
P.O. Box 25526
Juneau, AK 99802-5526
(907) 465-4190

Alaska offers high country hunters sheep and mountain goat hunts. Dall sheep permits are issued through either a lottery drawing or over the counter. Goat permits are issued on a registration system. All nonresidents must hire a licensed guide to hunt sheep or goats. Exceptions are made for nonresidents hunting with resident relatives within second-degree of kindred over 19 years old.

Alberta Environmental Protection
Natural Resources Service
9945-108 St.
Edmonton, Alberta T5K 2G6
(403) 944-0313

Alberta outfitters receive a quota of bighorn permits each year. Contact an outfitter first early in the year. Then, with his assistance, apply to Alberta for the sheep license. Alberta offers no goat permits.

Arizona Game & Fish Department
2221 W. Greenway Road
Phoenix, AZ 85023
(602) 942-3000

Arizona sheep permit applications can be submitted to the Department's Phoenix office between May 28 and June 18. Tags are mailed out on August 2.

Arizona Hualapai Wildlife Department
P.O. Box 216
Peach Springs, AZ 86434

Arizona's Hualapai tribe, at last report, has six desert sheep permits available each year. These do not have to be drawn through the regular Arizona drawing. The tribe handles their own drawing.

British Columbia Ministry of Environment
Wildlife Branch
Parliament Building
Victoria, British Columbia V8V 1X5
(604) 387-9731

Ask your outfitter for application advice.

California Department of Fish & Game
1416 Ninth St.
Sacramento, CA 95814
(916) 445-3531

California currently draws out nine bighorn sheep permits. One permit is auctioned, and no more than one of the remaining eight permits can go to a nonresident. Applications for the drawing are available in early June, and must be returned by mid-July.

Colorado Division of Wildlife
6060 Broadway
Denver, CO 80216
(303) 297-1192

Desert ram permits are available to residents only. No preference points are awarded. Rocky Mountain bighorn permits are available to both residents and nonresidents, as are goat permits. Up to three years of preference points may be used for bighorn and goat permits. The application deadline for both sheep and goats is mid-April.

Idaho Department of Fish & Game
600 S. Walnut St. Box 25
Boise, ID 83707
(208) 334-3700

Applications for both sheep and goats must be in Boise by the end of April.

Mexico Direccion General De,
Flora Y Fauna Silvestres
Netzahualcoyotl #109 1er Piso
06080 Mexico D.F.

For further information about desert sheep hunts in Mexico contact: Wildlife Advisory Services, Box 76132, Los Angeles, CA 90076.

Montana Fish, Wildlife & Parks
1420 East Sixth Ave.
P.O. Box 200701
Helena, MT 59620-0701
(406) 444-2950

Limited sheep and goat licenses are available. Hunters must apply before May 1 each year.

Nevada Division of Wildlife
P.O. Box 10678
Reno, NV 89520-3040
(702) 688-1500
(800) 597-1020 (nonresidents)

Apply for sheep and goat permits before the third Monday in April each year. Desert bighorn sheep and California bighorn permits are available for both residents and nonresidents. Rocky Mountain bighorn goats are restricted to residents only.

New Mexico Department of Game & Fish
Villagra Building
Santa Fe, NM 87503
(505) 827-7911

Apply for sheep permits by late-April each year. The drawing is held on June 3. Both residents and nonresidents have an equal chance in the drawings.

Northwest Territories
Department of Renewable Resources
Yellowknife, NWT X1A 2L9
(403) 873-7959

Ask your outfitter for license information.

Oregon Department of Fish and Wildlife
P.O. Box 59
Portland, OR 97207
(503) 872-5268

Apply for sheep permits by early March.

South Dakota Game, Fish & Parks Department
523 E. Capitol
Pierre, S.D. 57501
(605) 773-3485

Sheep and goat permits are for residents only. Apply by mid-June.

Utah Division of Wildlife Resources
1594 West North Temple, Suite 211
Salt Lake City, UT 84114-6301
(801) 538-4700

At this time goat permits are available to residents only. Applications are accepted in late January to the beginning of February.

Washington Department of Wildlife
600 Capitol Way N.
Olympia, WA 98501-1091
(360) 902-2515

For sheep and goat permits apply before the first week in May.

Wyoming Game & Fish Department
5400 Bishop Boulevard
Cheyenne, WY 82006
(307) 777-4600

For sheep and goat permits apply between January 1 and March 31 each year. Permits are drawn on May 22. Bowhunters must purchase an archery license after they win the drawing.

Yukon Department of Renewable Resources
#10 Burns Road
Whitehorse, Yukon Y1A 4Y9
(403) 667-5221

Permits are allocated to Yukon outfitters. For a list of outfitters, contact the Yukon Department of Renewable Resources.

Appendix 2:
Sheep Hunting And
Conservation Organizations

The following organizations promote the hunting and/or conservation of wild sheep in North America. Don't confuse these worthwhile organizations with anti-hunting, protectionist groups. This is not, of course, an all-inclusive list.

Arizona Desert Bighorn Sheep Society
P.O. Drawer 7545
Phoenix, AZ 85011

Boone & Crockett Club
The Old Milwaukee Depot
250 Station Dr.
Missoula, MT 59801

British Columbia Wildlife Federation
Darrel Winsor
5659 176th St.
Surrey, BC V3S 4C5

Foundation For North American Wild Sheep
720 Allen Ave.
Cody, WY 82414

Fraternity Of The Desert Bighorn
P.O. Box 27494
Las Vegas, NV 89126-1494

Grand Slam Club
Bob Householder
P.O. Drawer 6428
Phoenix, AZ 85005

Mzuri Safari Club
41 East Taylor
Reno, NV 89501

Nevada Bighorns Unlimited
P.O. Box 2417
Reno, NV 89505

North American Hunting Club
12301 Whitewater Drive
Suite 260
Minnetonka, MN 55343

Northwest Territories Wildlife Federation
Doug Barber
P.O. Box 501
Hay River, NWT X0E 0R0

Rocky Mountain Bighorn Society
P.O. Box 1086
Denver, CO 80201

Rocky Mountain Conservation Fund
Steve Beilgard
P.O. Box 156
Buffalo, WY 82834

Rocky Mountain Elk Foundation
P.O. Box 8249
Missoula, MT 59807

Safari Club International
4800 W. Gates Pass Rd
Tucson, AZ 85745

Wildlife Forever
12301 Whitewater Drive
Suite 210
Minnetonka, MN 55343

Index